Sharon
Thank you for
your support for
hopecam —
m —

# WHAT SPINS THE WHEEL:

## LEADERSHIP LESSONS FROM OUR RACE FOR HOPE

### BY LEN FORKAS

# WHAT PEOPLE ARE SAYING ABOUT
## *WHAT SPINS THE WHEEL*

"You could read this book to profit from the management lessons Len Forkas has gleaned from riding in Race Across America. Or you could read it for its insight into a little-understood endurance sport. But the real reason to read it is for its message of dedication, resilience, and hope. You are sure to learn something from *What Spins the Wheel.*"

—*Daniel Pink, New York Times Best-Selling Author of* To Sell Is Human *and* Drive.

"A tale that artfully blends a heartfelt mission, lessons in team building and leadership, and an amazing story of physical and mental endurance."

—*Patrick Phillips, CEO,*
*The Urban Land Institute*

"'Hard things are not put in our way to stop us, but to call out our courage and strengths. – Anonymous.' Len Forkas turns adversity into opportunity, teaching us that every challenge can lead to growth. We all need to be reminded that ordinary people can overcome extra-ordinary challenges. *What Spins the Wheel* offers a road map for embracing the extra-ordinary."

—*Chris Warner, Coauthor,* High Altitude Leadership

"The Hopecam story resonates for both the incredible work that the organization does for sick children and their families, but also for the broader messages that apply to teamwork and leadership in the business world. The story is one that every reader can relate to, and one that will leave every reader inspired and joyful at the end."

—*William Clark, President & Chief Executive Officer,*
*Savi Technologies*

"Does any parent really know how they will react when a doctor tells them that their child has cancer or some form of a life-threatening disease? What does a parent do? Do you bring life to a camera in the classroom that brings hope and connectivity to its users? Do you complete a grueling 3,000-mile bike race in eleven days? Do you learn leadership, team building, trust, forgiveness, delegation and cooperation while competing in the bike race? One parent, Len Forkas, does not only learn and do all of these things – he does them for his son, for his family and for people around the globe whom can all count themselves lucky to be a part of Len's world. This is not a story about what Len could have done, but a story about what he did!"

—*John Bucksbaum, Past Chairman, General Growth Properties, Inc. & Board Member, USA Cycling*

"The effort Len put into competing in Race Across America simply overwhelms anyone reading about his experience. His meticulous planning and execution is an inspiring story."

—*Robert E. Buchanan, Buchanan Partners*

"Whether you ride a bike or not, this real life story of Race Across America contains important lessons about running a business. It is an entertaining, enlightening and inspiring tale of a triumphant human spirit dedicated to a most worthy cause."

—*William H. Hudnut III, Past Mayor, City of Indianapolis & Director, Georgetown University*

What Spins the Wheel: Leadership Lessons From Our Race for Hope
By Len Forkas

Hopecam Publishing
Attention: Permissions Coordinator
12110 Sunset Hills Road, #100
Reston, VA 20190

Edited by Joanne Lozar Glenn

Cover, layout and interior design by Damonza.com

Printed in the United States of America.

ISBN: 978-0-9960969-1-1

*To Matthew, Elizabeth and Viena*

# CONTENTS

# ACKNOWLEDGMENTS

Any parent who attempts to train and prepare for Race Across America (RAAM) needs to have a very strong family foundation, as the preparation takes a tremendous amount of time.

Without the sacrifice and support of my family to plan, prepare, and train for Race Across America (RAAM), the journey would have been impossible. I dedicate this book to my son, Matt, who inspired me to push myself to new physical boundaries as I watched him endure with quiet grace the onslaught of treatments that kept coming at him each week and month during his two-and-a-half-year struggle to kill the beast called leukemia. To Elizabeth, who often felt like a single parent during the years that preceded RAAM, coordinating the everyday tasks that I couldn't do while either leading my team at work or training and planning for the race. Finally, to my daughter, Viena, who often went without my signature chocolate chip pancakes on weekend mornings while I was out on day-long training rides or the times when she needed help with homework late in the evening and I was asleep. I promise I'll make it up to you.

Few endurance athletes will admit that it's a selfish sport, but that's the reality. My family gave me their full support. Six months prior to the race I was training 25 hours a week, often away from home. The planning associated with assembling a volunteer team, raising charitable contributions, and executing the logistics for the race required another 15 hours a week. It was a second full-time job. Everyone sacrificed to make the race possible.

At the same time, I was leading the wireless company I founded while overseeing a non-profit charity. My staff at work, Jennifer Bond,

Linda Divalerio, Cris Hernandez, Terri Sutton, and Christian Winkler all stepped up to fill the gaps during my many absences. Robin Dvorak managed our blog posts, and the students at Flint Hill School prepared research on each of the towns we passed through for our blog.

Special thanks to past 2011 RAAM finisher Randy Mouri and his wife Susie for their excellent advice and support from the first day we committed to competing in the race through the moment we crossed the finish line. Thanks to Mary and Dr. Allen DeLaney for medical support and counsel prior to the race, and to RAAM race director George Thomas, athletes Paul Carpenter and Paul Danhaus who offered critical advice from their prior experiences. Dr. Andy Pruitt and the team at the Boulder Center for Sports Medicine provided expert bike fit assistance helping me avoid injury. Also, a special thinks to my endurance coach of more than seven years, Susan Hefler.

The race was supported by key financial sponsors including David Flanagan, Rob Stewart, Allen DeLaney, Jim & Sharon Todd, Scott Stewart, Steve Wiltse, and Kevin Reynolds. Weather support came from Earth Networks ("WeatherBug") who provided critical 24/7 updates. Medical and nutritional support was courtesy of the Fairfax County, Virginia, Fire Department and IAFF Local 2068 permitting two firefighters to join our crew. The Honorable Sharon Bulova, Chairman of the Fairfax County Board of Supervisors supported our race. Jim Strang, owner of Spokes Etc. provided the support for our bike gear, repairs, and mechanic.

Thanks to the individuals who sent 500 email messages of encouragement to my crew and me, especially the families of Hopecam children including the Eastman, Green, Rocca, Condoluci, McClain, and Blake families who sent multiple messages, some each day, to encourage our team. My sister Laurie and friends Jim Long and Mark D'Amico wrote messages almost every day.

I am grateful to the 15 reviewers who generously read and commented on the draft manuscript before it became this book: Mike Bonifer, Ed Cepulis, Steve Gladis, Lori Hatcher, Bill Hudnut, Greg & Pat Jacoby, Penelope Jones, Rachelle Levitt, Dick Michaux, John Moore, Diane

Naughton, Antonio Rodriguez, Lynne Strang and Alex Tremble. Both Elizabeth Sheley and Joe Fruscione provided copy-editing support. Last but not least, I would like to express my sincere gratitude to Joanne Lozar Glenn who collaborated with me weekly to write and edit this book, distilling and crafting 150,000 words into 70,000 so eloquently.

# HOW TO READ THIS BOOK

The book is broken into two parts. Part One is an Executive Summary for the reader searching for the top ten leadership lessons that emerged throughout the journey. These lessons have been distilled and summarized in compact and memorable paragraphs. If you were moved by the stories in Part One, then Part Two has all the details laid out in a chronological format that explains where and how these lessons emerged. Part Two provides background describing what happened between the worst day of my life, when I was told my son had cancer, to one of the best days of my life when I crossed the finish line of RAAM, winning my age division and raising over $300,000 for Hopecam. Chapter One is the story of how and why Hopecam was created. Chapters Two through Fourteen give daily descriptions of the journey. The stories are true, and they lead the reader through the ups and downs of the race events, with chapter summaries highlighting what we learned each day.

# TO THE READER

To this day I have a drawing by Professor Omar Faruque on the wall of my office. I had met Omar, a tenured professor, architect and landscape architect from Bangladesh, in my second year at the College of Architecture at Ball State University.

Omar was a passionate teacher. He challenged his students to reach beyond their own ideas of their potential. He believed his responsibility, as a professor was to develop leadership traits in his students, so he always assigned team projects to see who would emerge as a leader.

Often I found myself leading a team and proudly submitting our completed work to Omar for his review. One day after I'd turned in our latest project and was exiting the classroom with the other students, Omar motioned to me to stay.

"Leo," he said (he had his own nicknames for everyone, and despite my correcting him several times, the name stuck). "Leo, is this the best work your team can do?"

We had worked hard on the project. Architectural drafting in those days involved pens, rulers, protractors, circle templates, and compasses, not laptops or CAD software. Finished drawings had to be shot on specialized cameras resembling X-ray machines so they could be sized correctly for duplication or for binding into project books.

"Leo," Omar said, his dignified, deep voice emphasizing each word, "I believe your team can do better."

Omar shared the specifics of his critique with me and I later reviewed his remarks with my team. Omar wanted us to cultivate not only our architectural skills but an aesthetic for detail. Our team regrouped and asked Omar for an extra week to work on the project. We returned with a much-improved product and the satisfaction of having been given the opportunity to prove ourselves. Rather than teach us that lesson with a poor grade, Omar led us to see that we were capable of something better. Omar's validation was an incredible motivator. When others express their confidence in you, it reinforces your own determination and drives your resisting the urge to quit. Omar's critique of the team's drawing reminds me to always do my absolute best.

Racing in RAAM served as a clear example of how a belief in yourself, coupled with the support of others who believe in you, can lead you to succeed against extreme odds. This race would test me on many levels. Visualizing the goal of crossing the finish line was made possible through the belief in my team, just as Omar believed in me—and to remember why and for whom I was riding.

I had the luxury of choosing to put my body through a physical challenge. Children fighting cancer don't have the luxury of refusing chemo or radiation. My journey was filled with highs and lows and the moments you get through only with perseverance, relying on help from family, friends, and a medical team. Even though my race didn't equal the struggle these kids go through, I hope it demonstrates my passion for easing their burden. With each mile I pedaled, with every personal encounter I made, I hoped to bring greater awareness of the realities of childhood cancer and the resources of Hopecam, which is making a difference in the lives of these brave children. I want to thank Omar for instilling in me the perseverance not to quit. But most of all, I wanted to honor the Hopecam children who were the foundation of my inspiration.

# A HERO'S JOURNEY

Len Forkas is a hero by any definition I know. But like most heroes, he didn't intend to become one. Back in 2002, he was just a father who wanted to help his nine-year-old son beat cancer.

When Len came up with the idea of putting a webcam in the class-room and one in the home, it enabled his son to connect with his classmates as he underwent treatment at home. That technological break-through also marked Len's first step on his hero's journey. Soon after, he founded Hopecam and began helping hundreds of young cancer patients overcome their loneliness and stay connected to their friends—a funda-mental need for every human being.

Like all heroes dedicated to a cause, Len pushed himself to do more and searched for a way to elevate Hopecam's mission. His answer came in the form of Race Across America (RAAM), a 3,000-mile bicycle race considered to be one of the world's most extreme endurance events. Wolfgang Fasching, a veteran climber of the seven summits of the world and a three-time winner of RAAM, put it this way: "Everest is more dangerous, but RAAM is much harder."

Len figured a challenge of this magnitude would excite donors—and generate a level of funding that would take Hopecam to another level. Yet he also knew he couldn't meet his objectives without a team. Like every leader, his job was to excite, inspire, and motivate a wide range of friends, colleagues, donors and family so they would embrace his vision.

He approached his supporters in a way that would make an NFL owner want to recruit him to coach his or her team. The intense physical training and preparation required to compete in RAAM would intimidate any Olympian, but somehow Len never questioned whether he could do it.

Things did not all go according to plan, of course. As a friend once said, "Life happens when you're planning something else." In his book, Len shares his journey's twists and turns. He teaches us—clearly and succinctly—about the ups and downs of teams, how to gain trust, honoring roles and responsibilities, the power of gratitude, mistakes and forgiveness, risk and reward, and much more.

You don't have to be a cyclist to get a lot out of *What Spins the Wheel*. Established and aspiring business leaders and athletes of all stripes will come away with many useful lessons. It's also the kind of book you'll want to give to a new high school or college graduate, or to someone who wants to embark on a hero's journey. That someone may even be you.

—Steve Gladis, Ph.D., CEO,
Steve Gladis Leadership Partners

# WHAT SPINS THE WHEEL:

## LEADERSHIP LESSONS FROM OUR RACE FOR HOPE

### BY LEN FORKAS

*The brick walls are there for a reason. The brick walls are not there to keep us out. The brick walls are there to give us a chance to show how badly we want something… the brick walls are there to stop people who don't want it badly enough.*

—*Randy Pausch,* The Last Lecture

WHAT SPINS THE WHEEL
**PART ONE**

# EXECUTIVE SUMMARY

*Ask yourself, "Can I give more?" The answer is usually "yes."*
—Paul Tergat

ANY STORY WORTH telling is always two stories: the story of what happened, and the story of what it meant. This book is a story about the worst day of my life and one of the best days of my life, and what happened in between that made it possible for me to make a difference in the lives of kids who have cancer and other life-threatening illnesses. It's the story of competing in the grueling 3,000-mile bicycle trek known as Race Across America (RAAM)—and the mission-driven purpose that allowed us to succeed. Our team not only completed the race but also finished in eleven rather than twelve days, on top of placing first in our division. In addition to all of that, we raised more than double the pledged $150,000. And we not only produced an outcome that exceeded our objective, we also realized life and leadership lessons that forever changed us.

RAAM became a metaphor for everything I have learned as a business leader and endurance athlete about building a team and completing a mission. Like many businesses that are often subject to extreme market forces, with success or failure always hanging in the balance, we were sorely tested. The race, which begins in Oceanside, California, and ends in Annapolis, Maryland, is difficult not just because of the distance you have to cover in a small amount of time. It is difficult because the course itself—it is a monster that, over its 30-year history, has destroyed more than two-thirds of the rookie racers and more than half of the veterans—seems alive and hell-bent on preventing you from reaching your goal.

You are out there in the elements. You feel every degree of temperature change. In the desert, the sun is melting you. The headwinds are making you feel like you are Sisyphus rolling a rock up the hill, only to have it roll down again and have to start all over. Then you are in the Rockies, your extremities numbed by the cold. Finally you summit the highest peak and coast into the Great Plains, only to find the Kansas crosswinds acting like ropes pulling you back and forth and sideways. You have never ridden this far in a training ride and so everything now is uncharted territory. You don't know how your body will react. Now that your day consists of 20 hours of cycling and you get most of your nutrition in liquid form, even the smallest things—naps, the RV being five minutes late, a 50-calorie chocolate treat—become magnified out of proportion. The potholed pavement is booby-trapped. You constantly scan it for small things with big consequences—pieces of broken glass, chunks of jackhammered asphalt—that could cause you to blow a tire or toss you off the bike. And you haven't even gotten to the Appalachians yet, the final push that feels harder than even the Rockies because the hills, like going 15 rounds with the boxer Mike Tyson, just keep coming at you.

All of these conditions can be thought of as metaphors for the unexpected challenges, such as the Great Recession, that surface in a business environment. When it's impossible to do "business as usual" or sometimes even at all, coping with adversity becomes a core competency. In conditions like these, true power is in the mind.

RAAM taught us that no matter what the environment throws at you, if you have a mission-driven purpose and a high-performing team, you can beat the odds and make an impact. We did, and so can you. Here's how.

## BACKGROUND

My team of eleven volunteers and I entered Race Across America (RAAM) to raise money for and awareness of childhood cancer. My son Matt had been diagnosed with leukemia in 2002, when he was nine. The diagnosis was a brick wall. We had to find a way up, over, and past it.

It was a ten-year journey. On that cold January night when we first walked across the skybridge that connected the parking deck to the hospital that would become Matt's home during initial treatment, we felt the doors of our old life closing behind us. I didn't know what lay ahead, only that Matt was slipping away, having been stripped of the things that mattered to him the most: his friends, his school life, his normal routine.

When Matt got sick, we received many offers of help from friends and family. The best advice was the simplest: Find a way to help Matt feel like a normal kid while he underwent treatment. But how? It took me a while to come up with something, but when it occurred to me, the solution was as simple as the advice. Through mining my experience as the president of a wireless company, I realized we could connect Matt to his classroom and to his friends using a webcam and computer. We had to overcome some physical and school policy challenges—this was 2002, and virtual communication was not as common or as easy as it is today—but the results were fantastic.

It worked so well that I felt compelled to help other children who were fighting cancer. So I founded a charity, called it Hopecam, and entered endurance races to raise funds from friends for the webcams and laptops we would need. I'd built my athletic skills by doing exercise to cope with the stress of Matt's illness. Now I could use those skills to reach a meaningful goal.

Nine years later, by September 2011, I had successfully completed two RAAM-qualifying bicycle races. Several friends who were also endurance athletes encouraged me to give RAAM a try. Realizing that Hopecam was plateauing as a nonprofit, and that the national exposure from RAAM would help us raise awareness and financial resources to help more children, I decided to do it. That fall, I began building my team.

# LESSON 1. YOUR TEAM WILL MAKE OR BREAK YOU.

Competing in RAAM required the same amount of careful preparation that it takes to prepare for a major expedition or a new business venture. Without the right people who possess the right skills, an athlete simply will not finish.

To find what kind of people and skills were needed, I sought out and interviewed previous RAAM finishers, crew members, and race officials. All of them said the same surprising thing: The most important success factor was not training, equipment, or strategy. It was The Team. The RAAM veterans advised me to choose team members carefully. By nature, they said, your crew will be skeptical about you. You have to constantly prove yourself to them, and it will take longer to gain commitment to your objective until you've passed their test.

Based on that advice, I started building my team with people I'd known very well—longtime friends from my hometown of Cleveland, Ohio, and athlete friends I met through my exercise and endurance racing activities in Reston, Virginia, where I live. Former Marine and former Clevelander John Moore agreed to be crew chief. John has a chill vibe; he's less emotional than I am and a good listener. He would not only be the calm head in what would be a sometimes tedious 15-mph cross-country caravan, but his organizational skills would also shine as he meticulously sought out historical data from RAAM and put together logistics, timetables, and schedules for everything needed to successfully compete, such as calling in arrivals at time stations, checking race statistics, and developing nutrition and work schedules.

We decided to recruit three crews of three persons each, who would take turns working eight-hour shifts. One crew would work in the "advance van" that would ride ahead of me, booking hotel rooms for overnight rest breaks and running any necessary errands. One crew would work in the "follow van" that rode behind me. The follow van would hold supplies such as nutrition, a backup bike, spare bike parts, and all weather gear. One crew would rest while the other two worked, and then the crews would rotate. Most of our team would be generalists—people who could serve interchangeably as drivers, navigators, and go-fers. To fill the specialist positions (nutritionist, paramedic, bike mechanic, massage therapist, videographer), I relied on my friends' recommendations.

For a generalist or specialist, my criteria were a positive attitude, selflessness, and skills—in that order. Positivity came first because, as brain science is beginning to show, positivity creates what University of California professor Sonja Lyubomirsky called the "happiness advantage." The cliché of "work hard so you can succeed so you can be happy" has it backwards, Lyubomirsky pointed out in her best-selling book, *The How of Happiness* (Penguin, 2008). Instead, she says, positivity leads to happiness, which then leads to better performance.

John and I involved the generalists in the decision-making, recruiting, talking, and meeting with each of the specialists we interviewed. Each team member shared his or her thoughts about whether the proposed specialist would be a good fit, and we collaborated on the decision about whether to invite each person to join the team. Chemistry was everything. Chemistry was a core value. With each new team member we added, the foundational dynamic would change. We needed to ensure that each team member contributed positively to that dynamic, and that our values were in sync. So as we grew, I wanted buy-in from the group. I also knew that using referrals from trusted friends would create more than just buy-in: it would create a layer of accountability. The new recruit is accountable to the friend who recommended him or her.

My intuition about team chemistry and belief in attitude first, skills second, has always served me well in business, and it was critical in succeeding at RAAM. When you put positive, selfless people in a group, their selflessness allows them to bond; that bond creates a team that cares for each other like family. And if you have the right people, you never have to worry about motivating them. They motivate themselves.

## Lesson 2. Trust your team.

My team's selfless commitment to the Hopecam mission helped meld the shared sense of purpose that leads to high performance. But that was only the beginning. We had to use that commitment to figure out how to get a group of individual volunteers to work as a team.

From January 2012 to May 2012, we participated in RAAM trainings and practice rides on different sections of the racecourse across the country. I'd pick a training or practice event and ask specific crew members to meet me there. These trainings and practice rides were instrumental in familiarizing team members with their roles and with each other, and all of us with the race course and regulations.

We also participated in team-building exercises to help the get-to-know-you process along. For example, at the home of our hosts in California the night before the race, June 12, 2012, we drew pictures with crayons depicting the neighborhoods where we'd grown up. Sharing personal stories helps create the bonds that lead to trust.

As with any team, establishing trust happened over time. In the beginning, despite the schedules our crew chief John had labored over, things did not always go smoothly. Early in the race, for example, we had some issues managing the nutrition schedule and keeping the van organized. Nutrition was one of the key elements that previous RAAM finishers had said was crucial. It became clear that parts of the race plan needed revising. Our nutritionists explained to John that it would be better to allow them to work double shifts and take complete responsibility for the nutrition, even though they would be sleeping significantly less than all the other crewmembers and spending twelve or more hours a day stuffed into the back seat of the follow van.

John listened thoughtfully to the critical feedback from the team members, considered all the risks, and then made the difficult decision to throw out his well-detailed plan on how to run the operation. During the race, when different job responsibilities needed tending, John was also able to mold his message to each group or individual so that she or he would take ownership of the job. When team members take ownership of their work, worries about potential problems melt away.

What John did was to allow space for the three characteristics that, according to Dan Pink's book *Drive: The Surprising Truth About What Motivates Us*, are essential in every work environment to empower team members to do their best: autonomy, mastery, and purpose. The nutritionists were given the autonomy to do what they knew best when it came to managing my nutrition. They were masters of their trade, and they had proven themselves even before being asked to join the team, long before we left the starting line in Oceanside.

By encouraging autonomy, leaders empower their teams and build a two-way street for trust. When roles are honored in this way, mastery and dedication to purpose follow.

## LESSON 3. GRATITUDE ELEVATES PERFORMANCE.

It's important not only to honor team roles, but also to elevate those roles by expressing gratitude for what the performance of them makes possible. I learned this when I was trying to figure out how to approach team member Kaitee DeMonti about performing her job as massage therapist.

One morning, early in the race, I woke up with a stiff neck and swollen knees. This surprised me, because I was getting a massage each night after dinner, and it had always prevented any residual muscle problems. I questioned whether Kaitee was performing to her full potential. Massage is incredibly important to helping the body recover from the abuse of the race, and if she didn't step up her commitment to that role, we wouldn't be able to reach the finish line.

My initial thought was to reprimand her. My second instinct was to complain to John, our crew chief, about her performance, but that would be passing the buck. Luckily, while I was on the bike, another idea came to me.

Realizing that Kaitee would likely respond to positive reinforcement, I knew I had to elevate the status of her job. She was one of the specialists on the team, and the specialists were what John called the "difference makers." Was it possible Kaitee didn't fully understand the importance or value of her job in the grand scheme of things?

Validation—and heightened status—improves performance. To help Kaitee take ownership of her job, we had to help her visualize the positive outcome of her work. So that night, when I was eating my dinner just before she started, I asked Kaitee to sit on the chair beside me.

"Sure," she said. I waited to say more until she got situated and could look at me.

"I won't make it to the finish line without you," I told her. "I know it's hard to work on me in the middle of the night, when most of our crew is asleep. I'm asleep minutes after you start working. I have no idea what you're doing but all I know is that when I wake up I feel like I'm ready to start the day. What you do is so important. When we cross the finish in Annapolis one of the reasons will be because of what you're doing at night when no one is watching. You're doing a great job, Kaitee. Thanks for being part of our team and keep it up."

I never suffered a stiff neck again, and this interaction turned out to be a huge motivator for Kaitee, as I learned when I followed up with her about a year after the race to see how she was doing and get her thoughts about her RAAM experience.

"It solidified what I wanted to do," she told me. "I knew I always wanted to be in the field. Being able to experience and help someone achieve goals in that way, you looking at me and telling me I'm the reason you were able to make it to the finish line, made a huge difference. I want to work with athletes and say 'I did this. I helped that athlete win.' It changed me."

## LESSON 4. KNOW YOUR LIMITS. RESPECT THE EDGE.

Some of the most important moments of the race happened in the Rocky Mountains. The Rockies were not hard because of the climbs; they were hard because of the descents. Whenever I crested a hill, the lack of oxygen at high altitudes caused me to become drowsy.

One time, I drifted off while coasting downhill, heading straight for the edge of the mountain on my descent into Durango, Colorado. That afternoon, on the way to Pagosa Springs, I was worried that it would happen again. It didn't, but something just as frightening did. On a steep descent, hitting speeds in excess of 35 mph, my bike started shimmying as if a great hand had grabbed it with the sheer intention of shaking me loose from the bike and sending me to my death. Thankfully I regained control and made it safely down the hill, but we decided to retire that bike from the race and use the backup instead.

Those two harrowing events happened within hours of each other. Ahead was Wolf Creek Pass, at the Continental Divide and the highest point in the entire race course. It was already nightfall. It was freezing. The next rest stop was on the other side of the mountain, which we wouldn't reach until two in the morning. Most people would have stopped and taken Wolf Creek the next day. But I wanted to get Wolf Creek behind me.

The tension was incredible. Many team members were vehemently against the descent because of the obvious danger. I hadn't realized how much I'd depleted my reserves. My crew were biting their fingernails worrying whether I'd fall asleep on the bike and crash. I was mentally spent, fighting to keep my eyes open, and chilled to the bone. Even my three layers of clothes couldn't keep me warm. My hands were sore from constantly braking down the hill. We were lucky in the Rockies, or maybe we were blessed to have come through these harrowing events alive. When we reached the hotel, though, my knees were so swollen I could barely walk.

The entire race, but especially in the Rockies, felt like a regular tug-of-war between risk and reward. Some days we wanted to wake up and chase down other racers. Some days our goal was "Don't screw it up." It was much riskier to compromise our goal of finishing by going too fast and chancing a crash or other injury. None of our sponsors and supporters would criticize our team for coming in last, as long as we finished.

So we were always facing the question of knowing when to stop and when to take a risk and push on. On the one hand, there was the desire to persevere. Without perseverance, obstacles will crush you. On the other hand, there's the importance of respecting the fundamentals: to ride slow and steady, take regular breaks, and focus on your overarching goal. When you ignore the fundamentals and persist without respect for your limits, your poor choices impact your ability to achieve your goal.

The question of how to balance risk and reward is a prime question for athletes and for businesses. Here's what we learned: Our good fortune could have limits.

## LESSON 5. HONOR ROLES BY DELEGATING FEARLESSLY.

Without delegating, it's impossible for a leader to move to higher-level tasks. I could not have focused on racing my bicycle, for example, if I had to worry about implementing my own nutrition schedule, checking race statistics, verifying regulations, calling in arrivals at time stations or handling bike repairs. We deliberately chose specialists to whom we could delegate the responsibility for expertise we needed but could not provide ourselves.

The beauty of delegating is that it helps teams realize their own potential. Teams function at their best when leaders learn to suppress their power of authority, delegate fearlessly, and then honor the team members' roles. We had multiple opportunities to learn and relearn this lesson during RAAM.

One of the more memorable opportunities involved my nutrition team. We'd straightened out the nutrition schedule, and I was subsisting on a carefully calibrated, mostly liquid, 350-calories-per-hour nutrition plan. I was allowed one 50-calorie treat each hour of anything I wanted. One day, however, when I was bored from riding the windy, flat, endless landscape of the Great Plains, I craved a piece of chocolate even though I'd already eaten the one I was allowed that hour. The wind had been unrelenting. I was cranky, hot and bored. I was tired, but didn't want to take my usual five-minute rest nap to recharge. I challenged Ken, nutritionist and paramedic, to let me have another piece of chocolate.

Ken refused. He knew it would harm my performance. He stood up to me, telling me with courage and without fear of retribution what I needed to know without patronizing me.

It would have been easy for Ken to cave, to give me what I wanted "just this once." But he knew it would have led to other deviations from the plan. In his book *How Will You Measure Your Life?* author Clay Christensen talks about those moments when you are tempted to stray far from your plan because you've lost sight of the big picture. Ken saw the big picture and said, "No." His refusal to give me what I wanted challenged me to stick with my values of not second-guessing him or using my power to override him. Taking back that task by being critical or second-guessing my nutritionists for doing the job we had asked of them would have been devastating.

Honoring my team's contribution was not easy. I wanted that chocolate. The fatigue of racing had reduced me to acting like a toddler. But to be a good leader you have to acquiesce, especially when it's hard. Letting go and trusting your team to do their jobs is truly the only way to empower them. They can't truly "own" their jobs without this kind of empowerment.

But just because you are honoring roles and not second-guessing your team members' decisions does not mean that everything will always go smoothly. It also means accepting the risk of failure. For example, when my bike needed a critical repair during a planned sleep break, my bike mechanic had to execute a complicated and risky task within an impossibly short time frame. That operation could have had dire consequences, but Wayne had always demonstrated competence and single-minded dedication to performing his job. I had to trust him; my trust was amply repaid.

If you've selected your team members well, their assigned roles become part of the team identity. Then, when individual team members truly own the tasks that leaders have delegated, and leaders honor the team members' roles, the overall chances for successfully achieving an identified goal are substantially increased.

## Lesson 6. Mistakes will happen. Forgive and move on.

RAAM, like everything else in sports and life and work, is a rolling series of mistakes. During the race, for example, we often got lost and took wrong turns. Or I'd ask for something and not get it. Or the crew would make communication errors and then have to fix what went wrong.

Mistakes are normal. We are all human. Mistakes are part of life. What's important is what you do after making the mistake. You correct the error, you learn from it so it doesn't happen again, and you learn to forgive the mistakes so your team can continue to move forward to accomplish its mission.

When we missed turns, I had to promise myself not to get angry with my crew for making a navigational mistake. They felt bad enough for making what was a very human error. The good news was that we could put the bike on top of the van, drive me back to where we'd gotten lost, and start all over again.

When I lost my temper asking for what I needed—for example, a can of V8 juice that would provide some relief from my usual drink of powder mixed with water yet never appeared even after three requests— my crew had to forgive me for using foul language to make that request, an action I later regretted and apologized for. The team got the message and moved on. They were able to forgive me without harboring any ill will, and I vowed not to use that tactic again.

Then when the crew actually did take charge of getting me the V8, driving a team member to the nearest convenience store so he could purchase the drink and then mistakenly driving off without him, they not only had to acknowledge their own mistakes but also forgive each other. The team member ended up waiting at the store several hours for the crew to return and pick him up. The crew apologized, and the team member accepted their apology with grace and good humor.

"The focus was on you getting across the finish line," driver and navigator Ed Cepulis told me later. "We brushed off mistakes that didn't impact you and worked together to address the ones that did or could have. We wanted the race to be fun, but we kept the end goal in mind."

As Ed realized, it's important to have a positive attitude and recognize mistakes, but not get thrown by them. When you're "in it for the long haul," mistakes are inevitable. That's your opportunity to regroup. Good teams hold each other accountable, learn from their mistakes, forgive each other when they screw up, and move on without harboring any resentment. They don't point fingers of blame.

One of my closest friends, Kevin Reynolds, who is president of Virginia-based Cardinal Bank, uses a phrase that perfectly describes this approach: "Look forward, go forward."

## LESSON 7. POWER IS IN THE MIND AND THE BODY.

The willpower not to give up was most evident on the tenth day of the race. We were in the Appalachian Mountains. My team's nutrition strategy was beginning to show weakness. In addition, sleep deprivation was beginning to affect our entire crew. The mental fatigue of crossing the Appalachian Mountains is the final fatal punch that the race course has to offer as it attempts to demolish the racers. The cumulative effects of the desert heat, the thin air and high altitude of the Rockies, the crosswinds and the searing heat in the Plains, and now the steep Appalachians, were setting us up for a knockout round.

Here's what it's like: Your body is screaming at you to stop the sufferfest. Every muscle, every joint, everything in you wants off the bike. Motivation and willpower are the only things that keep you going. You have to want your goal more than anything else in the world. So you learn to persevere by hunkering down, cope by compartmentalizing anything—pain, fatigue—*anything* that interferes with reaching that goal. You tell yourself the winds will change, that every day is a new day.

In conditions like these, two things helped us through:

*Accountability.* Having made so many promises to so many children, donors, and crew members that we would finish the race, we used the power of "third-party accountability" to create self-induced fear, making the price of quitting so high that it would be unbearable to experience. That, in essence, is why giving up was so impossible to imagine.

*Grit.* Having the mental perseverance to compartmentalize and isolate pain. It helped motivate me to ignore what my body was telling me, which of course was "PLEASE STOP."

Because in the end it's not what is left in your legs or in your lungs but what is in your mind that gets you over that brick wall to where you want to go. Most athletes give up mentally well before their bodies have reached their physical limits.

Willpower comes naturally to many, but it also can be acquired through practice. The willpower and mental toughness that come from thousands of hours of physical exercise are subconsciously training both mind and body. You must believe in yourself and trust that you will make it through adversity. We did what Churchill long ago advised: "If you're going through Hell, keep going."

## LESSON 8. SEE IN OTHERS WHAT THEY CAN'T SEE IN THEMSELVES.

I learned this lesson on the final day of the race, when my crew chief John, knowing that my mind was even stronger than my 52-year-old body, dared me to chase down 34-year-old Stefan Schlegel, an accomplished endurance athlete who over a stretch of 50 miles had challenged me for the tenth-place position.

At the end of the race, I was riding on fumes and visualizing an ice-cold beer at the finish line. Then my tire flattened out. We pulled into a parking lot to fix it, where we encountered a dozen friends from work cheering loudly and chalking inspiring messages on the pavement. I began to shake hands and exchange hugs with the dozen or so supporters, but John quickly warned me to get back on the bike. Schlegel was gaining ground. Within a few miles, Schlegel passed me.

John and I are fellow athletes. We have respect for each other borne of having pushed each other to achieve difficult athletic goals. We each knew what it took to run a long race. I had often challenged him to do things he didn't think he could do, and vice versa.

John challenged me to overtake Schlegel. John could see in me what I couldn't see in myself—that as tired and depleted as I was, I could still challenge this younger athlete who passed me in a white blur of speed. So I pushed hard, sped up, and pursued him.

Then he passed me again. Again I pushed, caught up, and left him behind. If I hadn't been so exhausted, it would have been hilarious. Three times Schlegel gained on me, and three times I stayed focused on John's challenge to give my legs the strength to push forward. John believed in me. He knew exactly what to say to light a fire. This was a defining moment. How often have we watched a younger or less experienced competitor jump ahead of us in business? What we do at that juncture defines us. As a result, I was able to perform at my highest level ever, surprising Schlegel—and myself. I put so much torque on the bike I thought the frame might crack. But it held together, and I crossed the finish line ahead of Schlegel.

The final push to any goal can feel harder than everything else that led up to that point. That's when the faith others have in us can create a turning point. By seeing in others what they can't see in themselves, we can inspire people to achieve more than they ever thought possible. That's what John, my team, and all our supporters did for me. Because John saw something in me that my fatigue wasn't letting me see, I did what I'd never done before: surpass my physical limits and push through.

## LESSON 9. NOTHING BEATS A MISSION-DRIVEN PURPOSE.

When we started the race on June 13th we had one objective: to finish the race in the time allowed and bring in the $150,000 our sponsors had pledged to donate. We were not there to compete with the other athletes. We had one goal: finish. We were Team Hopecam. We were not about the personal glory. We just wanted to survive. We didn't want to take unnecessary risks or do anything stupid to jeopardize our objective.

To keep the mission "real," we honored the important role of connection. This was what Hopecam is all about—connecting children to life. We honored that by dedicating each day of the race to a Hopecam child and calling the child that day. Our phone calls let the Hopecam children know that they were remembered, and that we were, in a sense, taking them with us on the ride. All of us were deeply moved by the 500 stories that came to us by email from supporters every day, stories of the children whose lives Hopecam helped change. This shared sense of purpose—making life better for kids with cancer—galvanized our team.

We had understood from the start that we might need to "educate" people we met along the way. We set those wheels in motion by letting people know we were "Team Hopecam." We'd wrapped our van with our logo, set up media interviews in advance, and installed a GPS locator so people could follow our progress. We also took the time to talk with people on the course so they could get to know us and what we were about, even though we were in a race and had a goal to achieve.

Having a strong, well-stated mission—and a touchstone that keeps it "real"—fuels the willpower needed to fulfill a mission. We overcame all the challenges that the course threw at us and stayed focused on a mission-driven task that everyone believed in. All of this motivation to succeed was internal, proving once again what business analyst and writer Dan Pink says science has known for more than forty years and what business consistently ignores—that intrinsic motivation trumps extrinsic rewards.

"There's a mismatch between what science knows and what business does," Pink said in his TED Talk on "The Puzzle of Motivation." (July 2009). Contingent motivators (for example, monetary rewards for achieving a sales goal) don't work for carrying out the non-mechanical tasks that characterize 21$^{st}$-century business, and in fact might even do harm. In his talk, Pink quoted research by the Federal Reserve Bank of the United States that showed the higher the monetary reward, the poorer the performance.

Intrinsic motivation, or doing things that matter, is what leads to employee engagement. And intrinsic motivation comes from having that sense of autonomy, mastery, and purpose that Pink described in his book, *Drive.* When we have the sense of being involved in something larger than ourselves, productivity, engagement, and satisfaction go up, and turnover goes down.

How often do we run into rough patches at work that make us feel as though the pain and the distance ahead will never end? If we can create a mission-driven purpose that our teams can commit to and support, the desire to perform at a high level will become contagious and we will be able to accomplish any mission and surmount any challenge.

## LESSON 10. HIGH-PERFORMING TEAMS CREATE OUTCOMES THAT EXCEED OBJECTIVES.

RAAM tested my team and me. It pushed us beyond any previous capacities we had experienced in years of endurance sports. Yet the outcomes we realized were much greater than the objective we initially set.

Instead of just finishing the race, our team came in first in our age division, and tenth overall in a field of 47 competitors from 20 countries. Instead of finishing RAAM within the twelve-day time period, we finished in eleven days and four hours. Instead of raising the promised $150,000, we raised more than $300,000. On the last day of the race, one donor unexpectedly doubled what we had originally raised and wrote us a $150,000 check. "I give my money to a lot of charities without ever knowing how well they put their resources to work," he said. "If you run this charity half as well as your team supported you in competing in that race, I'll know I have made a good investment."

RAAM became not only the ground for observing leadership lessons in action but also a capstone experience for integrating a way to "give back to others" into an already full and busy life. Even though our team is now scattered to the winds, as is common in events like these, we retain the memory and the camaraderie of a team that was not only trustworthy and high-performing but also came to care about each other like a huge, extended family that included all the Hopecam children and their "villages" of supporters.

In the process, we were changed. Our crew chief said it reaffirmed his confidence as a leader. Our bike mechanic Wayne changed his originally skeptical perspective about racers who compete for charities and became a true ambassador for our mission, patiently explaining to irate motorists who sometimes got caught in traffic snarls behind our van "why we are following the guy in the orange and white spandex outfit." Our massage therapist Kaitee is now focusing her career on working with athletes. Our driver and navigator Ed said the race really showed him what he could achieve with determination, planning, and preparation. "If I'm better prepared I can have a better impact, whether in my personal or business life," he said. "I can always do more."

When we entered RAAM in June 2012, Hopecam was helping thirty children connect to over 800 friends at school annually, in the mid-Atlantic region. We ended 2013, the year after the race, doubling the number of connections. Fifty-five school districts in more than a dozen states and three countries have implemented the Hopecam program. When we started in 2002, our first connections took 10 weeks; now they take 10 days. Today, six thousand children in over 300 classrooms have empathy and understanding about childhood cancer. We often use the phrase *"Where the rubber meets the road"* to describe a particular situation. I believe that it's a perfect metaphor for what Hopecam is all about. We are not attempting to fund research to find a cure for cancer. We are attempting to relieve the suffering of one child at a time by combating the lonely isolation of homebound treatment.

## WHAT SPINS THE WHEEL.

One of the most frequent questions my team and I were asked to explain during RAAM was this: How, as a rookie team, were we able to do so well?

Think for a moment about a bicycle wheel. The spokes add strength to the wheel and when properly aligned, allow the wheel to "spin true"—i.e., with perfect balance. Now think of that wheel as a metaphor for the qualities that contributed to our rookie team's success: the role of chemistry and trust in team selection, training, and performance; the need to balance perseverance with a healthy respect for physical limits; and the importance of accountability, gratitude, forgiveness, and purpose to achieving more than what most people considered possible, let alone realistic. "Truing" a wheel to achieve perfect balance is an art and a science, and the same can be said about selecting and training a mission-driven, successful, high-performing team—then getting out of the way so the team can do its job.

In the 31 years since RAAM began, less than 300 solo riders have actually completed the race. As one of them, I couldn't have done it without my team. The members of my crew volunteered weeks of time away from their families during the planning, training, preparation, and execution of the race. Their effort and energy were extraordinary, and you will find their names throughout the book. Diana Nyad, who at 64 became the first person to swim solo without a cage from Cuba to Florida, said three things when she reached the shore: (1) Never ever give up; (2) You are never too old to achieve your dreams; and (3) It looks like a solitary sport, but it's a team effort. No one takes on a challenge solo, whether it's racing across the country or fighting cancer. Children who connect with Hopecam will tell you the most important part of seeing their friends on the webcam is the simple reminder that they have not been forgotten, and they are not alone. The lesson I learned from RAAM is that no one races alone.

WHAT SPINS THE WHEEL
# PART TWO

# CHAPTER 1

# SKYBRIDGE

*Matt, Elizabeth, Viena and Len Forkas,*
*December 2001*

*The ultimate measure of a man is not where he stands in moments of comfort and convenience, but where he stands at times of challenge and controversy.*

—Martin Luther King, Jr.

MY KIDS MATT and Viena were at school and I was settling into another ordinary January day at my office in the Northern Virginia suburb of Reston, just outside Washington, DC, where I own a wireless tower company. Matt was in fourth grade and loved the Power Rangers, his Game Boy, and playing basketball. He was a deadly three-point shooter. Viena was four and had made friends with her entire preschool class before the end of her first week. My wife, Elizabeth, was a full-time mom who kept everything in our household running smoothly.

We had just returned from a two-week vacation visiting family. This morning I was preparing for a few meetings, returning a few emails, and getting ready for an important interview with the selection committee for one of my volunteer commitments. After being gone for two weeks, work had piled up and I was digging out. We all know the feeling of catching up after a long trip away from work. My brain felt like a diesel engine on a cold day. It needed to warm up slowly before hitting the road. Easing back into work after time away with family and friends is not an easy task. Thankfully, I have a great team at work that kept everything moving during my absence. It felt good to be back.

Then the phone rang. It was Matt's pediatrician.

"Mr. Forkas, I'd like for you, Elizabeth, and Matt to come in to my office," the doctor said.

At first it felt strange to hear the doctor's voice on the phone. Doctors never call; it's always the staff. What was so important that we had to come to his office? Why couldn't he say what he had to say over the phone?

"Can it wait until after school?" I asked. "Matt's missed dozens of school days this year and I really don't want to pull him out of class one more time."

Matt had been sick a lot over the past six months. He'd been diagnosed with so many things: severe colds, then bronchitis, then Pertussis, even though he'd gotten the whooping cough vaccine as an infant. The previous December, Matt had begun to have headaches, and in January, his normally fair complexion began looking sallow. We were baffled. That morning, Elizabeth had taken Matt in for a quick blood test before dropping him off at school.

"No," the doctor said. "We need to see you right now."

I called Elizabeth and we agreed to meet at the pediatrician's office within the hour, after she picked Matt up at school.

When Elizabeth, Matt, and I arrived at the entrance, we had to decide which door to go in—the "well" door, on the right, where non-contagious children may enter, or the "sick" door, on the left. Our pediatrician had divided the lobby into two waiting rooms. Which fit our situation? We had no idea. Which door would you go through? Once we signed in the staff quickly escorted us to one of the exam rooms, where a nurse checked Matt's vitals and we waited for the doctor to arrive. Strange—the staff in the office were making more-than-normal eye contact with Matt. These were people we saw all the time for routine visits. Why were they giving us so much attention? Was it his "yellow" color? What did they know that we didn't? It felt awkward.

To make matters worse, after the doctor arrived in the examining room and greeted us, he asked Matt if he'd be okay waiting in the lobby while he spoke with us privately in his office.

"No problem," Matt said, then pulled out his Nintendo Game Boy and left while we walked into the doctor's office. The doctor closed the door behind us.

He looked down at the piece of paper in his hand. "We got the results of blood work from this morning," he said, "and Matt's white cell counts are abnormally high."

"What does that mean?" Elizabeth asked.

"A normal white cell count is 5,000. Matt's is 40,000. I believe Matt has leukemia."

I had no idea what to say. Nothing—nothing—prepares you for that kind of news. Elizabeth's face changed color and her body began to collapse, as if she was going to pass out. I reached to steady her.

*What had the doctor just said? How was that possible? Why Matt? There must be some mistake.* I was numb.

"I'm sorry," the doctor said.

"No!" Elizabeth said over and over again. She was sobbing. "No, No, No." I could feel her go limp so I pulled her closer and held her tighter, so she wouldn't fall. I could feel the warmth of her tears on my neck, as she regained her balance, steadying herself.

Matt's doctor said he'd consulted with a Dr. Greenberg, an oncologist he trusted. "We have a very good specialist in Fairfax, and we have already contacted his office," the doctor said. "We recommend you go there right now and they can speak more about what the next steps are. I'm very sorry."

Next steps. That's what we needed to focus on. We walked out the door to where Matt was waiting for us to take him back to school. But we wouldn't be going to school. At that moment, it felt like I had to suit up in a coat of mental armor to be strong for Elizabeth and Matt, because Matt was being condemned to a sentence that he didn't deserve. This wasn't like a scraped knee or a bad report card, trouble that was easily fixed. It was the most helpless feeling I could imagine. All I could think about was how far gone was he? What blood count is the right number for a cure?

So we did what we were supposed to do. We dried our tears and collected Matt from the waiting room. It felt like we were slowly spiraling into another world, a world where everything important and familiar faded into the background, and day-to-day worries and concerns seemed incredibly trivial. In their place, lots of unanswered questions and not knowing what would happen next beyond taking Matt to the pediatric oncology office for more tests.

How would I explain this to Matt and not make him fall apart?

"Hey Matt," I began, "we have to see another doctor for a closer look and figure out what's exactly happening with all these symptoms you've been having."

Matt was used to going to doctors' offices, so he just played his video game while we drove to the oncologist's office.

The oncologist showed us slides of Matt's blood cells. I don't remember the exact details of what he said, only that I needed to explain it to Matt myself. The oncologist left the room and gave us a moment.

"Matt, we have some bad news," I said. "This thing that's been making you sick is a cancer called leukemia and it will take some time to fight it," I said. Elizabeth was trying hard not to cry.

"What does that mean?" Matt said. "Do I have to stay home from school?" When he'd been diagnosed with Pertussis, he'd had to be quarantined for fear of infecting anyone until the antibiotics kicked in.

"No, it means we have to go home and get your jammies, like the doctor told your mom and me, so you can be in the hospital where they can figure out what to do next."

We drove home to gather Matt's belongings, stuffed them into a backpack, and then grabbed his favorite pillow so he'd have it when he was admitted to Inova Fairfax Hospital for a long stay. Matt also grabbed the handmade white quilt my mother had made for him with all the Mother Goose nursery tale characters sewn in. We traveled south on the Capital Beltway toward the hospital in the dark rush-hour traffic.

It was seven in the evening, just five hours after doctor's call, when we pulled our car into the hospital's parking garage. There were plenty of parking spaces. I guess few people check in at the end of the day. The winter wind blew through the dark gray concrete parking garage across from the hospital's pediatric unit. We rode the elevator up one level to the glass and steel skybridge connecting the garage to the hospital. The January cold had frosted the outside of the glass, though from that height we could see people driving up to drop off and pick up patients under the covered walkway. Most were new mothers leaving with babies wrapped up tight against the cold as they stepped out of their wheelchairs into the warm cars for a welcoming home celebration.

*Inova Children's Hospital Skybridge*

We walked through the small and narrow skybridge, then through the above-ground tunnel toward the steel doors of the hospital. With each step I felt our comfortable cancer-free world fading away and an unfamiliar universe of dangerous uncertainty looming ever closer. I kept reliving the conversation in the doctor's office, gradually realizing how all Matt's illnesses over the past year finally made sense, how they now fit together

What Spins the Wheel | 25

into a puzzle called leukemia, each thought clicking into place in slow motion, like how time slows down in the aftermath of a car accident.

As we walked I noticed Matt clutching a small two-inch statue of St. Matthew that my mother had given him for his First Holy Communion just two years before.

"Dad, am I going to die?"

That's a question no parent should ever have to answer. And that's when it all hit me, like a sledgehammer to my chest, and instead of being allowed to collapse under its force, I had to keep taking the blows.

"Not if I have anything to do with it, Matt." I pulled an answer from whatever place hope and faith live in the face of a threat. "Matt, most kids come through this and you're going to be one of those kids. Your mom and I will be with you the whole time."

The hospital doors opened as we approached, then slowly closed behind us as we walked into its labyrinth.

And so we entered the landscape of chronic illness, where everything is in the moment and everything you worried about before—returning emails and phone messages, meeting your next deadline, scheduling meetings—melts away. This was going to be a long road to travel. I didn't know it then, but Matt's question would launch me on a ten-year journey that would push me beyond physical and mental boundaries that I could barely imagine.

*

The first ten nights, I slept in the hospital chair next to Matt's bed, taking breaks in the morning when Elizabeth would arrive after taking our daughter Viena to preschool. We were consumed with the medical procedures, treatments, and doing what we could do for Matt. We called the parents of his friends and asked if they would allow their kids to come in and visit, to keep Matt entertained and help take his mind off the hospital drudgery.

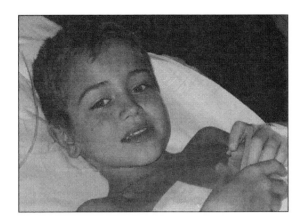

*Matt's first day at Inova Hospital*

Once the doctors settled on a medical protocol of chemotherapy, Matt's treatment sessions would be in two phases. The first, called "consolidation," would last a little over six months. Leukemia is a cancer of the blood, so the cancer cells had to be killed systemically. The doctors implanted a port in Matt's chest so chemotherapy medication could be injected directly into his main artery. We became experts at the purposes, dosage, and side effects of each medication, such as methotrexate, vincristine, and prednisone. Childhood leukemia has a 15% chance of developing in the brain, and Matt would also receive injections directly into his spinal column with a 3-inch needle, sending the cancer cell–killing medicine directly to the brain through the spinal fluid. There is no other way to get medicine into the brain because of an internal firewall, the blood–brain barrier, which prevents harmful and potent medicine like the injections Matt was getting from traveling to the brain when injected anywhere else in the body. In the second phase of treatment, Matt would undergo long–term chemotherapy.

Knowing the protocol, though, doesn't really describe what it means to go through it.

Matt would be homebound while the doctors lowered his immune system to allow for the medication to work. This meant that Matt would not be returning to his fourth-grade classmates. His treatment required that he be tutored at home, and he was very afraid of getting academically behind his classmates.

Not only would Matt be isolated, but the medicines would also have profound physical and emotional effects. Matt's face took on a moon-faced puffiness from the steroids. The week after the prednisone treatment, Matt ate voraciously to curb the intense hunger the steroids caused. The methotrexate injections also gave Matt mouth sores and made him stiff, sore, jittery, and anxious. His behavior became unpredictable. Once he climbed out the window of his second-floor bedroom onto the roof because he felt claustrophobic. Many times Elizabeth and I took Matt for drives in the middle of the night to help him relax and take his mind off the chaos that the chemotherapy medicine created in his mind. Then there was the stoic game face he wore when he had to undergo bone marrow extractions, the feeling of needles inside the cheeks of his mouth as a result of the cold sores induced by the chemotherapy, the strands of hair on his pillow as the treatment slowly made him bald.

When things like this happen to a family, everyone who knows your situation calls you and says the same thing: "If there's anything we can do, let us know." They mean well, and yet it strikes you as so repetitive. And it changes nothing. I don't mean to sound ungrateful, but after a few weeks, when the shock of his diagnosis settled in and our network of friends and supporters settled into their normal lives, the calls stopped coming. Anyone who goes through an experience like ours feels this. Many times the most important time to offer to help is months after the shock, when families are struggling to adapt to the new normal.

Matt soon became lonely and depressed. His friends played Saturday basketball games, attended sleepovers, and went to the movies without him. He felt forgotten by many of the most important people in his life: his friends at school. At the one time in his life when he needed his friends the most, he couldn't be with them.

It killed us to see Matt suffer. As a parent, I wanted to do anything I could to help my son. One day I received an email from the father of a business partner who was a professor at George Mason University, saying the same thing everyone else had said: *If there's anything I can do....*

This time I wrote him back. *Yes, there is something you can do,* I wrote. *I know what my son needs medically. What else does he need the most?*

He agreed to research the matter and get back to me within the week. When he called back he said, "I've spoken with the department chairs in psychology, education, health and human services, and social science, and they all said the same thing. He needs his friends, and he needs to feel normal."

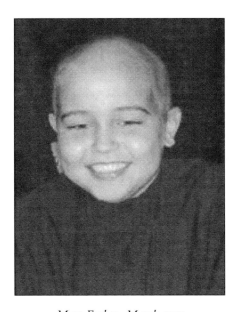

*Matt Forkas, March 2002*

It was that simple? Yes.

So I thought, *OK, friends at school, friends to visit...I run a wireless telecommunications company, I should be able to solve this communication problem. Maybe we can do it with a webcam.*

I was inspired. We could connect Matt to his classroom by live web video camera!

It was a simple idea, but a difficult task. Skype hadn't been invented yet. Video conferences for businesses were just emerging, but they involved cumbersome technology and expensive equipment. In 2002, no one had yet perfected instant messaging with video, like Google Chat or Facetime.

We had to be persistent, not just with figuring out the technology but also with getting the school to agree to our proposal. Schools are tough places when it comes to doing something new.

I floated the idea to the school's principal, who referred me to the administrative office. Matt's school system is the twelfth largest in the country, but thankfully it is also one of the most progressive. We were sent to the technology department, then to the legal department, then to homebound services in the social work division. Bouncing around in this enormous organization with over 20,000 employees and a $2 billion annual operating budget took some persistence. But the clock was ticking for Matt. In early March, as spring came closer, the restlessness and boredom of being homebound was grinding away at his psyche. His hair began to thin from the chemotherapy treatments. He was growing depressed. We had to move this forward. School ended in just a matter of months. I gave myself a deadline of April 1st to increase the pressure to make it happen.

Questions arose that needed answers. Did the school have the legal right to allow a camera in the classroom? What is the protocol for informing other parents that their children would be on camera over the Internet? Who else would be watching the classroom? Could predators hack into the connection to spy on children?

The list of questions and issues began to grow. The more we pressed, the more issues arose. It was like the Whack-A-Mole game: as we solved problems, more popped up. We needed a champion inside the school system with enough interest and credibility to help us cut through the red tape.

Our timing could have not been better. The school technology department had just received a grant from Verizon to implement technology in the classroom and the director was Robert Carr, a respected school tech administrator. We had found our champion. Working with Mr. Carr and Matt's principal, we cleared the legal and consent roadblocks, opened the school's massive firewall to allow the connection and, on April 1st, ten weeks after we started the initiative, we finally got permission to place a webcam in the classroom and one at home so Matt could see and talk to his friends.

The camera was installed in his classroom PC and we did the same on our home PC. We used a free program from Microsoft called NetMeeting. The first test was a failure. The firewall blocked all the images, and only our voices could be heard. The audio was so scratchy, it sounded like the first conversation between Alexander Graham Bell and Mr. Watson. We gave it another try a few days later, and the video was so choppy it looked like a strobe light was flashing at one frame per second. The following week, we had both audio and video working but the microphones on the web cameras were primitive, and it was almost impossible to hear clearly what was being said. Two days later, we had headsets with integrated microphones plugged into both computers, and we could finally test it with real children in the classroom.

You should have seen the smiles in the room when that first connection turned on. At last, Matt could see his friends and they could see him. Now he wasn't alone. The camera connection stayed available to Matt over the remaining three months of school. When his face ballooned from the steroids, his friends were there. All his hair fell out over time, and his friends were there with him as they talked and watched. There was a freak show going on inside his body, and they all witnessed it. They were part of it. They were *with* him as it happened. So when his face returned to normal and his hair started growing back, his classmates were there for that, too, because of the two-way camera.

The webcam connection was purely a social tool. But the most surprising benefits of the experience were what happened in the classroom. Children were learning about cancer in real time. It taught them empathy as they watched Matt struggle with the treatment's effects. They asked questions about survival, and about other forms of cancer and what it was like to be isolated. We were educating 28 children, sharing a life experience with someone they knew and cared about.

In late summer, the early stages of treatment ended. Matt still had another twenty-four months of chemotherapy treatment to complete, but his spirits returned when his medical team commuted his prison sentence of being confined indoors in July. After the end of the first phase of treatment, Matt's body was ravaged by the toxicity of the combinations of different medications. The worst part was over, though, and he was officially in remission, which meant that the cancerous cells had been killed.

The transition back to a more normal life began in June 2002. Matt swam at the local pool, rode his bike in the neighborhood, and played basketball with his teammates in our driveway. We had to buy extra groceries because Matt hosted sleepovers just about every night. But his muscles had atrophied after six months of inactivity. He was physically weaker and lacked stamina. So we hired a personal coach, Greg Wood, to work with Matt weekly to start the process of rebuilding. Greg became a close and trusted family friend.

During his absence, an instructor for homebound students visited Matt three times a week to help him stay current in his studies. Our friend Betsy Hubbell was a certified homebound instructor, and she registered to be assigned to Matt. Betsy understood that Matt's greatest fear was the risk of being required to repeat the fourth grade. During his treatment, he insisted on being dealt with the same as everyone else. He was invited to special all-star camps for children with cancer, where he could meet other children who were having the same experience, fighting the same battles. But Matt didn't want to relate to these others, or feel like "the kid with cancer." Matt wasn't ungrateful for being invited to share these special experiences; he just wanted his old life back.

In September, Matt was able to return to school. On his first day back, he walked in the door of his classroom with a full head of hair. His classmates started rubbing his new hair for good luck. They were goofing with him. They got it. They understood what he had gone through because they were along for the journey while he was undergoing treatment.

Can you imagine what it would have been like if Matt hadn't had the webcam connection?

\*

For a child with cancer, being apart from friends is like a prison sentence. It's like taking away a part of childhood. Having the webcam during chemo had made a huge difference in Matt's transition.

I started thinking. Because of our frequent trips to the oncology lab at Inova Hospital and the outpatient center while Matt was undergoing treatment, we had grown to know many kids who had cancer. Why not help them have the same feeling that Matt had when he connected to his classroom using the webcam? Happy, because he was with this friends again. *Normal.* This webcam idea was too good not to share. But we had a problem. Each computer cost $1,000. Connections cost $50 a month. Webcams were $100 apiece. How could we make it happen for other families without them going through the expense of purchasing the technology, which would just be another stressor? We needed money.

How and where could we get it? That's what I kept thinking about every time I went to work out. I had turned to exercise to cope with the stress of Matt's illness. I'd been a runner ever since I was in college and had exercised all my life. When Matt was born, I competed in my first triathlon, and then ran a marathon later that year. Over the years, I competed in Olympic distance triathlons and 10k races. When Matt was hospitalized, running was my stress reliever. Many turn to other outlets, some healthy, some not so much, to cope. Running shoes and a bicycle were my weapons of choice. The longer Matt's treatments went on, the deeper I dove into running and biking. And yet I couldn't run or bike away that question: how could we get money to help more kids with cancer stay connected to their friends?

In spring 2002, I decided to run the Marine Corps Marathon in Washington, DC, which takes place annually in October. To prepare for the race, I joined the 800-member Reston Runners Club (RRC).

That's when I met Anna Bradford, a devout and enthusiastic leader in the RRC and an experienced ultramarathon runner.

Anna said, "Len, if you can run the Marine Corps Marathon, you can make it through the JFK 50-mile ultramarathon that follows in November."

The RRC matches supporters with runners and coordinates teams of volunteers to "crew" by carting supplies like spare shirts, jackets, shoes, and extra nutrition not found on the race course at many of the eighteen support stations.

That's when it hit me: We could use the JFK 50 race to fund and kick-start a charity that could help other children with cancer make the same connection to school as Matt had.

I recruited two close friends, Ed Cepulis and John Moore—Clevelanders like me who had moved to Virginia years ago—to help me. Both quickly got on board. We printed t-shirts with Matt's picture on the back and called the event "The Run for Matt." We set a goal of raising $5,000 from friends and family members to fund the charity we would call Hopecam. The charity would provide webcams to connect homebound children with cancer to their friends at school, bridging the lonely divide during treatment. We would call it Hopecam because we wanted to send a clear message that it wasn't a matter of *if*, but *when*, a child would return to school. Asking friends for sponsorship money would be a fun challenge.

I called and emailed everyone I knew to help me raise the money. Rather than ask for money directly, I asked for sponsorships. "I'll do the hard work of training and running," I told them. "I really want to do this. Would you sponsor me?" By establishing a personal goal for myself and asking for sponsorships rather than for donations, we could avoid the quid pro quo that sometimes goes along with fundraising.

On the day of the race, John picked me up at 4:00 a.m. so that we could arrive at the Boonsboro (Maryland) High School gym, where the race would start at 7:00 a.m. The 50-mile course followed Route 40 toward and then along the Appalachian Trail, the C&O canal, and through the rolling hills of western Maryland, finally ending in Williamsport, a small town near the Potomac River. When we arrived, we found the Reston team immediately. They were wearing similar fluorescent yellow running shirts. My shirt read "50 Miles for Matt," and it was stretched over their many layers of high-tech outerwear fabric.

*JFK 50 Ultramarathon,*
*Boonesboro, MD, 2003*

Runners in the JFK race have twelve hours to finish. The windy 20°
F weather numbed my hands as we marched to the starting line, but by
the time we made it to the C&O Canal, the sun had warmed the air to
a balmy 45° F. The landscape's muted grays and earth tones made me
feel as if we were running through the set of a sepia-toned movie. Every
three to five miles, racer support stations emerged, featuring tables full
of free pretzels, potato chips, and drinks—foods with lots of salt like
chicken noodle soup. You don't want to over-hydrate and cause hypona-
tremia (too little salt in your system), which would make you headachy
and confused at best and could lead to seizures and/or coma at worst.

I ran the race in ten hours and twenty minutes. John and Ed had
met me along the way at 10-mile intervals, carrying a backpack that
held extra shoes and clothing and offering a lot of encouragement. At
the finish line, John handed me my backpack, which also held a bottle
of champagne and a few clear plastic cups to celebrate. This would
become my longstanding tradition for sharing victory with the team.
After a hot shower, a few slices of hot pizza, and a chicken drumstick,
John and I caught the bus back to Boonsboro High School, where
we'd left the car. As John took the wheel to drive us home, my legs

cramped into a twisted shape, and they stayed that way for the rest of the ride. That was okay. I'd completed one of the most unusual runs of my life and raised $5,000. We now had the funds to help at least five children connect to their schools during their treatment and relieve the loneliness and isolation by staying in touch with their classmates.

I realized we could keep doing what we knew worked to help kids with re-entry into school after cancer treatment. It was a first for Fairfax County, and probably a first in the country. Every week when we took Matt for treatment, we re-entered that part of the community that no one wants to join. Looking at the kids' faces, I couldn't help but think that they deserved to have a shot at normalcy while undergoing treatment, too.

We had already figured out how to work the technology. How hard would it be to duplicate? Other parents who didn't have those resources would be spared having to figure it out themselves while their minds were on just getting their kid through treatment. The challenge was the fear around using the cameras in a classroom. We were asked lots of tough questions and had to prove that the technology would not be misused. It had taken us two months to get the approval to connect Matt to his classroom, with the help of a cooperative principal and teacher and the IT coordinator. We used that success to pave the way for helping more kids.

*

Running ultra marathons each year to raise money for Hopecam became really magical—my friends would pay me to suffer. The more races we did, the more charitable contributions we received. After five consecutive JFK 50 races, we upped the stakes by signing up for the Ironman Florida in 2007. I hired a coach to write a training plan, learned how to mix distance workouts with speed training, and discovered the proper way to choreograph different workouts so my body had enough time to recover and avoid injury. My coach started performing special tests called VO2 and LT (lactate threshold) tests to make targeted improvements in the training regimen. With a heart rate monitor linked to a computer, we were capturing data and charting progress for analysis later. The transition to the next level of endurance sport performance was gradual, and by outsourcing this task to a coach, I had more time for balancing life's other responsibilities. The Ironman was an excellent lesson in the logistics of shipping bicycles, nutrition, bike supplies— basically in pre-thinking each transition—as well as a great opportunity to improve my efficiency riding a bike. The two hundred friends and supporters who sponsored me raised another $30,000 for Hopecam. This allowed us to bring on a part-time director and help a dozen kids a year. We created this wonderful upward spiral. Longer distance races resulted in higher fundraising results. More children were served as Hopecam's annual budget grew from $5,000 to $50,000 to $100,000.

*Crossing the finish line with Viena,*
*Ironman Arizona, 2008*

Encouraged by this success, we scheduled and completed four more Ironman races as an annual sponsored event, sprinkling in other fund-raising efforts such as banquet dinners, 5K family run/walks, and year-end campaigns. On the athletic front, I would schedule a marathon or Half Ironman to complement the training. My body had held up pretty well during all the rides and the training runs, and I discovered that

What Spins the Wheel | 37

my joints recovered quickly. I had become an expert at compartmentalizing, developing an ability to push past pain, isolate it in my mind, and press on. I'd learned to compartmentalize distance as well, another valuable lesson, and continued to better my times in each subsequent race. I'd also realized the value of taking off December and January to give myself a mental break to stay out late, sleep in, eat, and do whatever I wanted. I'd always force myself to get ready for race season by starting training while it was still cold in February.

In spring 2009, my friend Brian Daum invited me to join him and several other cycling friends on a two-day out-and-back bike ride between Reston, Virginia, and Cumberland, Maryland—nearly 260 miles. The challenge was not the mileage—28 miles further than the 112-mile cycling distance in an Ironman race—but the four steep 1,000–1,500-foot mountain passes between Hancock and Cumberland. Each hill in the Allegheny Mountains involved eight-to-twelve-percent grades, ascents significantly steeper than any hills in the Colorado Rockies, and long three-to-four-mile climbs with steeply curving descents before the next hill. But we did it. Over the course of the year, Brian and my new cycling friends (Bill Sickenberger, Joe Knill, and Steve Gurney) were together with me on weekend rides or connecting on the Tuesday and Thursday rides organized by the Reston Bike Club.

When the group decided to expand the ride to Rochester, New York, the following year, I suggested making it a charity ride for Hopecam. The team bought the idea, each member agreeing to raise $2,000 in exchange for Hopecam paying for hotels, meals, and transportation back to Reston. Hopecam director Jennifer Bond found a partner organization in Rochester and agreed to support a young girl recently diagnosed with cancer. The local television station turned out to capture the event.

The first part of the journey was the same route we had ridden from Reston to Cumberland in summer 2010. As we crested Town Hill in Little Orleans, Maryland, near Green Ridge Mountain, we stopped to admire the commanding view of the valley below. In our colorful orange and white bike jerseys printed with the Hopecam name and logo and the slogan "Ride for Hope: Reston VA to Rochester NY," we looked like a legitimate cycling team.

A few minutes after our arrival, a thirty-foot-long RV pulled up in the gravel parking lot at the top of the hill near our lookout point. Several expensive carbon fiber bikes hung on the rear rack. The colorful sponsor logos and large white signs proclaiming number 316 and the name Gerhard Gulewicz let us know that the RV was supporting a professional bicycle rider in some sort of race.

A demure brunette in her mid-thirties emerged from the RV and approached us. She agreed to take our picture. Then in a thick Austrian accent and authoritative tone, she asked us who we were.

*Reston to Rochester Charity Ride, 2010*

We proudly explained our journey and our cause. She explained that she was Gerhard Gulewicz' wife and that Gerhard was 170 miles away from completing Race Across America (RAAM) while holding on to second place. We had never heard of this race before.

"How far are you going?" the woman asked.

"Five hundred miles," one of us answered.

"And how long will it take you?"

"Four days." We said it proudly. We thought it was an aggressive pace.

The woman, on the other hand, quickly realized that we were recreational riders with no affiliation with bicycle racing and scoffed. "Gerhard could easily do that in two days!" She turned, walked back to the RV, and drove off to follow her husband.

We joked a lot about her response during the rest of the trip. Whenever we hit a steep hill, we shrugged our shoulders and said "Well, if we were as fast and strong as Gerhard, we'd be at the top already." But when we returned home after reaching our destination and our fundraising goal, we looked up Gerhard and realized that we were actually riding on the Race Across America course that day as the leaders were coming through. RAAM is a 3,000-mile cross-country bike race started in 1982 by four men in California. RAAM competitors ride one-third more mileage than the Tour de France in half the time.

*Bill Sickenberger and Len Forkas:*
*Sebring 400-mile, 24-hour race*

That November, Bill Sickenberger called me. He wanted to race in Florida's Sebring 12/24 ultra-cycling marathon. You ride as far as you can in 24 hours. It's not uncommon to do 400 miles in 24 hours. If you make it, you're eligible for RAAM, which has been described by *Outside* magazine as the toughest bicycle race in the world. Competitors ride from Oceanside, California, to Annapolis, Maryland, and have to finish in twelve days. To put the challenge in perspective, more people will climb Mount Everest this year than have finished the race in its entire 31-year history, and about half of all athletes who start the race do not cross the finish line. Wolfgang Fasching, three-time RAAM winner, author, and motivational speaker who completed the seven summits, once said: "Everest is more dangerous, but RAAM is much harder." To enter the race in the solo category, an athlete must finish at least one qualifying race. The Sebring 400 was such a race.

"Remember Gerhard?" Bill asked me. "I want to qualify."

"You're crazy!"

He was not listening. "Will you train with me?"

The race was in February. That meant training in December and January, when I usually took a break. I'd never trained much in bitter, wintry cold.

"What the hell? I'll do it."

Bill had a longtime friend from Orlando who agreed to crew for us. We both finished 400 miles before the 6:30 a.m. cut-off, riding nonstop through orange groves in the balmy central Florida sun, with the last 200 miles going around the historic 3.74 mile Sebring Auto Racing track 53 times in the darkness. We were now officially qualified to compete as solo athletes in RAAM.

With funds to sustain a full-time executive director for Hopecam, we anticipated a budget supporting more than 30 kids a year.

Seven months later, in 2011, my family gave me the green light to enter another RAAM qualifier in Saratoga, New York—the Adirondack 540-mile ultra-cycling event, ranked the 14th most difficult race in the world. I was so inexperienced that I didn't realize most people raced with crews. So, as one of the only riders with no crew for support, I rode four 135-mile long loops of the course, which added up to more than 30,000 feet of vertical elevation, equal to crossing the Rocky Mountains. Crossing the finish line in less than 48 hours with three hours of sleep, I once again qualified for RAAM.

"Forkas," Bill said. "You really should do RAAM. You're the only guy we know who gets stronger and faster the longer you ride."

The idea was intriguing. Hopecam was helping anywhere between thirty and fifty children annually, but they were mostly in the mid-Atlantic region. We had plateaued as an organization. The Hopecam board of directors supported the idea of doing something that would shake us up, create a platform to expand the charity to a much larger scale—to a nationwide scale. Competing in RAAM would spread our message to a much broader audience.

It wouldn't be easy. RAAM had a reputation as one of the most physically demanding athletic competitions in the world—a grueling 3,000 miles in twelve days. Most of the rookies drop out from the sheer fatigue of riding 250 miles per day, the minimum needed to finish before the cutoff. Many athletes hallucinate from sleep deprivation. If the brain-frying, 120-degree heat after 30 hours in the Mojave Desert doesn't dehydrate you, the oxygen-deprived, high-altitude Rocky Mountains crossing will destroy your legs. Headwinds in the plains are the reward for surviving the Rockies, only to be followed by an even more difficult challenge, the much less steep and shorter, but never-ending, Appalachian Mountain crossing. Some racers had even died. Bob Breedlove, a 53-year-old pediatric surgeon and five-time RAAM finisher, was struck and killed by a driver near Trinidad, Colorado, in 2005. Many racers are hospitalized from exhaustion, broken bones, dehydration, or oxygen hypoxia, to name just a few of the dangers on the race course. That course is designed to chew you up and spit you out.

But could we raise enough money to support children throughout the country as they adapt to the "new normal" of cancer?

I decided to do it.

## Lesson 1

When my son Matt got sick, we received many offers of help from friends and family. The best advice we got was the simplest: Find a way to help Matt feel like a normal kid while he underwent treatment.

Years later I read Sir Ken Robinson's book, *Finding Your Element*. Robinson suggests that using your strengths in such a natural way that things begin to flow is the key to creativity, happiness, and transformation. Reading and thinking about his message forced me to look deep inside myself and think about how I was able to use my strengths to a reach a goal—first, helping Matt, then later, helping other kids with cancer.

The best way to do this was surprisingly simple: using my experience in telecommunications to connect Matt to his classroom and his friends, then using my skills as an endurance athlete to raise the money needed to do the same for other kids with cancer.

Even if there is no immediate crisis in our life, it seems that all of us are striving to make a difference in the world, or as some people put it, "find our calling." American theologian Frederick Buechner used this metaphor to express a message very similar to Robinson's: "The place God calls you to is the place where your deep gladness and the world's deep hunger meet."

# CHAPTER 2
# GO BIG OR GO HOME

*The Starting Line Team.*
*Front row, from left: Brian, Ken, Wayne.*
*Back row, from left: Greg, Ed, Kaitee, Amy, Len, Bill, John.*

*Start by doing what's necessary; then do what's possible; and suddenly you're doing the impossible.*

—St. Francis of Assisi

WHEN I ARRIVED at RAAM headquarters at the beachfront pavilion in Oceanside, California, at 9:00 a.m., the line for picking up race packets was already long. Only two officials, seated on plastic folding chairs behind the desk, were available to register the more than 47 solo teams that would be competing in two days. Though I'd qualified twice for this race, it was my first time in an event of this magnitude.

Ask endurance athletes the best thing about racing, and they'll say "crossing the finish line." The second best thing, for me at least, is getting to the starting line. No more thinking about fundraising, training, equipment, or vehicles. Just riding my bike, something I love to do more than almost anything in the world.

Picking up the race packets was the first piece of official business before a long checklist of actions needed to gain the approval to reach the starting line. That afternoon at 2:00 p.m. we would need to pass the vehicle inspection test. We would have to rush to outfit the vehicles with the required reflective tape, identification decals, sign panels, and racer numbers. Half of our crew were still en route to the San Diego airport waiting to be picked up. I was doing my part by starting the registration process.

RAAM draws contenders from all over the world. Over its 30-year history, more than 25 countries have been represented in the race. Fewer than 200 solo and tandem racers have officially earned the title of RAAM Finisher. My team and I had trained hard for the past eight months, and I was determined that we, too, would be in the thirty percent of rookies who finish.

A group of seven people stood at the registration table, intensely listening to the instructions given by the elderly race official handing out packets. All seven were wearing red and grey jerseys and jackets with professionally designed logos and bright, bold lettering. The group looked like a seasoned NASCAR team

"Who are they, what's that all about?" I asked the young guy standing next to me.

He pointed toward a man at the edge of the group. "Do you see that guy over there?" He whispered the man's name. "He is competing in the Race across the West." This is the 1,000-mile version of RAAM that ends in Durango and is considered a warm-up race to RAAM.

I nodded. He must be some respected and tested warrior, I thought, to have such an entourage.

The guy filled me in on his background. "That's really impressive,"

I said, then looked more closely at the lettering next to the logo on the back of the jackets. "What does it mean, *Unfinished Business?*"

"Last year, he didn't make it out of the Mojave Desert," he said. "So this year, *Unfinished Business.*"

Well, good for him. He's about my age and has the guts to come back and avenge the loss. He'd brought his family and his young sons to support him. I could only imagine his disappointment in having had to drop out last year.

As I waited for my turn at the registration table and watched all the racers and their admirers milling about, it became clear to me that so often endurance races were all about the athlete—from the jerseys to the pampering from crew members to the reverence and respect everyone around the athlete had so proudly displayed—and the personal glory gained from reaching the finish line of this race. He was determined to show everyone that he could do it.

Eventually I made it to the front of the line, picked up my packet, and walked back to the car for the drive back to Poway, where my crew was finishing up last-minute preparations. As I was leaving, I saw Gerhard Gulewicz, the racer whose wife had first told us about Race Across America. I introduced myself and told him the story. "You're why we're here," I said.

I tried to explain how meeting his wife in 2010, then learning more about him and RAAM, was the first inkling that we could grow the Hopecam mission even bigger and expand its reach from local to national. By doing RAAM, we were swinging for the fences. It was go big or go home. But Gerhard didn't speak much English, and so it wasn't a long or involved conversation.

No doubt about it, endurance events can be all about the athlete and racing can be a really selfish sport. I knew that firsthand. I was a veteran Ironman, ultra-marathoner and, now, ultra-cyclist. I knew the kind of time it can take to train, time that would otherwise be given to loved ones. Yet exercise saved me when the stress of Matt's illness became too much. And the endurance events allowed me to fund Hopecam.

At least I could honestly say that our team had a very different mission. We were not focused on Len Forkas. We were not focused on finishing first. We simply wanted to survive long enough to finish the race. Our goal was to promote awareness about the mission of Hopecam and honor the courage of children with childhood cancer.

*

Our friends Larry and Elizabeth Fromm and their in-laws, Don and Jeanne Ing, had graciously offered us their houses in Poway for the three nights prior to the race. Besides hosting us, they let us park our vehicles in their driveways, where we'd been working feverishly on getting them ready. Larry had also let me drive his old Lexus to Oceanside to complete the registration details. Our preparation would have been very different and a lot more difficult had it occurred in the parking lot of Motel 6, where we'd originally booked five rooms for the crew.

Poway is known as "the city in the country." Its suburban streets had a relaxed atmosphere. From the Fromms' house we had a sweeping view of the canyon, and the Ings' house was situated on Rancho Bernardo Golf Course. Just like in the reality show "Survivor," our large group had been split into two "tribes" of the younger team and the older team. Being situated in two houses actually helped us adjust to each other more quickly.

Even though our resort-like lodgings were great and our hosts' hospitality unmatched, we were stressed. Ever since my team and I had arrived in Poway, it had been "game on." We'd been working nonstop getting everything organized, provisioning the vehicles, and assigning responsibilities to crew members. Every action was critical and the clock was ticking.

The 25-foot RV, equipped with bed, shower, kitchen, meeting table, and bathroom, would serve as my team's home base during the 3,000-mile race. One van, wrapped bumper to bumper with our colorful Hopecam logo and the names of our thirty-plus sponsors, would serve as the follow van. We had paid a driver to bring the vehicle with most of our gear to Poway. Two weeks before the race, Joe Knill and

I had outfitted the van in my driveway with speakers, bike racks, and strategically positioned storage cabinets for holding bins full of gear, food, drink mixes—everything needed to support me while I rode. The other van, "unwrapped" but otherwise identical with magnetic stickers identifying it as part of the Hopecam team, would serve as the advance vehicle. The advance van would ride ahead of the rest of the team and me, and its crew would be responsible for booking hotel rooms and providing other supplies when necessary. The advance van was our redundancy plan. If the follow van broke down, we could easily transfer its contents to the advance van and continue with the race.

We planned to have eleven team members work in mostly three-person crews: one crew in the RV, one in the advance van, and one in the follow van. Shifts would be rotated so no one team member would be overworked and all would have time to recuperate and refresh. After all, this was essentially going to be a 15-mph caravan across the country. Traveling at that speed could feel exhausting. It would be important for the crew to be fresh, rested, and alert.

Building a team is one of the toughest and most challenging aspects of competing in RAAM. I had learned much about what it takes from interviewing dozens of previous RAAM racers like Randy Mouri, who had completed RAAM the year before and who also happened to live fifteen minutes from me in Reston. Randy had been into endurance cycling for many years and had completed numerous qualifying races. Laying out his road map over beers in Chantilly, Virginia, Randy and his wife Susie, an endurance athlete who had run ultra-distance races including a 100-mile race in Europe, handed over the owner's manual to the race they had successfully completed in 2011. They gave me volumes of navigational manuals, training plans, nutrition plans, and schedules. Most importantly, they gave me contact information for many other riders they'd consulted before they began the race.

We interviewed them all and asked what advice they'd give a rookie. We asked about the unexpected events they'd experienced and how their teams handled them. We asked them what they'd never do again. Although we sprinkled in detailed questions about nutrition, training, equipment, and crew selection, we were searching for the deal-breakers lurking in the mix of all the thousands of details required to execute a well-run race. What they told me was surprising. The most critical success factor was not nutrition, or the right gear or proper training. Nothing was more important than the crew. We had to have the right people supporting the race. Three key characteristics emerged: (1) Positivity, (2) Selflessness, and (3) Skills. In that order. There were many people that we interviewed to join our all-volunteer army of eleven members, but not all were chosen. Some had strong skills and a positive attitude but big egos, and others had various combinations, but we refused to compromise on these three criteria. In Jim Collins' book *Good to Great,* he uses the metaphor of filling seats on a bus to describe the importance of the caliber of people on your team. He talks about having the right people on the bus. If you have the right people you never have to worry about motivating them.

Among the right people on our bus would be a crew chief, back-up crew chief, two drivers, a navigator, a "go-fer," a bike mechanic, a massage therapist, a paramedic, a nutritionist, a media and communications person, and a videographer.

It would be critical to surround myself with people who shared my commitment to Hopecam. For that reason, I'd asked long-time friends John Moore and Bill Vitek, another fellow Clevelander, to serve as crew chief and back-up crew chief, respectively. John had competed alongside me in endurance sports. John and I met in 1996, sharing an interest in mountain biking, ultra-marathon running, and Ironman distance triathlons. There was no one I trusted more to lead our team. Bill had known me since I was eighteen and had been best man at my wedding. Three years later, he asked me to be his best man. He was also an entrepreneur and one of the most dedicated and unselfish leaders on the team. I was confident he'd do whatever was needed to take good care of the crew and ensure their smooth functioning.

John and Bill, along with other crew members, would drive the van, serve as navigators, and run errands if needed, including preparing nutrition bottles, doing laundry, or even emptying the RV's septic tank. They were our generalists. It was easy to recruit them because many were the very same friends who encouraged me to do this race in the first place. They were the first to volunteer when I approached them. Yet we also needed specialists with skills so unique that it seemed all but impossible to recruit people who shared the same belief in my commitment to finish as my longtime friends.

This is the dilemma that many small business owners face when building a team. Small teams must have strong chemistry. You have to select people whom you know will bond. Recruiting volunteer specialists required a lot of intuition and trust, making decisions with imperfect information. You have to trust your gut. In his book, *Blink,* Malcolm Gladwell talks about the "feeling in your gut" that occurs when making a crucial decision. It is the product of a complex algorithm running through your brain at speeds beyond comprehension. This physical feeling of positive or negative emotion is intuitive and powerfully accurate.

We relied on friends recommending friends to recruit these specific crew members—massage therapist, paramedic, nutritionist, bike mechanic, and videographer. This is the strongest form of shared trust, because the new recruit is accountable to the friend who recommended him or her. The RAAM veterans we had interviewed had always said the same thing: the key to any strong crew is always the people. One "bad apple" can impact the psychology of the entire crew. If we could recruit the right mix of creative problem solvers, we would be able to overcome obstacles as they appeared.

We recruited Ken, our paramedic, and Greg, our nutritionist, five months before the race and included them in the practice runs. This gave them a chance to work together on what would be required to ride a great race, until it was so familiar that it became routine. We studiously avoided prima donnas. We lost sleep at night worrying that we would have to make last-minute picks, as had happened to a previous RAAM athlete who didn't take his commitment to his crew very seriously. At the starting line, only two of the six members he'd recruited showed up—riders need a minimum of four. He found two people the day before the race at the registration facility who wanted to crew for a team. He signed them on, and the next day after the race began his entire team became ill from *Salmonella* poisoning. One of the new recruits had brought along his pet iguana without telling anyone and stored it in an ice chest when they crossed the desert. The crew used the same ice to mix drinks. Everyone was poisoned and dropped out at 400 miles.

Prospective crew members face apprehension, too—for example, that the rider will flake out on the crew. Think about it. There is much uncertainty and risk for a volunteer joining an unknown team for a two-week road trip. One athlete was so abusive to her crew that they abandoned her on a mountaintop in Colorado. Still another athlete, delirious and sleep deprived, fell in love with his massage therapist half-way through the race, making her so uncomfortable that the crew chief allowed her to leave and catch a ride to the finish line with another racer's team. Athletes like these seemed to be in the race just to see if they could pull it off. There didn't seem to be a sense of a larger purpose, and it seemed they had little respect for the magnitude of the task.

Similarly, when team members have not fully subscribed to a mission, the entire team feels the effect. For example, one team member, a mature medical practitioner, was egotistical and refused to help with small chores, such as cleaning the RV or doing laundry. He was so self-righteous and he so annoyed the crew members that they became negative and cynical.

One of the things we did to prepare for the race was to hold conference calls every two weeks from January to June. I was clear with my team about our mission. I also took my commitment to them seriously by investing both time and resources to ensure they received the proper training. In December, I had arranged for seven of the early recruits to get a first-hand look at RAAM by attending a seminar in Boulder given by George Thomas, five-time RAAM finisher and this year's race director, allowing them to learn the ins and outs of the race.

After the seminar, we scheduled three training rides of 500, 730, and 750 miles—in March, April, and May, respectively—on three different segments of the RAAM course. My goal for the training rides was to see the course and build a mental map of what we would encounter, encouraging our drivers and navigators to make mistakes in the practice, when it didn't count, to reduce errors during the race. These practices involved three different crew members at a time who would serve the dual function of getting me in shape while allowing my team to gain some critical driving skills so they would not run me over. It worked like a mini boot camp and the crew members formed a quick and lasting bond from the shared experience of being together without much sleep for several consecutive days.

We ran the training rides and pre-training events like projects. The mini teams had homework assignments before we departed, such as studying maps, making checklists, and shopping for storage bins for the van. We set mileage targets, as well as clear beginning and end dates, so we could sustain our focus. By delegating the support roles to the team early, the volunteers took ownership of the tasks well before the race started.

*Oceanside, CA: Official Vehicle & Gear Inspection*

This was a lot to ask of the crew. They would themselves need physical endurance, strong concentration even when fatigued, special expertise, and the ability to get along with others. It's one thing to take two weeks off for RAAM, but another to ask these volunteers, as I did, to take a four-day weekend to fly to a portion of the course. It was essential, however, that they learned how to follow me in a support vehicle for twenty hours a day practicing the techniques needed to successfully support a solo rider without breaking the policies of the race's thick rule book, in order to avoid mistakes that could cost our team a time-out penalty.

So, when fitting out the van in Poway became unexpectedly complicated, I trusted that John, a great leader with a great sense of humor, would handle it. My role was to ride, not to micromanage.

The rider was of course the other critical factor in how well a team performed. After seven months of rehearsal and dozens of interviews, I had learned that the common point of a breakdown within a team is when the members lose faith in the rider. Team members are rational people. They know that crossing the finish line is something that only half the riders will accomplish; rookies cross less than one-third of the time. So it's quite natural for a team to start the race with a lot of skepticism.

I was a real outlier in the world of endurance cycling, showing up for this race as an underdog. My training had been limited by having to balance the demand of operating my wireless company, serving as president of the Hopecam charity, and being around my family long enough to be considered a responsible parent and husband.

Our team was banking on our commitment to our families and Hopecam to sustain and focus our effort during the race. And we were banking on what Ed Cepulis, team member and long-time friend, had shared with me after the seminar with George Thomas. "It was one thing to commit to you but another to commit to each other," he said. "Everyone showed commitment early in the game. The entire team was looking forward to the challenge, not only of the race itself but also of the preparation. And the stories I read and heard about the kids that were being helped gave us a common purpose."

Even people who know the Hopecam story and understand its mission marvel that people so willingly volunteered to join the crew, essentially giving up two weeks of their lives to ride cross-country (and at 15 mph in the follow van) through deserts, mountains, and plains, with little sleep, and subsisting on mostly road food. For some, like Steve Gurney, our media person, it was curiosity coupled with the ability to "support a good friend and a great cause."

John, Ed, and others told me that they saw it as a chance to share a challenging adventure with friends. "A good friend asked me for support and I had to give it serious consideration," John said. "Also, an all-consuming project is an honest pleasure for almost anyone, I think. Allowing the noise of work, 24-hour news, home repairs, and the hundred other daily interruptions to fade [in exchange for] being able to focus one hundred percent on an adventure that also has a higher purpose is a rare treat."

*

When I returned from registering in Oceanside, the crew was in a flurry of last-minute vehicle preparation. Most people had flown in Monday afternoon and came into a frenzy of organizing. We had underestimated the amount of work needed to get ready for inspection, and now everyone was playing catch-up.

On top of that, fitting-out the vehicles with provisions and equipment, a set-up we'd copied from a British racer who placed second a couple of years ago, had taken longer and was more complicated than we anticipated. I was sorely tempted to add my advice, because I felt the time pressure and I wanted it done right. But I mostly kept quiet. John had already impressed me with how well he was already managing this group of people as a team, many of whom hadn't met each other before this weekend. And yet John was responding appropriately to individual differences and perspectives. I didn't want to disrupt his chain of command.

Ken, our paramedic and Greg, team nutritionist, were working inside the follow van, which would contain a driver, a navigator, and a nutritionist who would sit in the back and act as utility fielder and "go-fer." I knew Greg from the gym in Reston, where he'd once worked as a personal trainer. His expertise had impressed me, and because of his experience working with high school athletes, I'd approached him to work with my son after his treatment. Matt had desperately wanted to get back to playing basketball but his muscles had atrophied from the cumulative effects of chemotherapy. Greg prepared a program for Matt to follow, but made it fun by cracking jokes and always ending each session with a ten-minute game of one-on-one hoops. Now thirty-two, Greg was working his way up the fast track in the Fairfax County Fire Department and earning a coveted spot on the Urban Search and Rescue Team, which assists natural disaster victims worldwide.

Ken was Greg's firefighter colleague and a paramedic. A twenty-four-year-old power lifter from State College, Pennsylvania, he'd dreamed of being a paramedic since he was 14. He showed up wearing his signature baseball hat, a hunter camouflage design, with a bullet split from his first deer kill pinned to the shade. He had cut a groove across the cartridge so it looked like a clothespin and would easily slip over the stiff shade of the baseball hat.

Greg and Ken had spent hours the day before precisely determining the best places for each of the provisions—nutritional supplies, bike parts, clothing, and electronic devices—so they would be in easy reach. Now they were filling the empty bins, then securing the drawers with bungee cord bands attached to small hooks so the supplies wouldn't spill when the follow van took a sharp turn.

While Greg and Ken worked inside the follow van, Wayne, our twenty-eight-year-old bike mechanic, tuned up the bikes for optimal performance. This was my first time meeting him. Ed, who had been living in Boulder, Colorado, had found Wayne through his local bike shop. Ed, John, and I interviewed Wayne in a 30-minute conference call in April. Affectionately known as "The Wrench," Wayne tightened every screw, micro-adjusted the derailleurs, and went through his mental checklist the way a fighter pilot goes through a pre-flight ritual. Six-feet-four and as laid back as his shoulder-length curly brown hair, he'd have to then lift the bikes (we had brought two bikes with us—one to ride, one to serve as a backup) and firmly mount them to the top of follow van's bike rack, where mounting forks accommodated three spare wheels. We planned to place the fourth spare wheel we'd brought in the back seat of the advance vehicle.

We wanted to get video footage of me leaving the starting line, so Wayne helped our videographer, Amy, find the optimal place on the bike to mount her camera. We had to do it this way because she would be crewing in the "follow" vehicle, which was not permitted during the first twenty miles due to traffic congestion and the risk of forty-eight cyclists departing at one-minute intervals and jamming the roads. By mounting the camera on the bike, she hoped to get footage of me leaving the starting line in Oceanside and capture the riding experience for the first twenty miles.

*A team barbeque the night before the race*

That evening, after all the prep work was done, the Fromms hosted a barbecue for us and we completed one last team-building exercise. It's an exercise I love—everyone is given crayons and a piece of poster board and asked to draw the house and neighborhood where they grew up. Crayons take you back to your childhood, and drawing what amounts to a cartoon of your neighborhood leads to lots and lots of storytelling. Although I was friendly with at least half the team, they didn't all know each other. This exercise would be a good way of getting to know where we all came from, especially since we'd been working so hard to get everything ready that there wasn't much time to get acquainted.

It was interesting to watch the different drawings appear. After fifteen minutes we went around the room and explained our drawings. John drew a map of a dozen blocks and included the elementary school and the five-and-dime where he bought sodas and candy. Ken's drawing was more rustic—a stop sign, a paved road—to reflect the rural community where he was raised. Some drew soccer fields, others backyards where they'd spend a lot of time in tire swings suspended from trees.

Doing an exercise like this creates a common denominator for a group. The stories each team member told helped cement the bonds that had already begun to form by working together to get the vehicles race-ready.

Months earlier, I had shared my story with each crew member as they had signed on to support my mission. We were not the veteran group of seven I'd seen at the registration desk in Oceanside, but we were just as strongly, if not more strongly, committed. We were here for Hopecam. We were riding for all the kids Hopecam had helped and all the kids that, with our sponsors' donations, we could help in the future. With Amy's help, we would videotape a special message dedicating each day of the race to one of them. Kids like Alex Green, Justin Condoluci, Stefano Rocca, and Shannon Eastman. Kids like my own son, Matt.

Later that night, I reflected on everything that had brought us here and all the racers like Gerhard who had done battle with this course, rated by *Outside* magazine as one of the highest-ranked and most difficult ultra-endurance events in the world.

Racers like Gerhard get the glory. But the truth is, I was jealous of all my team members. My work on the bicycle would be lonely. They were going to have a shared experience—enjoying each other's company, solving problems, and working together as a unit—that would be remembered for many years to come. My job was different. I would see a fraction of the experiences they would have as members of the crew. My sole responsibility was to ride the bicycle. That was only a small piece of what needed to happen for us to have a successful finish.

"Nothing can take place without you working together to solve problems, be resourceful, anticipate the unknown, and adapt to the varying environments we're going to encounter," I had told my team that night, after we'd finished the team-building exercise. "That's how we will make it to the finish line."

The truth is, too, that I did not envy that they'd be sitting for hours in a car that was traveling fifteen miles an hour, following the route book and mixing nutrition drinks to hand off to me on the side of the road every thirty minutes. And I didn't envy having to be responsible for making sure that each of the three vehicles was at the right place at the right time with the right people doing the right thing.

That last day before RAAM was all about the importance of having the right people on the team. We had trained together, lived together, and meticulously planned for every possibility imaginable together. We had a clear mission and purpose. We would be reminded every day that we were racing for a child, dedicating our every effort to helping more children. We had been blessed with the hospitality and friendship of the Fromms and the Ings, who welcomed eleven strangers into their homes and treated us like family.

Like the astronauts in Tom Wolfe's book *The Right Stuff*, I kept praying I wouldn't "screw the pooch." *Dear God, don't let me make a stupid mistake and blow this mission.*

The world's toughest bicycle race was starting the next day.

## Lesson 2

Accomplishing a mission requires a team that is purpose-driven and committed to the goal and to the team leader. Building that team is one of the toughest challenges any athlete or business-person faces. "Nothing is more important than the people on the team" has been said so often that it feels like a cliché. But it's a cliché because it's true.

To pick the right people, look for three characteristics: positivity, selflessness, and skills, in that order. When seeking candidates, it helps to rely on trusted friends' referrals, because it builds in a layer of accountability. The new recruit is accountable to the friend who recommended him or her. Then trust your gut about whether these people share your commitment to your cause.

If you have the right people, you never have to worry about moti-vating them. They motivate themselves.

---

*You give new meaning to "When I see an adult on a bicycle, I do not despair for the future of the human race" (H.G. Wells).*

*—Roger Winston*

*Go Len!! We are very proud of you!! Ride safe and we'll keep watch on your progress.*

*—Heather Harwood*

*Godspeed to you, Len! Way to use the athletic gift God gave you to bless others! I pray health, joy, and a comfy bike seat for you!!*

*—Jill Coleman*

---

# DAY 1
June 13, from Oceanside to Brawley

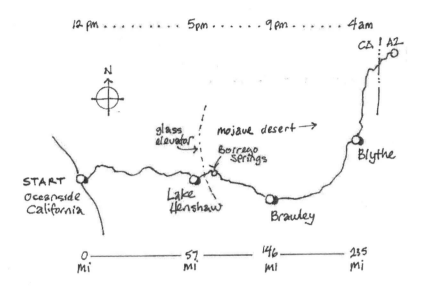

TODAY WE RIDE FOR ALEX

| START | END | START | FINISH | DISTANCE | TOTAL MI. | ELEVATION |
|---|---|---|---|---|---|---|
| Oceanside, CA (PDT) | Lake Henshaw, CA | 12:28 PM | 4:43 PM | 56.8 | 56 | 5,104 |
| Lake Henshaw, CA | Brawley, CA | 4:43 PM | 9:20 PM | 88.7 | 145 | 2,274 |
| Brawley, CA | Day 1 Sleep Break | 9:20 PM | 3:20 AM | 89.8 | 235 | 2,991 |
| Day 1 Sleep Break | | 3:20 AM | 5:30 AM | | | |

# CHAPTER 3
# ADAPT AND PERSEVERE

*Let me tell you the secret that has led me to my goal. My strength lies solely in my tenacity.*

—Louis Pasteur

THICK CLOUDS HUGGED the normally sunny coastline of San Diego County when our team began preparing to set off for Oceanside. This phenomenon of cool, sometimes foggy air with drizzle was typical for June and more pronounced this year because of La Niña. The locals call it June Gloom.

I placed a quick call to Alex Green, the eleven-year-old child we were riding for today. Alex was recovering from the surgery he'd had to remove a cancer called a "Wilms Tumor" from his lungs and around his stomach and pancreas. The procedure was very risky. The weeks of radiation treatments he had received blasted away most of the cancerous tumors but had left him weak. His arteries were also weakened from the radiation, making the procedure very risky. During surgery, his aorta was accidentally cut and although the surgeons repaired the tear, it took more than 45 minutes to get the blood flowing to his legs. Constricting blood flow for too long has dire consequences. When he'd left the hospital, Alex was paralyzed below the waist due to the surgery, unable to move his legs. Being an athlete at heart, he figured out ways to do what he wanted to do, whether that meant hoisting himself unsupported into his wheelchair, popping wheelies, or even snowboarding. Alex even played hockey on a specially designed sled with other young paralyzed athletes. Dedicating day one to Alex was easy.

"Today our crew is heading out on this race course in a couple of hours inspired by your bravery," I said. "No matter what life tosses at you, nothing stands in your way, and we are all going to take that same attitude with us over the next two weeks." Alex's family wished us well and promised to follow our progress on the race blog.

It was my intention to connect with a Hopecam child each day of the race, to share what was ahead of me that day. That connection was also a way to remind me of their courage so I could carry it with me on the ride. Alex had a long journey ahead of him. I wanted to dedicate Day 1 to Alex to honor and respect his strength and ability to adapt, to persevere.

After the call, John grabbed some chips and pretzels for me, in case I needed anything salty, and we said our goodbyes to our hosts. John, Ed, Amy, and I would ride in the follow van, while Bill Vitek drove the RV and Greg Wood the advance van. Before we left, Kaitee, our massage therapist and, at twenty-one, our youngest crew member, asked, "Len, is there anything you're worried about?"

I thought for a minute about the question. "I try hard not to worry about things I can't control, and the things we can control are in the hands of our crew."

I had confidence in my crew. Yet I was still not entirely comfortable with what essentially amounted to delegating power and control. When Greg and Ken were setting up the van in Poway, Greg had called me a perfectionist. He was right. It was hard for me not to take over the set-up when we got there. I cared about how the inside of the van looked and functioned. Despite our practice set-ups months earlier, Greg had been spending hours trying to figure out where to put the drink mixes and how to use the hooks, safety belts, and anchors so the two forty-pound water coolers, the ice chests, and all the other gear and supplies would stay in place. I kept worrying. Would we be ready in time? Would the supplies be accessible when I needed them? Would everything be there, or would something be forgotten or left behind?

It was hard to stay out of it and let Greg and Ken do the work. I had to remember that they cared as much about doing their jobs well as I did. It was built into their personalities, and it showed when we stayed with our hosts in Poway. Greg, for one, could not stop cleaning up the kitchen. Our hosts repeatedly asked him to relax and let things be.

"I can't," Greg always said. "When I'm at the firehouse and I make a mess, I clean it up."

Finally he got the van fitted out to his satisfaction—everything that needed to be found was within a 90-degree turn of the person seated in the back, who would get me whatever I needed during the race.

Now there was nothing left to do but get to the starting line. During the ride, John and I tested the GPS transmitter that linked to the iPod on the dashboard, checking the device to see if our location was tracking to our website. John had found a device called "SPOT Connect" that would pinpoint our location every ten minutes on a virtual map linked to www.hopecam.org where our friends could track our exact whereabouts and read our daily blog. Amy sat in the back recording the drive to the starting line while Ed drove and John and I discussed the day's logistics.

Only this handful of the crew needed to travel from the starting line. John, Bill, and Greg would take the first shift in the follow van. The RV and advance vehicles and their crews would take a different path and meet us in the late afternoon at the base of the foothills along the western wall of the Mojave Desert. At that point we'd become a three-vehicle caravan traveling together for the remainder of the race.

We also set up the radio units we would use to stay in touch in case cell phone service was too spotty, or even nonexistent. My crew rigged an earpiece for my right ear, keeping the left ear open and making it possible to hear cars approaching, and tucked the microphone that was built into the earphone wire inside my shirt collar. We had done it this way on the practice rides, and I'd become accustomed to listening and riding at the same time without incident. I checked my emergency kit one more time: spare tube, air pump, micro multi-tool, a $20 bill, and a laminated copy of my health insurance card and driver's license.

Then I glanced at the holy card that Sister Therese of the Poor Clare Colletine's had given me when we met in May. Ten years ago, my mother had reached out to her when Matt was diagnosed with leukemia. She and the eighteen cloistered sisters prayed in shifts around the clock for Matt to be cured. Before my departure for RAAM, I dropped by the convent in Cleveland, Ohio, with three boxes of Malley's chocolate-covered pretzels, a Northeast Ohio favorite, to tell them about the race and to ask them to pray for me and for the safety of my crew.

"Len, remember that you are starting on a very holy day, the feast of St. Anthony," Sister Therese told me. St. Anthony was the patron saint of lost items, someone to pray to if you were searching for hope to locate someone or something. He was also known as "the saint of miracles." Quite appropriate given that the odds for finishing the race were incredibly low.

I wasn't sure how much to read into her remark, although many of my friends thought I had lost my mind in preparing to do this race. We had high hopes for RAAM, but I liked to think St. Anthony and Sister Therese would be our insurance policy on the long journey that lay ahead. It seemed that keeping the holy card in the follow vehicle would be a good idea, just in case my crew had a hard time locating something that I might need.

When we arrived, Gerhard Gulewicz and the other race veterans were lining up in the pen near their support vehicles. They are not big or overly muscular. They win because they never stop pedaling. Our designated spot, 443, was wedged between vans for Ireland's Joe Barr on my left and Italy's Luigi Barilari on my right.

It was like being at a miniature Olympic event. Endurance cycling is almost a national sport for many smaller European countries. As it is in the pits before the Indy 500 race, other crews were buzzing around the vehicles, taking down bicycles, fine-tuning the colorful lightweight carbon fiber bikes that weighed less than the lightest bowling ball, pumping up tires, lubing chains, and shifting gears then listening for the click-click sound indicating all was well.

Wayne had done a fine job of cleaning up my bike. All white with a few sections of gray along the fork and central top tube, and slick with clean, white tape on the handlebars, it looked like a white knight's horse getting ready to head into battle. That's how being an athlete in this event felt. Instead of armor, we were putting on gloves and helmets and sunglasses. Instead of war paint, sunscreen to prepare for the brutal rays that lay ahead.

*At the starting line*

While music played, friends, families, and crews mingled, wishing everyone well. My good friend, fellow endurance athlete and Hopecam board member Scott Stewart was there with me minutes before we departed. Scott and I had competed in four ironman races together and he was the first to step forward and pledge $10,000 in sponsorship money to kick off the fundraising effort. We would see Scott again in West Virginia as we approached the last stage of the race. The announcer counted down to the moment when the riders were asked to move from the pen to the starting line. A little after noon, the program began with a soloist singing "The Star-Spangled Banner." At 12:15 race director George Thomas began introducing each athlete. The rookies get to start first. I rolled up to the starting line with my follow van inching forward just a few feet behind me. Our van had received a lot of attention because of the bold blue and orange Hopecam logo. When Thomas got to me, he asked me to share a few words about Hopecam. Then it was 12:47. Time to take off.

It felt like a huge burden had been lifted from my shoulders. The logistical decisions were all now on the shoulders of my crew. The first 24 miles of the race are totally self-navigated. The crew and I would start on separate routes because of the course's initially serpentine trajectory, but we'd meet later in the day. I headed east down the bike path, following the river toward the mountains of Southern California where 3,000 miles of the most beautiful landscape in the world lay waiting for me and my crew, all of us finally tracking in the same direction.

*

The further we got from Oceanside, the warmer and sunnier the weather became. My crew had taped a cue sheet of instructions on where to turn on the bike handlebars. I knew the course well because our first practice-training ride had started in Oceanside. Back then we began before sunrise. After six miles the course turns left over the bridge. On the practice ride, I had made the unfortunate mistake of cycling three miles in the wrong direction, arriving at the entrance gate to the Camp Pendleton Marine Corp Base. The Marines guarding the gate were naturally suspicious of a spandex-wearing cyclist heading straight toward the gate at 5:30 in the morning. They helped me find the missed turn, and I took this as a good sign. John Moore had been stationed at Camp Pendleton more than 25 years ago when he was a tank mechanic in the Corps. Getting lost and then back on track with the help of a U.S. Marine could be a good omen.

All the practice and preparation were paying off within the first hour. Pedaling through familiar territory in Southern California, I recalled in clear detail each twist and turn of the roads away from Palomar Mountain and the coastal valley toward the desert. Familiarity dissolves fear. The other racers and I passed one another frequently during these first twenty miles. Men in cowboy hats directed us at the intersections.

I felt confident knowing I had my cue sheet, two water bottles, and my emergency repair kit in case of a flat or a mechanical problem.

Two minutes into the race, and unbeknownst to me, my crew missed a turn. Luckily, they recovered quickly and met me at mile 24, the section of the course along the Old Castle Road where crew teams and their vehicles were waiting to commence the next 2,976 miles of full support driving behind the rider. Dozens of vans were pulled to the side of the road. My crew switched out my water bottles with four fresh, cold refills, and sprayed sunscreen on my neck, a routine that would we'd repeat over and over again during the race.

As we slowly climbed Highway 76, Palomar Mountain to my right, the road became more and more narrow and flanked with steep embankments. I was melting from the effort of climbing 2,500 feet on this five-mile stretch of switchbacks in the afternoon sun. We were on our way to our first time station stop, Lake Henshaw. RAAM has 54 Time Stations, or tracking points for racers, spaced forty to ninety miles apart across the 3000-mile course, where racers must check in to report their arrival times.

The road conditions on this stretch, and over the first 1,000 miles of the race, require drivers to "leapfrog." And that's when we ran into trouble.

Typically, a van follows a rider until a car gets caught behind the van and cannot safely pass. When cars start stacking up, the van driver must pull over, or drive past the rider and then pull over—or leapfrog—to let the traffic flow normally. Race officials treat traffic delays seriously. The first occurrence earns you a fifteen-minute penalty, the second a thirty-minute penalty, the third an hour, and the fourth, disqualification. Delays from a bicycle race build up a lot of anger among local residents, and upset drivers take out their anger on the cyclist.

At this point Ed was driving the follow van and having difficulty finding places to pull over safely. It was late afternoon, ninety-degree heat. I had only one water bottle left on my bike rack and the follow vehicle was at least a mile or so ahead of me on a steep hill. I pedaled for what seemed like an eternity with no sign of my crew.

My throat grew more and more parched and I started to feel dizzy as I climbed the steep eight percent grade hill. One of the most dangerous aspects of the race is dehydration. It's common to underestimate not only the heat but also how much energy it takes to climb out of California over the Sierra Ridge toward the Mojave Desert. Where was my crew?

John had selected Ed as the first driver, but had forgotten that he'd not attended any of the practice rides due to scheduling conflicts. He had never practiced leapfrogging. At first you might think, "How hard could it be? Cars stack up and you pull over." But when there is no place to stop safely the driver must pass the rider and look for a safe spot. Ed found one far ahead of my location, but I couldn't see it. I passed driveway after driveway on the steep hill.

After fifteen minutes without water I pulled over and called them on my phone. "Where are you guys? Why did you go so far ahead of me?" I was getting angrier by the minute. I knew the road conditions were rough but I had counted dozens of safe places where Ed could have easily pulled over to wait for me had he known what to look for.

They had just turned around, they said, and were heading downhill to find me. When I rolled up to the side of the van they apologized, but I was still angry. They'd made a needless mistake. I had learned a lesson in 2006 about stupid mistakes when I ran a marathon in a shirt I hadn't pretested for comfort on long distances; it had constricted my breathing as if I'd been wearing a boa constrictor. However, it had also taught me that the stupidest mistakes are also the avoidable ones. I learned never to experiment with gear before a race.

I wish I had remembered that lesson when John and I discussed the driving shift schedule. Ed shouldn't have been driving…he was the wrong person in the wrong place at the wrong time. Rule number one in RAAM is *never* try something new the first time in a race.

"Ed, you know I love you," I said with a wry smile as he rolled down the window. "But don't ever #@% do that again."

I hated having to be so stern so early in the race, but being sick and dehydrated when it was completely avoidable was a mistake that our team could not afford to repeat. I hoped to make the point without causing the team to fear me or become overly cautious. I was trying to balance making suggestions for improving our work together with a lot of validation at appropriate times, while holding the team accountable.

No one seemed to blame me for being fried and parched in the mid-day sun for a half-hour. They knew that making mistakes that are easily avoided would have a compounding effect later. And I had prepared them—that there would be times when I'd be upset at one thing or another during the race, but I hoped they'd remember it was "tired Len" talking. To their credit, the crew turned the leapfrogging debacle into a learning experience.

They also reminded each other of the "two-thirds rule," which we had learned to follow during the training rides. For the first 1,000 miles of the race, two thirds of the time the support vehicle should be behind me, and one third of the time in front. It's a lot easier for the crew to see if the rider is in distress if they have driven past the rider. Every driver on our team had learned this during the training rides, except Ed, because he couldn't participate in the training rides. In the excitement of the start, we had forgotten to tell him.

*

We arrived at Time Station 1 at Lake Henshaw at 4:45 p.m. and called in our location to the race officials. Twenty miles later we climbed another 2,000 feet before descending 3,000 feet down eight miles of a two-lane, switchback road into the lowest, hottest, and driest place in North America. This famous segment of the course is referred to as the Glass Elevator. At the highest point, the temperature was 85° F at 6:30 p.m. At the bottom: 105° F. Welcome to the Mojave Desert.

As we approached the peak, I saw John standing atop a huge pile of boulders, waving me on. The view from the apex is breathtaking. To the west lies the green valley of the Sierra Nevada. To the east is the most desolate place in North America, where many pioneers perished trying to make it to California's coastal plains. It felt like we were descending into a furnace, the heat slowly increasing with each hairpin turn. This was an extremely difficult descent and critical to navigate before nightfall. Despite the problem with leapfrogging, we stayed on schedule and rolled into Borrego Springs where we rendezvoused with the rest of the team. The shifts then switched and we headed southeast toward the Salton Sea and Brawley, California.

The first time we'd passed through Brawley on a training ride, our gear was housed in three cardboard boxes. It was the second stop in our first practice ride and the crew had wasted time fishing for items needed during the ride. We realized we had to perfect the layout, something we worked on during the other two practice rides.

My interviews with athletes who had done RAAM had revealed that, to be effective, it's best to have several teams within the overall team, with everyone pitching in on a shift. Most teams have two shifts of three people: a driver, navigator, and nutritionist. The larger teams have nine people on the crew so there can be three eight-hour shifts. That was our plan: to have three shifts and have the crews fulfill dual roles. For example, the bike mechanic could also be a navigator, the massage therapist a driver, and the blogger a nutritionist. One shift would always be "on break" resting or using private time for writing email, reading, or just doing nothing.

But the crew began challenging our plan, based on what they'd observed about what had worked and what had failed during training. The basic issue was that some roles had higher risks for my overall performance than did others.

A key risk area was nutrition. When we'd reached Prescott, Arizona, during that first practice ride in March, with just 67 miles to go to complete the ride, we pulled up to a shopping center with a big sign overhead that read "Chipotle." I was starving. My day started in Parker at 5:30 a.m. and over the past 36 hours we had covered 443 miles. I asked my team if it would be okay to have dinner there. They agreed.

I ordered a chicken, rice, and bean burrito for dinner. We all sat down next to the sidewalk in front of the restaurant. After being so hungry, it felt incredible to peel back the aluminum foil and scarf down that burrito. When the crew was ready, we headed north toward the town of Cottonwood. I pulled out of the parking lot. That is when I felt the blood from my brain race to my stomach to digest the 600-calorie bomb that I had wolfed down in five minutes. It was like taking a sleeping pill. But I had sixty more miles to cover.

Darkness was falling as we merged onto a busy intersection that felt like the entrance to a freeway. The road merged from the left lane, so we had to cross over oncoming traffic to make it safely to the curb. My eyes were getting droopy and I could barely see the road as the cars honked at me or at my follow van. When I finally reached the shoulder, it was almost impossible to hold the handlebars straight. I was weaving left and right as the fatigue slowed my pace. My head felt like a bowling ball. It was like a slow-motion dream. Cars were flying by my left side, one by one traveling in excess of 50 mph, and I was worried about drifting into that lane.

I had read the story about four-time RAAM finisher Bob Breedlove who (it was believed) weaved into oncoming traffic and was then struck and killed. I stopped the bicycle and pulled over.

"Something wrong, Len?" Steve Gurney asked.

"Yeah, I need something with sugar. I am really tired."

"All we have is this jar of jelly," Greg said, holding it toward me with a spoon.

I ate the entire jar of jelly.

Then, for a brief moment, I fell asleep standing up. My crew desperately searched for anything they could find in the van that had sugar. My brain felt like all the blood had been drained from it. Finally Greg found a box of a dozen large peppermint Chiclets that finally jolted my brain awake. The rush of sugar felt like the electrical charge from a defibrillator. I managed to finish the rest of the mileage we set out to cover before midnight, and we all learned a valuable lesson.

Now that we were doing the race for real, the nutrition issue came up again. Greg and Ken started the discussion on the importance of consistent nutrition after they looked at the nutrition log for the first 100 miles. Not only were Greg and Ken experts at physiology who had

What Spins the Wheel | 73

extensive first aid and triage skills, they were also both body builders with extensive knowledge on the use of supplements to rebuild torn muscles. They were livid when they saw the entry in the nutrition log stating that I had eaten a submarine sandwich two hours before the race started.

Ken and Greg approached John with their idea. Nutrition, Greg said, would be the most critical element to keep consistent.

"He's going to crave other food, and if someone else is in charge of logging the nutrition, most likely Len is going to bonk," they told John. Bonking was cycling jargon for running out of the kind of fuel needed to stay alert and functional. Runners call it "hitting the wall." Glucose and carbohydrate stores go way down, electrolytes get out of whack.

John said he'd think about it. He wasn't convinced of the value of burning out Ken and Greg by making them the only ones responsible for my nutrition.

"C'mon, John, if our team screws up his nutrition and we don't accurately log everything that goes in and out of him, he's going to slow down and eventually bonk," Ken repeated.

Greg started lobbying other members of the crew, explaining his logic. He found allies in everyone who'd witnessed the Arizona burrito incident. He talked to John again.

"We have to adapt, John," Greg said, meaning that the shifts should be adjusted. "The nutrition logbook is complicated. Given the heat, Len is going to burn muscle instead of fat if we don't manage his calorie intake."

John spent a lot of hours working out shift crews and timetables. He reassured Greg that he'd think about it. For the time being, though, the watchwords became "Beware the burrito."

*

By nine at night, the desert temperature had cooled to ninety degrees and we caught a westerly wind that propelled us toward our destination. Several times the crew had to follow my hand signal—a system we'd developed on one of our training rides—to back off and create more space between the front bumper of the van and the rear wheel of my bike to avoid blocking the tailwind that was gently pushing me eastward. The strong tailwind made following a sort of dance. If the van was too close behind the rider, it blocked the tailwind, negating its advantage. It was a constant approach-recede balancing act between maximizing performance while preserving safety.

The ride from Brawley to Blythe, where we arrived at 3:20 a.m. for my first sleep break, was relatively refreshing—the temperature was a balmy eighty-one degrees. The advance van had secured three hotel rooms for the crew. I stripped down for a quick shower and was handed a plate of chicken and rice to eat while Kaitee, our massage therapist, worked on my legs.

*Borrego Springs, CA, where follow van &*
*RV crews meet up for the first time*

It was a great first night. We'd hit a record average speed of 20.2 mph covering the 89-mile segment from Lake Henshaw to Brawley, our second time station stop. My speed eventually evened out to a 16.6 mph pace. We had passed through one of the most spectacular sections of the course with mile after mile of sand dunes, although we could see none of it, no light at all, not even the taillights of my competitors.

Sometimes beauty and opportunity are all around you, even though you can't see them. I was remembering Alex, the day's Hopecam child, whom I'd talked to that morning. Alex just picks up everything that life throws at him and throws it right back. In his mind, the whole experience with paralysis is just a temporary setback. How many adults would love to have an ounce of the determination that flows through the veins of that little warrior?

When George Thomas, the RAAM director, had asked me to say a few words about Hopecam at the starting line, I said that we were riding for children who have cancer. They have a similar journey that requires perseverance and strength. The only difference is that they have to finish. I can stop at any time.

I prayed that I'd have the same determination and strength to finish the race that Alex had about finding ways to do what he wanted to do.

Before drifting off to sleep, I asked for no more than sixty minutes of rest so I could get back out and enjoy every minute of the cool air. I was up at five, eating breakfast and talking to my morning driver, Bill. With a few quick adjustments to the bike and the lights, we were back on the road at 5:30 a.m.

## Lesson 3

Even with extensive preparation for a mission, things will still go wrong—or at least need to be adjusted once the mission launches. Some of these are things we could have foreseen, such as how we learned about needing to fine-tune our lineup and have the right people in the right places at the right time. We made a mistake by having a rookie driver take the wheel on the very first segment of the race.

Other things will become clear as you implement the mission in real time. We began to realize, for instance, the importance of the nutritionist role to the rider. The empowerment that came from having delegated this responsibility to only two crew members allowed them, even though they were young firefighters drilled to respect the chain of command, to challenge our crew chief to rethink his lineup and make the nutrition role a specialist task, shaking up his well-prepared shift rotation.

Through it all, we kept our focus on our mission. A huge part of that was honoring the important role of connection. We were taking Alex Green "with us" on the journey that day. Just as my son Matt's webcam visits with his classmates at school kept his friends with him during his journey even though he could not be there physically, and kept him from being alone, our connection to Alex Green let him know that he, too, was not alone.

Finding a touchstone that "humanizes" your mission makes it easier to keep that focus.

---

*Let the games begin! Here is to an awesome start!*

—Laurie Forkas

*Len, you are an inspiration to all of us who try every day to be better persons, or change our lives and venture into the unknown, but most of all because your great endeavor and sacrifice is being made not for yourself but for Hopecam and the children it benefits. Pace yourself and ease into this thing. Good Luck.*

—Mark D'Amico

*Hope for the best. Have a good race. See you at the finish line. My mom wants to know if you are going to come in first place.*

—Ian (age 9), Nick (age 9), and Thomas Cox (age 6) (Laurie's children)

# DAY 2
June 14, from Blythe to Prescott

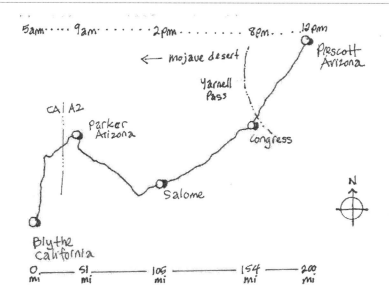

TODAY WE RIDE FOR JESSICA

| START | END | START | FINISH | DISTANCE | TOTAL MI | ELEVATION |
|---|---|---|---|---|---|---|
| Blythe, CA | Parker, AZ | 5:30 AM | 8:42 AM | 51.10 | 286 | 1,565 |
| Parker, AZ | Salome, AZ | 8:42 AM | 2:00 PM | 53.70 | 342 | 1,615 |
| Sleep Break | | 2:00 PM | 4:20 PM | | | |
| Salome, AZ | Congress, AZ | 4:20 PM | 7:44 PM | 49.00 | 395 | 1,448 |
| Congress, AZ | Prescott, AZ | 7:50 PM | 12:10 AM | 46.20 | 441 | 4,708 |
| Day 2 Sleep Break | | 12:10 AM | 5:07 AM | | | |

# CHAPTER 4

# SUFFERFEST

*When going through Hell, keep going.*

—Sir Winston Churchill

THERE IS A word for days like this one: Sufferfest.
WeatherBug, the second most popular online weather information service after The Weather Channel, was forecasting brutally hot, windy, and miserable conditions for today's desert crossing. WeatherBug had agreed to support us during the ride with twice-daily updates and 24/7 access to a meteorologist to guide us as we crossed the country. This support was critical. How you deal with winds and storms can make or break your ride. If there's a sustained 20 mph headwind and I'm near a rest break, for example, I'll go to sleep early. If there's a strong tailwind and I'm scheduled for a long sleep break, I'll take a quick nap and ride all night.

When we departed from Blythe early that morning, along a relatively flat course that followed the Colorado River into Arizona, temperatures were in the low eighties.

By 8:40 a.m., we encountered a 20 mph headwind as we rode uphill for the next 50 miles. Every pedal forward was an effort. Pedaling against this section with a strong headwind felt like there was a rope connecting my bicycle seat to the follow van, and I was towing it. Little did I know that the next five hours would be one of the most memorable experiences of the entire race course.

Unlike yesterday, dehydration was not my issue. My team had stored lots of ice-cold water and nutrition bottles, and we'd figured out a system for getting me what I needed. Today's issue was overheating my core temperature. In the Mojave Desert in June, temperatures move from the eighties to the nineties to the hundreds. Today's forecast: 105° F.

In the sun, 105° F really feels like 115° F. When you stand still on the pavement for more than two minutes, the bottom of your sneakers starts to melt. My crew was spending as much time as possible in the shade, and even they felt like they were melting. On the bike, it feels like being in a toaster oven. The sun bakes you from above and the asphalt cooks you from below. The bike's wheels heat up. Everything radiates heat, and you're feeling as cooked and malleable as that wavy air you associate with mirages. Except this isn't a mirage. It's real.

If I had been built like some of the skinnier cyclists, overheating wouldn't be such a concern. But at 5'10", 187 pounds, it was an issue for me. The heavier you are, the more muscle you carry. The more muscle you carry, the more likely you are to run the risk of heatstroke. Your body's muscle tissue is composed mostly of water, and as your core temperature rises, your brain swells. There is less blood in your muscles because blood is a coolant and is redirected to tissue closer to your skin to cool you down. As core temperature rises, muscles get fatigued, and breathing becomes painfully difficult. Heatstroke symptoms begin with disorientation, then headaches, followed by seizures, and eventually coma. When your throat is parched and your skin feels like it is cooking and the possibility of heatstroke is as real as every push of your pedal against the hot desert wind, it's easy to start freaking out.

This is the point when many people quit. They get fixated on the pain of the present moment instead of looking past it and realizing that better days are ahead. In business, it's the ability to hunker down and survive crappy economic times knowing that even if you have done everything in your power to minimize the suffering, you still have to endure.

Churchill got it right: "If you're going through Hell, keep going." Stop thinking about the pain. Just get through it.

Our team was prepared to endure the Mojave Desert, because we could draw from our experience on practice rides, and from developing the mental confidence and toughness that comes out of familiarity with similar challenges. In a half-Ironman race I'd done in June 2009, in Cambridge, Maryland, the heat index was well over 100° F. It was so hot and sticky at 6:00 a.m. that the volunteers who wrote your race number on your arms and legs with permanent magic markers had to give up because athletes were sweating so profusely. The marker wouldn't stick and it was a worthless task. That day, after a 1.2 mile swim, I biked in the unrelenting sun, then headed out for a thirteen-mile run in even hotter shade-less conditions. My body remembered that feeling. It also remembered that I had survived it. Competing in hot endurance races made crossing the Mojave Desert less fearful.

Every five minutes my team handed me ice-filled tube socks and ice-cold water bottles. I draped the tube socks around my neck to cool it and keep my core temperature down. There was a possible downside: the melting ice could drip into my bike shorts, combine with bacteria, and create saddle sores. Today was so hot that the melting ice evaporated before it hit my waist.

The water bottles served two purposes. One was to keep me hydrated. The other, like the tube socks, was to function as an external cooling system. I was wearing white arm coolers made of white stretch fabric wrist to elbow. The fabric acts like a sunscreen and at the same time absorbs water. The company that makes these coolers is called RecoFit and the owner, Susan Eastman Walton, is a neighbor of our crew chief, John Moore.

Some of the water my team handed me I drank. The rest I poured on my forearms, which cooled the network of veins and arteries carrying heat throughout my body. After soaking the arm coolers thoroughly, I would resume pedaling only to find that they were dry in about 10 minutes.

For five hours nonstop, my faithful crew created a virtual assembly line of six people cranking out freezing cold drinks while I burned through the equivalent of a week's worth of sunscreen. The follow van would pull far enough ahead of me—like we did when we leapfrogged in the beginning of the course—to stop and let a team member holding a bottle step out onto the pavement. It was like a well-rehearsed dance:

I get within sight of the crew, I throw my empty bottle on the road, the team member starts running backward, I pedal forward, the team member hands off the bottle like in a relay, I grab the bottle and stuff it in the bike's holder, the team member picks up my discarded bottle and runs back to the van, I pedal past them, the van leapfrogs again for another round. It was a synchronized symphony. It was beautiful. It got me through.

And today at least, I didn't have to worry about saddle sores.

But biking against the relentless wind was a struggle that just wouldn't end. I could not change the force coming at me, so I decided to improve my form on the bike to be as aerodynamic as possible. I started thinking about my pedal stroke and how efficient my cadence was. As I turned over my pedals, were my heels flat so I wouldn't waste energy?

*Thirty hours in the Mojave Desert*

Having good form consumes a lot of brainpower. But it's also a way to filter out thoughts like what time it is, and how many miles you have yet to go. There are so many rational reasons to quit, to allow environmental factors to influence your resolve to move forward, to make you want to stop and wait for them to recede before you go on.

Jessica, the second-grade immigrant child from Ghana for whom I was riding that day, was on my mind. She had recently moved to the

United States and after only a few months in her new country she was diagnosed with liver cancer. We were both in the desert that day—me in Mojave, she in her own social desert. I was planning to call her on my lunch break, ask her how she was doing, and tell her how I was doing. Radiation and chemotherapy treatments are like the hell of the desert. They send heat searing through Jessica's body, tormenting her.

How could I even entertain the idea of quitting while riding that day for Jessica? I'd signed up for a race. The twelve-day clock was forever ticking in the back of my mind. I had to finish. I'd promised my sponsors I would. I had 150,000 reasons to come across that finish line—one for every donated dollar. I wanted to raise awareness and financial resources for Hopecam. I wanted more kids with cancer to have what Matt had had—a connection to friends at one of the scariest and loneliest times of their lives.

In their book, *Willpower*, Roy F. Baumeister and John Tierney explore the idea of how self-control is similar to a muscle. It can be exercised. The nine years of prior endurance athletics increased my physical capacity to press on and do an increased volume of exercise, but it was the mental capacity to endure greater and greater challenges that gave me the ability to draw strength during the challenge of the desert heat. Willpower is not an inherited trait as much as it something that can be acquired, as the authors so eloquently report. Willpower also involves the ability not to notice—or at least to ignore—the pain that goes along with challenges, a trait that seems hardwired in me.

In tough conditions, sometimes personal flaws become extremely useful. Mine is a tendency not to notice things. My wife, for example, is completely amazed at how good I am at this. One day she'd bought a beautiful orchid plant and placed it on the center of our kitchen counter. After dinner, when I was cleaning up the kitchen, she said, "Do you like the orchid I bought today?"

I looked at her. "What orchid?"

She rolled her eyes, pointed to it, and walked away. It had been right in front of me all along.

When racing, I often did not notice some of the outrageously difficult conditions right in front of me. A teammate might say, "I can't believe you just plowed up that hill so quickly," and the truth was I simply didn't remember the hill or plowing up anything.

It's as if some filter screens out my fear, such as when Matt got sick. The armor went up, my voice got quiet. Somehow the words to reassure Matt that he was going to survive appeared. Everything else faded away. Over the years, I learned that pain becomes isolated—whether it was in a race or when watching Matt go through chemotherapy. Pain is compartmentalized. It's not about looking away or turning your back on it. Instead it's about trying your best to take each negative or challenging event and put it in one of two buckets:

**Bucket One:** the factors you can do nothing about because you have no control or power to change them.

**Bucket Two:** the factors you can do something about like relieving the pain or changing the circumstances that were the root cause of the negative situation.

Today our team was in an arid, desolate, and blindingly bright landscape. Sunscreen dripped into my eyes, dust choked my breathing, tractor trailer trucks sped past me kicking up dirt, gravel, road grit, and grime. These were things we had *no control* over. They went in Bucket One. In Bucket Two, the elements we had *some control* over, we put the poor, bumpy pavement called hard tack – a mix of gravel and tar glued to the base road pavement. I credit my team's critical thinking skills for this one. My team could relieve the effect of the Arizona hard tack's vibration on my wheels and handlebars by letting one third of the air escape from my front and back tires. Reducing tire pressure softened the ride and thereby the vibration of the road that was burning out my forearms. Lower tire pressure also meant slightly slower speed, but it was worth it. Smoother flow is a good tradeoff for loss of speed when you factor in the wear and tear on the upper body when riding hard tack. You just have to remember to pump them up when you hit smooth pavement and start pedaling faster again.

My team was always offering other creative solutions to problems, sometimes broadcasting them on the loudspeaker attached to the roof of the follow van and sometimes simply pulling up next to me on the road and shouting or handing written solutions out the window. But I had to ask my team to stop a couple of them, like their cheering from the sidelines along the lines of "You are almost there!" It's not exactly a helpful reference point. Likewise, when John sprayed me with water, trying to keep me cool as I was pedaling: although I appreciated the effort, all it did was mist my glasses.

*Mojave Desert stop to re-inflate tires*

By the time we all pulled into the next time station, I was mentally and physically spent. It was only 2:00 p.m. My speed had dropped to an average of 11.5 mph, but the two-hour sleep break in the air-conditioned RV felt so good. We knew the road would break north eventually, the wind change direction, the desert come to an end.

*

At 4:20, when I was ready to get to work again, the temperatures were dropping. It was a subtle shift, but when your body is engaged in nonstop physical work, it becomes acutely aware of even the smallest environmental changes. I could tell that it was just below 100° F. Each degree of drop was like a vise slowly releasing my neck from its grip. Now we had a mild tailwind. We made it to Congress, Arizona, Time Station 6, in about three hours, and kept going east toward the town of Yarnell, which sits atop a 2,000-foot vertical climb to a high mesa. It's one of the most challenging sections in the state.

It probably seems crazy to say that after fourteen hours of tough desert heat I looked forward to that climb. A dozen switchback turns and a steady four – to six-percent grade that becomes an eight – to ten-percent grade at the peak have made Yarnell Pass one of the most famous sections of the RAAM course. But leaving Congress at dusk to face down the Yarnell hill was something quite beautiful. The toughest section of the race was behind me, the vise grip of heat on my neck was releasing with each push from desert to mountain.

Adversity or opportunity is always a matter of perspective. Many years ago I learned that it was futile to look up ahead when climbing a long twisting hill, like Yarnell Pass, preferring to look down and attempt to mentally detach from the suffering. Looking up to another switchback turn was simply too depressing. Finally cresting the hill after an hour-long climb was like being released from a prison cell.

The stars were out, and I was looking forward to a fast 25-mph descent. The only recognizable forms were the tall evergreens. My worry now was the crew following me and their mental fatigue from having to drive fifteen miles an hour, or, in this case, eight to ten as we first climbed, then braked as we descended, losing more and more light the longer and further we went. Night diminishes the view of the hills in front of your wheels. Anxiety rises when cars stack up behind you and you know that some of those drivers have just come from a late night at the bar. Local cyclists had been killed on roads like these.

During the day, navigators are not as challenged as they are at night, watching like sentinels for the first inkling that my form is beginning to wobble or weave—a sure sign of dangerous fatigue. We were all acutely aware of the risks of falling asleep and veering into oncoming traffic, so

I took frequent five-minute naps in the van or in the RV to recharge whenever my eyelids started drifting shut.

Riding in total darkness is transformative. The darkness makes it seem as if you are wearing blinders, like race horses. Darkness filters out distractions, narrowing the field of view and magnifying the immediate. Specific elements that would normally go unnoticed, like the texture of the pavement and the brightness of lights as you approach a small town, are magnified. The sound of passing trucks and the whoosh of the wind that follows them. The bright high beams of the headlights of approaching cars that can be detected well in advance of their arrival. My follow van and its three crew members carefully positioning their location to protect me from an errant driver. Of course the best part of riding at night was the cooler temperatures and refreshing air.

When we completed the five-mile descent on the moonlit twisty and bumpy highway that rolled right into Prescott, Arizona, the nightlife was in full swing. At this point it wasn't drivers I was concerned about. It was the temptation of breaking routine in this hip and trendy mountain town and giving in to the desire for a taste of a cold beer. If ever we all could have used one, it was then. Hot, sweaty, and sunburned, my crew entered into the nutrition logbook eight gallons of freezing cold liquids with only two bathroom breaks. Thankfully our hotel was two miles from town.

*

Today's Sufferfest was the most painful experience I'd ever had on a bicycle. Fighting to keep hydrated and stay steady during that 50-mile segment at such a slow pace was just depressing. It took every ounce of willpower to focus and just keep going. But we did, and we survived our first true test. Plus we were in the top third of the field overall and in the middle of the pack in my division.

A race coach once told me that it's never the fastest person who wins these endurance races. It's the athlete who slows down the least. Success in many races results from achieving a negative split, meaning the first half of the race is slower than the second, and you are feel strong at the end of the race.

Yes, I was determined to finish—that was the focus. And sure, I wanted to be competitive, but I also didn't want to get sucked into stretching myself too thin in exchange for a podium finish.

And yet, while Kaitee was working on moving blood through the muscles and smoothing and stretching them out, I started thinking about what that race coach had said. And I started thinking that when all the others were speeding up, I wanted to slow it down. I wanted to have that negative split and feel strong at the finish line.

## Lesson 4

Willpower comes naturally to many but it is a skill that can be acquired through practice. Willpower and the mental toughness that comes from the thousands of hours of physical exercise are subconsciously training both mind and body. Most athletes give up mentally well before their bodies have reached their physical limit. Our commitment to press on was mission based. Our mission was to help children with cancer so that more could have access to what Hopecam delivers.

Having a strong, well-stated mission creates the fuel that drives willpower. Just as nutrition was a critical element in fueling my body, the mission of helping these children was the mental fuel that sustained the will to not give up. How often do we run into rough patches at work or with our families or relationships and feel like we are in our own Mojave Deserts? When the pain and the distance ahead seem as though they will never end? If you believe in your mission and are committed to reaching it, you will find the willpower to endure. The headwinds eventually will shift, as they did in my case, becoming a tailwind that pushed me toward Congress, Arizona.

*Great planning, great practice, great support, great cause, great ride!!!*

—Dick Michaux

*Dear crew... hate to ask, but would you mind singing the following to Len.... Macho macho man....I want to be a macho man. When I sent Len that singing birthday card a few years back I had no idea the impact it would have on him!*

—Laurie Forkas

*Go Len! You are AWESOME, brother. Tailwind should be at your back for the next 3000 miles! The Longs (Jim, Molly, Mary & Megan) are all praying and pulling for you!*

—Jim Long

*The desert is tough. But you're tougher. Drink. Peddle. Drink. Peddle. McGuire Woods is cheering for you.*

—Preston Bryant

# DAY 3
June 15, from Prescott to Mexican Hat

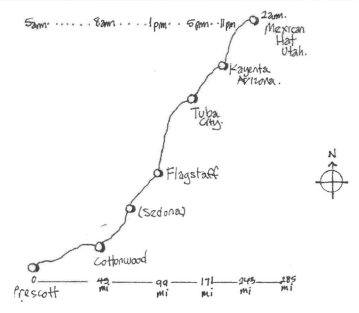

TODAY WE RIDE FOR DANIEL

| START | END | START | FINISH | DISTANCE | TOTAL MI | ELEVATION |
|---|---|---|---|---|---|---|
| Prescott, AZ | Cottonwood, AZ | 5:07 AM | 8:20 AM | 44.70 | 483 | 2,452 |
| Cottonwood, AZ | Flagstaff, AZ | 8:23 AM | 12:46 PM | 54.00 | 536 | 4,728 |
| Flagstaff, AZ | Tuba City, AZ (MDT) | 12:48 PM | 4:50 PM | 71.90 | 608 | 1,696 |
| Tuba City, AZ (MDT) | Kayenta, AZ | 5:23 PM | 11:08 PM | 72.20 | 680 | 2,455 |
| Kayenta, AZ | Mexican Hat, UT | 11:17 PM | 1:41 AM | 42.00 | 725 | 1,073 |
| Day 3 Sleep Break | | 1:41 AM | 6:02 AM | | | |

# CHAPTER 5
# THROWING OUT THE PLAN

*I think a hero is an ordinary individual who finds strength to
persevere and endure in spite of overwhelming obstacles.*

—Christopher Reeve

THE MOUNTAINS CONTINUED as we climbed north through
Cottonwood and then Sedona on our way to Flagstaff. Joe Knill
and Steve Gurney, two new members of our crew from Reston, would
join us sometime mid-day, in Flagstaff. Joe, the ultimate utility fielder,
could and was willing to do anything needed. Steve, a gifted writer, would
feed reports from the road that would be posted on our blog. Our team
would be complete.

Though the morning air mist, courtesy of the change in altitude,
was cool and refreshing, the day did not start off well. I had woken up
with a sore neck. How was that possible? Our nightly routine involved
me showering, eating some solid food, and lying down for a two-hour
massage. Usually Greg worked on my IT (iliotibial) bands and Kaitee
on my shoulders and neck. I always fell asleep during the massage. So
how did I have a sore neck if Kaitee was massaging me properly? On top
of that I had water on my knees. They were puffy and swollen. I was
beginning to freak out. My knees looked like softballs. I was in trouble.
I had 7,000 feet of climbing to do between Prescott and Flagstaff. How
was I going to keep riding if my knees looked like that?

Then I had a thought: Kaitee had developed a good friendship with
one of the other young crew members with whom she had a lot in

common. They were working the same hours. Was it possible that once asleep, she figured she was done and took a break with her friend?

The problem was, massage is essential for helping your body recover from the abuse it gets from riding the bike twenty hours a day. It's normal to develop water on the knee. It's normal for your feet to swell up to two shoe sizes bigger than normal. One of the things every RAAM athlete worries about is getting Shermer's neck, a condition that can incapacitate a rider because the strain it puts on the neck muscles completely fatigues them, making it impossible to hold the head upright without support.

If you get Shermer's neck (named after RAAM athlete Michael Shermer), your head flops over like a Raggedy Ann doll. There is no gradual warning sign of this ailment. It's about two hours from when the rider first feels the extreme neck fatigue to when the neck completely gives out. Shermer's neck is a game-ending event for most RAAM athletes. Wearing a neck brace is a risky option because it limits your vision. Riding with a brace becomes extremely dangerous. Michael Shermer's neck gave out in the 1991 race. He finished by riding while propping up his head with his hand.

Greg, Kaitee, and I had put together a neck-stretching program and massage schedule that we thought would keep my neck muscles strong and flexible. I knew how my body felt when it got the proper amount and kind of massage—and when it didn't. I knew I'd have to talk to Kaitee. I just didn't know when or how. So I put that problem in the back of my mind for the time being, trusting a solution would come.

I was glad that my crew had let me sleep three and a half hours that night, the longest sleep break I'd had so far, to prepare for today's ride through one of the most mountainous areas of Arizona. I needed every minute of it. I'd slept less than three hours total the first two days, just to make it through the desert, and I was beginning to feel the effects of sleep deprivation, even though I'd trained myself to function on only four hours of sleep a night and even though by nature I'm one of what science calls "the sleepless elite"—people who require fewer than six hours of sleep to function normally, according to an April 2011 article by Melinda Beck published in *The Wall Street Journal*.

The "sleepless elite" constitute from less than one to as much as three percent of the population. The article suggests that a genetic variation explains these sleepers' different circadian rhythms. The pattern is observable in childhood and often runs in families, these individuals having a "sort of psychological and physiological energy that we just don't understand" according to a neurologist quoted in the article. Besides being able to get a lot done on very little sleep, they tend to have a high tolerance for pain and push right through obstacles without the setbacks that stop normal sleepers.

My sleep cycle is 60 minutes instead of the typical 90–120. That means that I can recharge my battery faster than most other athletes. The previous January, I had put myself on a "sleep diet" of four hours each night, no matter how much training I had planned for each given day. By the time I'd arrived in Oceanside, I had physiologically adapted to craving only four hours of sleep.

Charles Duhigg writes about this in his book *The Power of Habit*. Through sheer repetition, it is possible to create "reflexive behavior" by repeating certain patterns. He describes the "habit loop," which is when an environmental cue turns into a normalized behavior. In my case this was the habit of waking up at 4:00 a.m. The alarm would go off and, like one of Pavlov's dogs, I would immediately spring up from bed and start preparing for a two-hour bicycle ride as part of my training regimen, without thought. It was never a choice when the alarm buzzed at the early morning hour. The alarm rang. I went right to the spot where I had set out my clothing the night before. Got dressed and went right to the bicycle. No thought. No choice. I just did it.

Today was no different. It was still dark at 5:00 a.m., so I turned on the lights mounted to the handlebars and my headlamp. Nothing. I pulled over, released the handlebar light from its mounting, and snapped off the helmet headlamp, then handed them to the team in the follow van that pulled up next to me.

"I brought three of everything," I said. So my crew handed me a replacement battery for the bike and a new headlamp, which has a battery built into it.

Nothing. Again I handed the battery and headlamp back to the crew. Again, nothing. All three batteries and all three headlamps were dead.

Thankfully the sun was just rising and I could see well enough.

"Fellas, I'm not pointing any fingers at anyone but how many of these lights do I need to buy to get one that will work when I need it?"

Whose job was it to charge the lights? It's not very complicated. And it was only the third day of the race—what other mundane tasks had not been assigned? What's going to fail next? It felt as though things were beginning to slip through the cracks.

"If this were ten o'clock at night, I'd be screwed," I said.

*Steve Gurney and Joe Knill join crew in Flagstaff*

There is nothing worse for a mentally prepared rider than to be grounded for something that could have been easily avoided. It's in the WE CAN CONTROL THIS bucket. It's not the same as a navigational mistake, when our crew is tired or we miss an important sign along the highway. If just one person had accepted ownership of the task or created a process to ensure that charging the lights was on a checklist, things like this wouldn't happen. In professional football, the saying goes, the team that makes the fewest mistakes typically wins. This incident felt like a 10-yard penalty for delay of game. How many more mistakes would our team make between now and the end of the race?

I couldn't dwell on that now…what I could control was my progress toward the peak of the Woodchute mountain range in the Jerome State Park. Grueling, unrelenting, with short twisting-turning sections, the road seemed to sprout a never-ending array of yellow signs with arrows pointing left, then right. In the light of day these signs can be hard to see. But at night or in the pre-dawn, their reflective coatings are like a little voice shouting out *just a little further, a little more, just a little more.* I felt like saying, *stop already.* I know the road is going to bend, where else can it go?

*Two crew teams meet near Tuba City*

Even though I am a strong climber, there is nothing fun about stomping up a hill at 10 mph. It is dreadful. Your quadriceps start to burn, the soles of your feet begin to heat up from the force on the pedals. Mentally, it is exhausting to be on the bike pumping out so much effort to go such a short distance with no end in sight. This is a tormenting 30-mile uphill grind.

Finally after two-and-a-half hours going up, I see ahead, in a clearing like a mirage in a desert, there was this beautiful sign, unlike all the rest. It is my favorite road sign of all—a picture of a truck heading down a big black triangle representing a steep hill. In my mind a beam of light shining down from the heavens illuminates this sign. It means only one thing. You are at the top of the hill, and should get ready to grab two handfuls of brakes because you're in for a wicked downhill descent.

Today, this road launched into a twelve-mile, 3,500-foot drop. This is where the car companies film the sports car commercials. The freedom, the open road—but miss a turn or blow a tire at 45 mph and you will catapult over the guardrail over the cliff into oblivion, where it will take a team of rescue workers to recover your body and what is left of your bike.

*

RAAM, we were discovering, is a mix of moments. The "sufferfests," like when we crossed the Mojave Desert. The highs of being surrounded by stunning scenery that was both natural and man-made. The irony of always being ten or twenty miles from famous landmarks like the Grand Canyon that we couldn't tour because they weren't on the pre-designated race route. The unexpected camaraderie at some time station stops. The good sportsmanship was heartening, such as when we missed a turn after Cottonwood. The backup van of the competing Czech team supporting Jiri Hledick, a racer in our same age category, followed us, its lights flashing. They had chased us down for over a mile to tell us we were going the wrong way. We missed a critical turn and they helped us.

During my afternoon rest break I ducked into the RV, showered, and changed into a new shirt and shorts (kit). Wayne, our mechanic had to tighten many of the screws and bolts on the bike after that long climb because of the amount of force it took stomping on the bicycle crank lurching up the hills. In just a little over a half-hour, my team had me back out riding the next leg toward Kayenta, while our videographer drove ahead to film the landscape between Kayenta, Arizona, and Mexican Hat, Utah, our goal for the night. Amy would do anything for a shot. She was a professional in every sense of the word. She'd climbed onto a 20-foot tall pile of gravel to capture the absolute desolation of the moonscape we were riding through. Now she was on a mission to capture every angle of the dry and parched "Painted Desert."

Amy had been filming everything she could, including our daily dedications to Hopecam children. Earlier she'd filmed the dedication to one of my favorites, twelve-year-old Daniel Shank-Rowe. He's a very likable kid. On one special occasion, while Daniel was homebound undergoing treatment, two entire fifth-grade classes lined up, one by one, in front of the camera and told Daniel jokes. They then formed a line and each gave high-fives to the classroom web camera, delighting Daniel, but ultimately breaking the camera. It was a small price to pay for a moment of joy in a sick child's life.

Daniel was featured in the video that was used to recruit sponsors to support our fundraising goal. There is no better way to share the benefit of a service than to ask for a testimonial from a customer. Daniel was one of the first kids to use Hopecam, and this articulate twelve-year-old has spoken publicly about his experience in a way that makes Tony Robbins look subdued. His testimony was heartbreaking. Amy completely nailed that interview and his story was compelling to many donors before the race.

Amy took care of posting the daily dedications on the website. These were the other moments that made RAAM more than just a race to the finish line. They reminded us of why we were riding. And they were our way of letting these Hopecam kids know we were serious about the inspiration they were to the team and me.

*

By this third day of the race our team was beginning to establish a groove. They'd overcome initial confusion about roles and responsibilities and worked out doing mundane tasks like laundry and cleaning the RV. As crew chief, John led by example. He did whatever needed doing, including emptying the RV's septic tank.

Individual crew members were also stepping up for specific tasks. When Joe heard about the battery and headlamp debacle experienced that morning, he stepped up. "It's my job from now on," he said. "I will make sure that this never happens again." Joe took ownership of the problem. He spoke with our crew chief John and they added "charging lights" to the advance crew's list of responsibilities. We never had another dead battery the entire trip.

Around this time, John began following a pattern that he would keep throughout the race. He'd see to it that I made it down for the evening and that the morning crew had everything they needed to roll until 10 a.m. He then rotated sleeping between the RV, hotel rooms, and his hammock.

Bill Vitek, our second in command, drove the follow van during the morning shift, usually paired up with Greg or Ken in the nutrition spot in the back seat and Brian, Steve, or Joe as navigator. Bill often drove until the lunch break, about a nine-to ten-hour shift. Ken later told me that Bill Vitek slept even less than I did: He was always giving up his bed for another crew member and made it his job to worry about my safety.

Every morning, John's first priority was to determine the errands the advance van would need to run to keep our caravan moving. Typically by ten the advance van and the RV had pulled up stakes at the hotel and passed me en route to the lunch hour time station to set up.

*Firemen Greg Wood & Ken Gates*

John brought the crew together every morning and discussed the next few hours' important tasks, such as doing laundry, shopping for supplies, and scouting hotel rooms for the night's stay. We had made a commitment to the team that we would not go cheap on accommodations. Every night we rented three hotel rooms so each member of the team could have a warm bed and a hot shower before starting the next day. Many teams rent an RV for that purpose and rotate sleep schedules so that there is always a resting/sleeping shift. We knew that over time, fatigue from a sleep-deprived crew would contribute to navigational errors—or worse. The safety of the crew was paramount and the money for the additional rooms was an easy expenditure to justify. Having hotel rooms was especially fortuitous during the early days of the race, when Ken experienced a severe two-day case of elevation sickness compounded by fatigue from the negative effects of sleep deprivation. Though during the day he slept in the RV whenever he was not mixing nutrition bottles, he at least had a comfortable bed at night, which always makes being sick while away from home a little more tolerable.

*John's whiteboard*

It was during these first few days that we realized that we couldn't operate on the original "three static crew rotation" plan that John had worked out. He'd wanted to have two of my long-time friends, Bill and Greg, people I'd be more inclined to take direction from, operate as sub-crew chiefs on two shifts.

But the nutrition issue resurfaced.

Logging calories was important, but at first we didn't realize how specialized it really was. Nutrition? Sure, mix it and write it down. Greg and Ken counted every calorie, but when a new person joined the shift, the logging fell apart. And when Greg heard that someone had given me one-third of a sub sandwich the first day of the race, he nearly lost it. "If that happens," he said, "then we have learned nothing about the first practice ride where you almost got hit by a car in Arizona because of eating that burrito and almost falling asleep."

It became a bit of a showdown on how to break up the teams and focus on specialization. John didn't want to overwork anyone by having two people perform a three-person job. He was worried that someone would burn out.

The earlier lobbying by Greg hadn't been completely successful, so Ken joined the lobbying efforts. They continued to work on convincing John that they could handle the nutrition by dividing that one job planned for a three-person shift rotation between the two of them.

"We're firemen," they said. "We train to work under less than optimal sleep conditions."

Since they were two of the younger members of the team and had great stamina, the argument was that much more persuasive. They also reasoned that there would be fewer screw-ups if they were the only two doing that work.

In the end, the argument made sense. As John listened to the different discussions about this that were going on while I was on the bike, he rethought his original three-shift, three crew members per shift plan, and changed his plan.

"We came to realize that we didn't have three crews. We had four specialists—Greg, Ken, Kaitee, and Wayne," he said. "The rest of us were just chauffeurs."

His management problem then became how to make sure the right specialist was in the right place at the right time, and then using the "chauffeurs and go-fers" for support. He changed from line management to using a matrix to manage the schedule.

We laughed about the low-tech way he ended up doing it—stopping at a Walmart to pick up a magnetic board and magnetic stickers. He wrote everyone's name on a sticker and twice a day moved those around on the day's "to do" list as needed to indicate the day's schedule. Then he'd snap a photo with his smartphone and share it with the team, so everyone had a copy.

Adjusting the schedule became more an art than a science. Though initially there was some confusion while everyone got used to working with each other, the new system worked. The saving grace in getting things done, whether it was booking hotel rooms or picking up parts, doing laundry or emptying the RV's septic tank, was that everyone was clear on the mission.

"Everyone understood what the end goal was," John said. The other thing was flexibility. "The plan that we drew up was not something we stuck to precisely."

*Kaitee DeMonti*
*Massage Therapist*

In fact, one of our crew had talked to the German team supporting rider Holger Roethig. This team had done the race several times. "It's good to have a good plan, then work to perfect it," they said. "Then you throw the plan into the trash."

How often do business leaders create business plans to attract investors, or obtain financing only to launch their business while rarely revisiting the document that helped jumpstart the initiative? Plans force the authors to think through multiple possibilities and scenarios. It's an essential tool in critical thinking, and we had no shortage of critical thinkers on our team, including our leader, a seasoned technology executive and business development expert.

The planning process wasn't wasted. It was a good way to think through all the variables and all the details. "Developing a plan is a great way to understand what you are doing," John said. "Holding the plan wasn't the goal, though. The goal was to cross the finish line."

So we made good use of the specialists. Wayne kept the bike in tip-top shape, fine-tuning the derailleurs, tightening up loose parts and inspecting the bike, scanning for problems that might cause trouble every time I was on a break, which meant that a lot of his shift happened during the early hours of the morning. He also always had to be within close range in case anything went wrong mechanically.

Ken mixed nutrition bottles and tracked what I was eating so that I'd have the fuel to sustain the effort without mental fatigue. Greg also managed nutrition, he and Ken pulling really long shifts to make sure that even the smallest things—such as making sure that anyone handling the ice wore gloves to avoid bacterial contamination—were taken care of. This meant that Greg and Ken would work 30 percent more than other members of the crew, but they were firefighters and accustomed to working double shifts. What made me feel confident was the commitment and complete ownership that our crew exhibited toward their job during the race.

The other specialty, of course, was the bodywork provided by Greg, who besides being a paramedic was also a physical trainer, and Kaitee, who'd been trained in sports massage. Greg was strong and could apply the force needed to release the lactic acid in my IT bands so that I'd be pain free and ready to ride the next morning. He was so strong, in fact, that at first I had to bite a towel to distract myself from the force of the pressure with his hands. Greg used the active release technique (ART) of pressing with his thumbs along the IT bands that run from my hip to the knee. This is not a pleasant procedure, as he pushes out all the built up lactic acid using very hard pressure. It feels like someone is taking a 50-pound rolling pin to your legs.

The advantage to the new plan and to mixing up the shifts was that the team didn't bond in small sub-units and become insulated from one another. This also avoided any competition between shift crews. For example if one team strays off course more than once, they get a reputation for being the "lost crew" between the other two shifts. It can create animosity.

Instead, the whole team pulled together as one unit and worked hard, and everyone picked up the slack whenever something needed to be done. Yes, specialized skills matter, but attitude and selflessness—and commitment to a clear sense of purpose—are what's most important for effective teamwork.

*

By the time the follow van and I reached the Painted Desert between Kayenta and Mexican Hat, darkness was falling. It was great to see that most of the crew—those in the advance van and the RV—had driven ahead and could experience this landscape. It was by far the most picturesque along the entire course and full of multi-colored boulders stacked on top of one another in huge pillars and columns. We wouldn't get to the hotel until around 2:00 a.m. but the slow sunset and the gradual decline of the oppressive desert heat were incredibly energizing.

We continued straight east to the next time station of Mexican Hat, 42 miles away, where a warm bed and a hot meal awaited me. Most of our team had already settled in at the San Juan Inn, which was built into the cliffs of the San Juan River valley, when I arrived at the parking lot. I climbed the stairs to my room, a two-bedroom apartment, and wanted to laugh. John had strung his hammock on the balcony, and the room was wall-to-wall people, fast asleep. It looked like a frat house party had just ended and I had missed out on all the fun.

Fortunately, while on the bike an idea had come to me about how to approach Kaitee. I had to let her know how important her job was to the outcome of the race. If my body didn't get the recuperation it needed before the next day's ride, there was a good chance I'd get injured in a way that would prevent us from reaching the finish line.

So that night, when Bill brought my dinner, a plate of pasta, as I settled myself on the bed, my back supported by the headboard, I asked her to sit on the chair beside me.

"Sure," she said. I waited to say more until she got situated and could look at me.

"I won't make it to the finish line without you," I continued. "I know it's hard to work on me in the middle of the night, when most of our crew are sleeping. I'm asleep minutes after you start working. I have no idea what you're doing but all I know is that when I wake up I feel like I'm ready to start the day. What you do is so important. When we cross the finish in Annapolis one of the reasons will be because of what you're doing at night when no one is watching. You're doing a great job Kaitee, thanks for being part of our team and keep it up."

I'm not going to lie. My first instinct had been to reprimand Kaitee and reiterate her duties, especially since we had discussed these responsibilities months before the start of the race. It would have *felt* like the right thing to do for maybe a minute or two, but I could imagine watching the reaction from this 21-year-old volunteer as I criticized her lack of effort.

My second instinct was to complain to John, our crew chief, about her poor performance and let him deal with the problem, but that would be passing the buck. During my 20 hours on the bike—plenty of time to think long and hard about this—I came to the realization that showing gratitude would be the best way to change Kaitee's outlook on her role. There are many ways to motivate, and experience has proven that without some sensitivity, I would wake up the next day and she would be in a car catching the next flight home from the closest airport. After our talk, I never had to mention it again. She stepped up, and everything fell into place.

## Lesson 5

When team members take ownership of their work, worries about potential problems melt away. Apprehension is replaced with trust. This third day showed many examples of that sense of ownership by our team members. Joe stepping up to promise that there would always be a fully charged battery to power my lights at night. Ken and Greg convincing John to allow them to work double shifts and take complete responsibility for the nutrition, knowing that they would be sleeping significantly less than all the other crew members and spending twelve or more hours a day stuffed into the back seat of the follow van. Kaitee discovering how important her role was as the massage therapist and recognizing the responsibilities and importance of her role.

Improvisation when faced with the unexpected is another key factor in dealing with the obstacles that occur when trying to accomplish a mission; the ability to improvise is the mark of a true leader. John's leadership skills shone, for example, as he listened thoughtfully to the critical feedback from his team members, considered all the risks, and then made the difficult decision to revise his well-detailed plan on how to run the operation.

This give and take allowed team members to begin trusting one another and sharing their thoughts without fear of being criticized. These small, incremental moments behind the scenes began forming the foundation of close personal relationships between the team members.

*Len—as I go about my business I keep thinking that you are still on your mission and I am amazed. Love seeing your progress! Keep it up! See you soon.*

—Lisa Rother

*Glad to hear that you are still moving and looking good. I agree... a huge thank you to your crew and their families :)*

—Laurie Forkas

*Go Len!! Just keep thinking about all those wonderful children who are counting on you. As you have said before, they can't stop until they finish fighting their cancer, but you can stop but I know you won't because you are on a mission and have a passion!!! So keep turning those wheels!!*

—Kim & Kaitlin Knill

*Liked the story about your competitors helping you out on the way to Flagstaff. Those Czechs ARE class acts!*

—Robin Dvorak

# DAY 4
## June 16, from Mexican Hat to South Fork

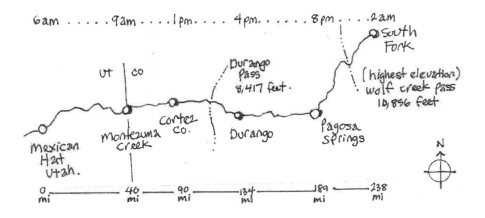

6am . . . . 9am . . . . 1pm . . . . 4pm . . . . . 8pm . . . 2am

South Fork

Durango Pass 8,417 feet.

(highest elevation) Wolf Creek Pass 10,856 feet

UT | CO

Cortez Co.

Montezuma Creek

Durango

Pagosa Springs

Mexican Hat Utah.

N

| 0 mi | 40 mi | 90 mi | 134 mi | 189 mi | 238 mi |

TODAY WE RIDE FOR TREVOR

| START | END | START | FINISH | DISTANCE | TOTAL MI. | ELEVATION |
|-------|-----|-------|--------|----------|-----------|-----------|
| Mexican Hat, UT | Montezuma Creek, UT | 6:02 AM | 9:14 AM | 39.70 | 764 | 2,469 |
| Montezuma Creek, UT | Cortez, CO | 9:15 AM | 12:37 PM | 50.20 | 814 | 2,892 |
| Cortez, CO | Durango, CO | 12:37 PM | 3:57 PM | 44.80 | 859 | 3,068 |
| Durango, CO | Pagosa Springs, CO | 4:12 PM | 8:31 PM | 54.60 | 912 | 3,327 |
| Pagosa Springs, CO | South Fork, CO | 8:31 PM | 2:00 AM | 48.20 | 960 | 4,047 |
| Day 4 Sleep Break | | 2:00 AM | 7:02 AM | | | |

# CHAPTER 6
# RESPECT THE EDGE

*When you are at the end of your rope, tie a knot and hang on.*

—Theodore Roosevelt

OUR LONGEST TRAINING ride had been three consecutive days in these very same hills in Utah and Colorado, about a month before the race began, when there was still snow on the ground. From this day forward, everything would be one great big science experiment in new physiological territory, especially since we were headed toward Colorado's Rocky Mountains. Many of the athletes who drop out of RAAM do so because they don't make it through the Rockies.

I prepared myself for a monster of a day. What I concentrated on, after shooting a few pictures of the follow vehicle as we headed out of Mexican Hat, was getting my groove back on the bike. That morning, Brian had kicked me in the butt.

"Forkas," he said, "What is taking you so long to get moving?"

Everyone knew I was a slow starter. It usually took me an hour to hit my stride. "Dude, I'm just waking up. How about a little sympathy?"

"If you're looking for sympathy, I'm afraid you picked the wrong support team."

Brian was our math guy. He could calculate our locations and then predict when I'd roll into each time station. He'd clocked me at an average 13 mph, far below my target of 15 mph. I needed to pay more attention to maintaining my pedal stroke and to keeping an efficient form. That's what happens when you ask a CFO of a start-up tech company to join your crew. Today would be bittersweet—we'd say goodbye to Brian Daum, who had both work and family commitments and so needed to catch a flight from Durango back to Washington, DC. But we knew that he would later join us at the finish line.

By the time we got to Cortez, Colorado, a little after 12:00 p.m., we'd already climbed 5,000 feet. The next goal was a 2,000-foot climb on our way to Durango, the first major mountain pass and the highest elevation on the race course so far—8,300 feet. But before cresting that pass we had to navigate the first major downhill incline, a 1,500-foot broadly curving descent.

Our team had practiced in these mountains less than four weeks ago, and although it was familiar, the effects of the higher altitude were slowly kicking in. The first symptoms are headaches, as the brain adjusts to having less oxygen. Thin air feels like a vise is clamped down on both sides of your temples, slowly tightening, squeezing your head. At first it's almost imperceptible, but the feeling builds with each pedal stroke ascending the long uphill.

The trees were now receding, thinning as we climbed. The absence of trees is a good indicator that you are passing through higher elevations. The trees simply can't survive on this windswept landscape. My heart rate was higher now although my speed was the same as earlier in the day. Thin air requires more output. As we crested the top of the hill and began coasting down the long, slow, curving descent, the follow van behind me, the view majestic, I found myself getting more and more relaxed, feeling great, expansive. Then the unexpected happened. My brain shut down.

The pressure from the change in altitude as I was descending was releasing its clamp on my head. No longer having to work so hard, my heart slowed from its climbing rate of 115 to its recovery rate of 90 beats per second. I could feel the blood draining from my head. Without realizing it, I dozed off, traveling more than 100 yards at 25 mph. A few seconds later, my eyes flashed open. I was headed straight for the guardrail at the edge of the cliff. Over that guardrail was nothing but air, trees, and rocks.

*Steep descents in altitude*
*(Photo courtesy of Pawpro Media)*

In the fraction of a second after opening my eyes and processing all the new information entering my brain I thought, *"This is it. How am I going to stop in time? I am so screwed."* My hands clenched the brakes and pulled hard to the left, as hard as I could pull while still staying upright on the bike, my eyes glued to the horizon before me. This was how my race was going to end? Pitched into a guardrail and hurled over the side of a mountain? I prayed for my brakes to work in time. Hitting a guardrail at any speed was going to send me to the emergency room. *"Please don't let me crash,"* I prayed.

I continued clenching the brakes and pulling to the left. Finally the wheels stopped turning. I came to a complete stop just in time. Stepping off the bike, I leaned it against the guardrail, then climbed into the follow van's passenger seat. My heart was racing and I was trying hard not to show that I was shaking uncontrollably.

"I'm going down for a five-minute nap," I told the crew.

"Len, you're less than twenty minutes from Durango," they said. Racers had to reach Durango within a specified time limit or be disqualified from competing in the rest of RAAM.

"I need to sit down for a few minutes." I'd managed to stay upright on the bike when I'd blacked out, so the crew hadn't seen me wobbling. They had no idea of what just happened, and I wasn't going to tell them. It was embarrassing and frightening at the same time. Let them think that this is just one of my normal five-minute naps. Let me just lean back in the passenger seat, crank the A/C, pop in my ear plugs, and sleep.

"Why don't you keep going and take a longer rest there. We can give you oxygen." Before the race, we had taken good advice from a medical doctor who had been on Randy Mouri's team the previous year. He'd given us a full medical kit that came with a tank of oxygen and instructed the paramedics on how to use it.

"Guys, just work with me," I said. "I only need five minutes, just wake me up in five."

I didn't want them to worry. I also didn't want them to bench me, not so early in the race.

Thirty seconds later I fell asleep, my thoughts drifting to what Sister Therese had told me in Cleveland. "Len," she said, "everyone has a guardian angel that travels with you to lend a hand when you need it most. Don't forget once in a while to show some appreciation and remember that your guardian angel is always there for you."

*Did my guardian angel wake me up before I hit the guardrail at Durango Pass? Or was it the spirit of one of the kids I was riding for that day, carrying that child with me, keeping me safe?*

I'd never know. Five minutes later I jumped on the bike again and finished the descent in ten minutes.

*

Durango was important not just because it was the first of the mountain passes and the first major RAAM milestone. It was important to me personally because months ago Ned Overend, one of the investors in my company and a world-famous mountain bike champion who lived in Durango, helped us arrange an interview with local media to spread the word about Hopecam. Ned is a founding father of the sport of mountain biking.

My advance crew had set up a Hopecam tent in Santa Rita's Park where a reporter from the *Durango Herald* and I would be able to talk during my ten-minute rest break. Durango was one of the few towns that had an interest in following our progress, thanks to Ned's influence. He'd validated our mission with well-timed phone calls and emails. It proved to all of us the power of having a local connection in the towns that we serve, as well as showed the impact third-party validation can have on motivation. It also reminded me of how many of my own crew had come together through connections others made for me.

*An interview with the Durango Herald*

We did a lot of multitasking like that during the race. This particular interview meant a lot to the team, our driver and navigator Ed told me later, because it made the whole race more personal and brought the mission home. "Yes, it was a race, and yes, we were a team, but [RAAM] was about the children," he said.

Today we were riding for Trevor Blake, a generous eleven-year-old who was fighting neuroblastoma, a rare cancer that begins in the nerve tissues of the adrenal glands, neck, chest, or spinal cord. In treatment for his third relapse, Trevor decided he wanted to bring a treasure chest full of toys to other children who were also hospitalized and undergoing cancer treatment and let each child choose one to brighten the day. His dream became a nonprofit organization: Trevor's Treasures. He and his family travel in an RV to oncology clinics and hospitals in the mid-Atlantic area and personally deliver gifts to these children. I couldn't help thinking about what a fine young man his parents had raised.

And because we were thinking about Trevor and Stefano and all the Hopecam kids and missing our own kids and families, and because it was the day before Father's Day, we ended the interview by snapping a picture of all the "dads" on the crew standing next to the Hopecam tent.

*

We departed Santa Rita Park a little after four, moving east toward the remaining two major mountain passes that would take me over the Continental Divide. Halfway up the first pass I took a quick sleep break in the RV. Oxygen and rest—that's what I needed for the descents down both passes toward Pagosa Springs. I didn't want to black out again.

Kaitee worked on my shoulders and neck while I slept with an oxygen mask covering my face. After fifteen minutes I was rested and ready. Then, for the second time that day, trouble.

We'd just crested Yellow Jacket Pass, elevation 7,400. On the downhill face, hitting speeds over 40 mph, the front wheel of my bike started to vibrate, then wobble left and right, which became more and more pronounced. A few seconds later the rear wheel began to wobble.

The color drained from my face. This same thing had happened three or four times before on training rides and we could never figure out why. We'd asked our mechanics, wheel manufacturers, and industry reps, and no one had ever experienced it, nor did they have any answers.

The vibration got more and more intense, the kind of intensity you can see and hear in tuning forks. The bicycle began to shake violently. *Dear God, please do not throw me off this bike in the middle of the afternoon and end my race.* I kept squeezing the brakes in a desperate attempt to slow down and stop the vibration. If I braked too hard I would be thrown over the handlebars. *Dear God, please do not throw me off this bike.* But the bicycle was heaving back and forth. It was as if some invisible monster were shaking the frame. *Not here. Not here in the middle of Colorado.* I didn't want to be the next RAAM fatality, the bike skidding sideways at high speed, the skin on my arms and legs peeling off as I careened across the blacktop with my bike in front of me bouncing, and my head, protected with what is left of my cracked, shattered helmet tap, tap, tapping the road, the helmet's white plastic shell holding together the glued-in large chunks of hard Styrofoam. *Please do not end my race, not here, not now.*

*The crew decides to press on to*
*Wolf Creek Pass, Durango CO*
*(Photo courtesy of Steve Lewis, Durango Herald)*

On a practice ride two months earlier in the Catoctin Mountain Range in Pennsylvania, I'd blamed the bike shimmy on the wind gusts that blew across the frame and the bicycle's deep dish wheels. Though incredibly aerodynamic, my Zipp 404 wheels were very susceptible to cross-winds, making them shake and become hard to control. Was it the wheels this time?

But there were no wind gusts today.

The same shaking had happened for a few seconds when we were in Arizona. When we'd asked Wayne to inspect them for over-wear on the ball bearings, he said they were fine. It had to be the bike. Something was wrong with the frame. It might have cracked.

Every muscle in me was straining to hold the bike vertical.

The seconds seemed like minutes until I was finally able to decrease the speed and regain control of the bike by slowing to a normal speed, and then to a stop. My forearms felt like concrete and I had to pry my hands, which were holding a tight grip for what seemed like an eternity, from the handlebars.

The follow van caught up with me. They had seen me struggling to stay on the bike as it bucked and heaved. John stepped out of the van and walked toward me. His face was white.

He said, "We thought you were a goner" and shook his head in disbelief, speaking as if he had just witnessed a terrible accident. Twice in under four hours I had nearly crashed on a steep, high altitude rocky mountain descent.

"What the hell happened?"

I explained that there was something terribly wrong with this bicycle. This had happened again—the same thing that had almost cost me my life in Maryland in April, and before that in Virginia on a ride with Joe in March. Each time the event occurred, it was on a steep, downhill road at speeds exceeding 35 mph.

"I'm done with this bike," I said.

Thankfully I had heeded Wayne's advice in May and ordered a similar but less expensive Trek 5.9 Madone bike with identical parts. We retired the Trek 6.2 on the roof rack of the follow van, and put the spare bike into service.

After Wayne made a few quick adjustments, I was riding toward Haystack Mountain and Chimney Rock, in the Devil Creek State Wildlife area. Like a quarterback who's thrown his fourth interception, my trusty starting bicycle had hit the showers before halftime. Later that night while I was sleeping Wayne tore the wheels apart but could find no explanation for the wobble.

Now my fate was in the hands of the backup bicycle.

*

We reached Pagosa Springs just as the sun began to set. My team and I had made the decision to forge ahead to the next time station at South Fork. I was plenty tired, but it was too early for me to go to sleep. I knew that if I could get to South Fork, I could get Wolf Creek Pass behind me. We'd have to climb an eight-mile, six-to seven-percent grade (runaway truck ramps have a six-percent grade) to get over Wolf Creek Pass. This was the toughest climb of the entire race course over the route's highest point. We were heading over the Continental Divide, 10,857 feet—more than two miles—above sea level.

*The crew near Durango Pass*

That week, forest fires were burning all over Colorado. The state had experienced one of the worst droughts in history, and the pungent smell of smoke was everywhere, making it hard to breathe. I managed two miles in thirty minutes—a 4 mph pace—then had to pull over. I couldn't push one more pedal. I set down my bike, and climbed into the follow van with the air conditioning set to full blast even though the temperature was only sixty-five degrees when we'd started. I had nothing left. The searing heat and the day's harrowing events had pummeled me.

What Spins the Wheel | 117

The crew woke me after five minutes. I mounted the bike and started climbing again.

It began to dawn on me that my competitors were probably sleeping, conserving their strength to avoid burn out. And there I was, climbing this monster of a mountain at midnight. Would I be able to stay awake for the screaming-fast switchback descent awaiting me on the other side? Unlike the broad sweeping lines at Durango, the switchbacks at Wolf Creek were tight, steep, narrow, and dangerous.

I pushed one pedal at a time, my feet stomping down with all the force I could muster, over and over again. What had I been thinking? I felt like Sisyphus trying to push a rock up the hill. We climbed higher and higher, repeating the 30 minutes to pedal, five minutes to sleep routine. The temperature had dropped to thirty-eight degrees, but my shirt was soaked with sweat. I was burning up from the output. My throat was parched and my eyes stung from the smoke. The air was so thin that it felt like I was breathing through an oversized milkshake straw.

But I had to keep going. The RV and eight members of my crew were waiting for me at the peak. My crew in the follow van was desperate to help take my mind off the misery. They read one of the many emails that came through our blog. This one was from Alex Green's family. It couldn't have been read at more perfect time:

> Just as a child and his/her family battles cancer, push on harder
> when the road gets hard, with each step you pedal think of our
> children's battles. What you are doing is amazing, it is more than
> any race, and it represents the unbearable struggle we go through
> as parents watching the children [fight] this difficult battle.

As they finished the message I could see the tail lights of the RV parked at the crest of the hill marking the continental divide.

It was around midnight when we finally reached the summit. When I got off the bike, they all applauded. John was on the phone with the WeatherBug team in Germantown, Maryland. Coincidentally, their head-quarters are in a master-planned development that I built in 2000 called

Milestone Business Park. Talk about a small world. The night team was partying in my honor.

I couldn't party yet. We had a choice to make: do the 20-mile descent into South Fork or sleep in the RV at 11,000 feet. The cold chilled my bones, reminding me of the time I rode so hard and in such cold weather that my fingertips were numb for two weeks. I was wiped out, but going down the hill seemed to make more sense than sleeping at this elevation.

*Midnight descent from the*
*Summit of Wolf Creek Pass*

Some have called me relentlessly positive and upbeat. But even I was not immune to fatigue and the after-effects of two brushes with death on this punishing course. And here we were at the top of another even more dangerous descent. Would the altitude, which had never affected me before this race, again shut down my brain? Would I be headed for another crash, and if so, would I wake up in time, before anything bad happened? Was that how my Hopecam mission was going to end, with me flayed and broken on the side of the road, another RAAM fatality?

There, at the top of the Continental Divide, was what used to be my favorite sign—the yellow diamond with the image of a truck on top of a black triangle and the words "steep downhill grade." Now the sign seemed ominous rather than friendly. I looked at it straight on. Go or stay? I was dreading the descent. Dreading it. Snow was everywhere. I climbed into the RV, took off my cleats, and slept for fifteen minutes, this time with an oxygen mask on my face. I was taking no chances.

When I awoke, I was so tired that my crew had to help me dress. They piled on spandex pants, two long-sleeve base layers, my cycling jersey, heavy winter-weight gloves, insulated boot covers, and a warm Windstopper insulated jacket, clothes you'd wear if you were going snow-boarding. I started racing again, but two minutes later the wind chill of a 30-mph descent in thirty-eight degree temperatures made me stop and pull over. I needed another long-sleeve shirt.

It was pitch dark. John led in the RV so that I could follow the brake lights at a safe distance respecting the race rules. In the dark, the mountain loomed on my left like a predator, waiting for a moment of weakness. I continued down the mountain, passing Wolf Creek ski area on the right and sign after sign of a truck with its black wedge of cheese underneath. The hills and switchbacks were never-ending. Left, right, left, right. My wooden fingers struggled to brake hard enough to hold the bike's speed to 20–25 mph. I was grateful for the RV's flashing tail lights ahead of me to regulate my speed, grateful for the freezing cold wind that kept me awake. Maybe I could make it safely to the bottom. Though it took fewer than sixty minutes to make the descent, it felt like hours as I fought off sleep, clenched the handlebars, and shifted my weight with every turn in the bitterly cold air—until I could finally slide onto easy, straight, Route 160 along the Park Creek River.

Ten miles of rolling terrain remained before entering South Fork. My legs felt as if someone had taken a baseball bat to my knees. I arrived in the parking lot at 2:00 a.m., feeling completely drained. My crew had to help me dismount, once again prying my hands from the grip that had locked onto the handlebars. In the grey light of the street lamps, my knees looked swollen to the size of grapefruits. My crew supported me as I walked into the hotel. They propped me upright and helped me as I staggered into the open door leading to the hotel room.

The team knew just what to do. They helped me strip off the three layers of clothing so I could shower. They gave me a quick meal, then laid me on the bed, propped up my legs under two stacked duffle bags, and packed a five-pound bag of ice on each knee. They were working like a triage unit in an emergency room, with my two firefighter pals, Greg and Ken, moving around with purpose. The room felt like it was spinning. Kaitee started to massage my feet and legs, working to release the lactic acid that had built up. Greg began his high-pressure IT band technique, pressing with both thumbs on the quadriceps from the hip to the knee using all of his weight to move the lactic acid. Normally this caused me to writhe in pain, but I was so spent I fell asleep during the procedure. My crew worked on me for a record three hours before calling it a night at 5:00 a.m. I slept in this "Z" shape for four hours.

At the time, I hadn't realized what a bold and strategic move it would be to take Wolf Creek Pass at night. My goal was just to get down without injury. We later learned that our one decision to press forward had given me a lead over my competitors.

And for us, that was when the race not just to finish, but to finish first, began.

## Lesson 6

The day's events pointed out the importance of "respecting the edge," which we had to do if we were to survive this demon called the RAAM race course. We could not cavalierly push our resources—physical or mental—to the brink.

The question for all athletes and for business leaders as well, is when and how do you learn to balance risk and reward? When you push too hard, there can be dire consequences. Ken and some of the others had been vehemently against descending into South Fork because of the obvious danger. I hadn't realized just how much I'd depleted my reserves, and there were no hospitals...if I crashed Ken would have to put me back together.

We were lucky. Or maybe we were blessed, given moments of grace from a guardian angel or simply the spirit of the children like Trevor Blake whom we "carried with us" as we pushed forward on the RAAM course.

Sometimes, despite all odds, a bold risk can create a turning point. The decision to take Wolf Creek Pass was the turning point in our race. We started in Oceanside with the goal of just surviving the race before the twelve-day cutoff. When we ended the day in South Fork, we were in first place in our division. We realized that we were not just riding; we were now competing.

Still, we needed to remember to run our own race, and respect our own physical and mental limits. We were in it for Hopecam. If we didn't finish, nothing else would matter.

*Hi Len, it's Shannon. Yesterday was my last day of school. I'm excited that my summer has started. I got my report card yesterday and I got all As and Bs and I knew you would be proud of me so I'm having mom help me send you a message. I'm proud of you too for all the biking you've done so far. I hope you aren't too tired and I can't wait to see you at the finish line.*

—Shannon Eastman

*Keep peddling, Len. We are behind you in Texas! You are an inspiration to all of us. May God be in you and surrounding you.*

—John Walsh

*Hi Len. Ron, mom and I are thinking about you and your ride. Stay strong, we are praying for your safe return. Remember Dad is with you. We love you. Godspeed.*

—Deb Forkas

# DAY 5
## June 17, from South Fork to Kim

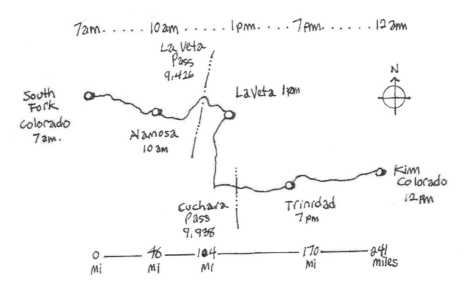

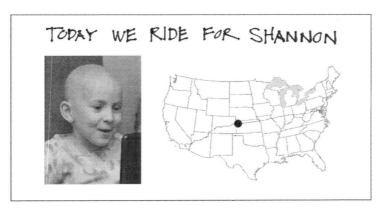

TODAY WE RIDE FOR SHANNON

| START | END | START | FINISH | DISTANCE | TOTAL MI. | ELEVATION |
|---|---|---|---|---|---|---|
| South Fork, CO | Alamosa, CO | 7:02 AM | 9:33 AM | 46.60 | 1,007 | 1,175 |
| Alamosa, CO | La Veta, CO | 9:42 AM | 1:00 PM | 58.40 | 1,065 | 2,053 |
| La Veta, CO | Trinidad, CO | 1:48 PM | 6:30 PM | 65.70 | 1,131 | 3,854 |
| Trinidad, CO | Kim, CO | 7:00 PM | 11:04 PM | 70.80 | 1,202 | 1,856 |
| Day 5 Sleep Break | | 11:04 PM | 2:40 AM | | | |

*Photo courtesy of Jai Photography*

# CHAPTER 7
## IT TAKES A VILLAGE

*You can survive on your own; you can grow strong on your own; you can prevail on your own; but you cannot become human on your own.*

—Frederick Buechner, The Sacred Journey:
A Memoir of Early Days

WHEN I WOKE after snoozing for what seemed to be an eternity—over four hours, the longest rest break so far—I was shocked. Our crew had done the impossible—rebuilt me while I was sleeping. I went to sleep imagining I'd have to pop Advil like Skittles to move without pain. How could it be possible to push so close to a physical limit and not pay the price in the morning? *My crew.* The painfully swollen grapefruit-sized knees from last night had shrunk back to normal size and the redness was gone. Fully expecting to need two people to help lift me out of bed and on to the bicycle, instead I was standing up without pain.

After getting dressed with a warm layer of arm and leg covers and stepping outside into the cool 60-degree sunny morning at 7:00 a.m. I wanted to give bear hugs to everyone in my crew who was still awake. Every one of the eleven members of my team had stayed up last night until well past 2:00 a.m. waiting to see me come in after cresting the continental divide. I remembered nothing. Last night was a big blur.

Now there they were…my morning crew shift was waiting, smiling. It was Father's Day, I was in first place in my division, and there was a 20-mph tailwind pushing east. I wished everyone a Happy Father's Day, thanked them for restoring me, and mounted the bike. After a brief five-mile climb, we'd have a 40-mile descent ahead on our way toward Alamosa. We averaged a whopping 20 mph courtesy of my guardian angel's gift of a tailwind.

We'd all been tireless, sleeping only when we could, even the crew. Bill Vitek, who was always willing to do anything needed to make life on the course smooth, became known as the "night owl" because he was always the last to turn in. Greg was known to grab fifteen-minute catnaps between working on my legs at night and pre-filling water bottles so they'd be ready for the next morning shift. Wayne maintained the bike in the early hours while I was sleeping so it would be in top condition for the next day's ride.

So this morning was going to be their catch-up and rest morning while I pushed onward. On that flat straight road, I phoned my family to tell them I was still alive and would miss them this Father's Day. I also wanted to thank my fourteen-year-old daughter Viena for that morning's email.

> "Happy father's day daddy! You are the best "fasha" ever. I am so blessed and grateful. You are the most determined person I know. You never give up and that's what makes you so strong. Well that and the fact that you are a crazy triathlete! You've always been there for me, and I want you to know how much I appreciate it. I hope you have a great father's day even though you will be riding your bike all day, but you deserve it. I made you a father's day gift and I can't wait to give it to you! You do so much for our family and all your friends, but you never ask for anything in return. You're such a good man. You have so many people who love you because of how much you care for others and help people. I love you because you're everything a daughter could ever ask for. I've been checking your blog every day. By the way I've been showing my friends too! I'm so lucky to have a dad that I can show off to my friends! Stay strong and remember, I love you more than anything, I miss you and happy father's day."

Today I was riding for another special and strong young lady, Shannon Eastman. Shannon was four when she was diagnosed with cancer. She went through treatment and then went into remission. Months later, after a routine checkup to check her white blood cell counts, she heard the worst thing that any cancer patient can hear after enduring treatment, news that was even more dreaded than a relapse. An entirely *new* form of cancer had appeared in Shannon's body. Tasked with a new regimen of medications and treatment, she used Hopecam as a lifeline to connect with her friends at school. Her aunt had sent me an email describing how Shannon "proudly showed me her computer [as she] signed on and joined her Chinese language class…with lots of hellos and giggles from both sides of the screen." Shannon and I had been interviewed on Washington DC's Fox 5 network a few weeks before the race started in June. One of my favorite videos is Shannon lifting my 14-pound bicycle in the studio right before her interview with the morning news anchor.

Hopecam's director, Jen Bond, always said that Shannon had a "village" supporting her, demonstrating how critically important staying connected is to a child undergoing treatment for life-threatening diseases. The Eastman family gave us so much support during this race that there is not enough room in this chapter—or this book—to properly thank them. Shannon wrote me daily emails that my crew read to me, usually at night, over the loudspeaker on the follow van. These messages—hundreds of them from Shannon, her sister, mom, and extended family and friends—did more than anything to make our mission real to us and bring our purpose home.

*

After South Fork, we learned not only that we had placed first in our division, but we were in fifteenth place overall. John started crunching the numbers and realized that maintaining our lead was a possibility as long as I kept riding at the same pace. At that point, the mood of our team shifted. "Everyone on our crew became an athlete," Ken said, "everything took on an edge. Concentration intensified, excitement became palpable."

It was hard not to let that excitement distract our team from running the race the way we had planned. At one point our crew turned off the GPS tracking device called "findmespot"—technology that let a GPS transceiver broadcast our location onto a website that we then linked to the Hopecam page—to stop announcing our departure time to our competitors. At other times, we would say "forget about the other racers." We didn't want to increase the risks of making a stupid mistake and not finishing.

*Eric Burt and Wayne*
*Smith at Kristi Sports*

Father's Day was about to give us all another gift—a 20-mph tailwind from the mountains in the west, which upped our average speed to 19.4 mph—and then take it away when the tailwind shifted to crosswinds. The bike wheels had rims that were 1.5 inches wide, aka "deep dish," which made them aerodynamic—except in crosswinds, where they are a detriment. Wide rims in cross winds slow down the bicycle. Wayne would say, "Okay, we'll just stop Len, and quickly change the wheels to the stock wheels." This switch would allow wind to flow through the wheel instead of pushing against the wheel. We had brought these wheels to Oceanside to load in the follow van for situations just like this one.

But when the crew looked for the stock wheels, one was missing. We all remembered what John said when we were standing around waiting for the race to begin. *You always forget something. It's just a matter of whether it's something really important.* The wheel we needed most, we learned, was accidentally left behind in the Fromms' garage.

We called Ed in the advance van and gave him, Steve, Kaitee, and Wayne an assignment: see if you can purchase an extra set of wheels. Steve and Ed were both in their late forties. Kaitee and Wayne were both in their early twenties. Ed laughed, and said that the people in this small town might think we were like characters in the television show "Modern Family." It did not hurt that Ed and Steve, who were probably the funniest on the crew and always quick with a smile and something positive to share, enjoyed goofing around.

Father's Day on Main Street in Alamosa, a small town of 8,000 people, was dead except for the one propped-open door at Kristi's Outdoor Sports. The locals call this store *"the REI of the San Luis Valley."*

The store wasn't officially open, even though the door was propped open. Four employees were inside, using the holiday to prepare provisions for a backpacking trip. They remembered our team from our previous training ride when we passed through in May. We explained why we were there.

"Don't know if we have what you need but go in the back," one of the employees said. "If you find something, we'll see if we can sell it to you."

They found nothing, so Wayne walked to the back of the shop and rustled around. The owner, Eric Burt, was in the back. Wayne went into full sales mode. He told Eric about Hopecam.

"Hmmm," Eric said. "I do have a set of wheels one of my customers wants to trade out."

"Okay, we'll take 'em," Wayne said.

"I should call my customer first," Burt said, but he couldn't reach the customer who had just swapped out his used stock wheels for brand new deep dish Zipp wheels like mine. "Can I call you tomorrow?"

"Nope. We need them right now." Wayne said.

Wayne tried to negotiate a loan, but the owner was reluctant because technically the wheels didn't belong to him. They tried to negotiate a price, but that didn't go so well either. Wayne offered to mail the wheels back if the owner wanted them returned.

We really needed those wheels. The alternative was driving to Pueblo, 120 miles northeast and in the wrong direction, since we were heading southeast. Besides, we knew the wind would kick up as soon as we left the foothills in Trinidad, Colorado, before we reached Kansas.

Finally, Wayne offered $200, a very fair price, and the owner relented. "Well, he's a good customer," Burt said. "Hopefully he'll accept your story and your offer."

The team left addresses and phone numbers so if the trade wasn't okay, the customer had some recourse. And as it turned out, the customer was happy. "He got money for wheels he didn't even want without having to do any legwork to sell them," Wayne said.

We were incredibly lucky. It was a big victory, not just because we got the wheels, but because, as Steve said later, it was a case of old-and new-school generations working together. The team was again finding its groove.

*

The next leg, to Cuchara Pass, was the very last climb in high altitude. At 10,000 feet, this mountain was the third highest of the course. The course rises up almost 3,000 feet over twenty-five miles before cresting the front face of the Rockies' eastern foothills.

This part of the course snakes between amazing geological formations—one looked like a 90-foot-tall, 600-foot-long Stegosaurus—many of them made when prehistoric magma forced its way through the Earth's crust and hardened into igneous rock. The temperatures were in the mid-90s as we set out, but we had a breeze from the southwest. That breeze was comforting even though the wind was not blowing in our direction, slowing the pace. When a rider is in climbing mode, the wind is less of a factor. It's like having two annoying injuries to contend with—say, a blister on your heel and stiffness in your neck. One will cancel out the other.

Our crew would be waiting for me at the top, enjoying the scenery and celebrating reaching the last mountain pass in Colorado. With the exception of a few rolling hills, the rest of the ride would be mostly downhill until we reached the Ozark Mountains in Missouri.

*Cresting Cuchara Pass*

As I climbed, I looked to the side and noticed a green SUV with a familiar face peeking out the window. It was Ed Cepulis' wife, Julie, who had driven up from Boulder with their three kids and golden retriever, stepping out to cheer for me on the long climb up. Ed lived near my home in Vienna, Virginia, before relocating to Boulder several years ago. We met during a cleanup day at our sons' preschool fifteen years before. Matt was great pals with Ed's son Mik, and the other children as well.

"Julie! What are you doing here?" I said, trying to catch my breath.

"Here to wish Ed a Happy Father's Day," she said.

"I'll meet you at the top!"

She smiled and drove on to surprise Ed and to meet the rest of the crew.

That she'd take a road trip of 230 miles over three and a half hours to surprise Ed on Father's Day just speaks to the support we all had from family members—and from friends who have become family. I was thinking specifically of Bill, who'd been with John, Kaitee, and me on the training ride through Cuchara Pass the previous month. Bill and I had known each other since we were 19 and I consider him one of my closest friends.

Bill had been driving the van through Cuchara Pass the night of the practice ride. The mountaintop was covered in mist and the light rain afforded little visibility. It was near nightfall and I could see very little of the landscape. After we met at the summit, I bundled up in wet weather gear for the rainy descent. I was just coming up to speed when a bull elk leaped onto the road and stopped right in front of me.

Bull elk average about 700 pounds, and this one had ten or twelve points on its antlers. It stood there staring at me. I grabbed the brakes and stopped about twenty feet in front of him. It looked like the elk was about to charge. I quickly turned my head to see if the van was nearby. Thankfully they were just pulling up behind me. Had the others seen him? I turned back toward the animal, but he was gone. Vanished. To the left alongside the road there were two female elk, his herd mates. He must have been protecting them when he saw me coming with my bike lights.

We pulled over to the side of the road for a few moments while I tried to calm down.

Less than a mile later, a small herd of mule deer ran across the road directly in front of me, and I pulled over again. "It looks like nature's got it in for you today," John said.

John and I talked and decided since there were hardly any cars on the road—we'd seen one about every thirty minutes—the van would lead me down the mountain. This way the van could clear the road of any more animals and give me the advantage of following their path. By the time we got to our Trinidad hotel it was almost midnight.

I slept four hours and then got ready to complete the third day of the practice ride. As I tiptoed around the room so I wouldn't wake anyone, a phone rang in the adjoining room. Who would be calling these guys at this hour?

Bill stepped out a few minutes later with a tear in his eye. His father had just passed away. What an irony that we were together when his father passed, just as we had been together through sheer coincidence in Cleveland when my father passed away four years previously.

"Let's stop here, Bill, and get you home."

*The Cepulis family.*
*From left: Mik, Ariana, Ed, Julie, Aiden and Cricket (dog)*

"No, it's okay, Len, it can wait," Bill said. He thought quietly for a moment as I prepared my water bottles for the early morning solo ride.

"There is nothing that's going to happen there today that I am needed for," Bill said, then paused. "Do you remember that elk last night?"

In that frame of mind, Bill and I decided the bull elk was a totem. Native Americans believe that totems are symbols related to ancestry and family connections. The bull elk is thought to be a power animal, representing stamina, strength, and agility. Bill's father, like my father, had been a large, strong man who worked well into his seventies and eighties, until dementia and Alzheimer's eventually claimed him.

Now, only a month after Bill's father died and we'd first crested

Cuchara Pass, we were seeing a cheerful family reunion on the top of the mountain. While the handshakes and introductions were going all around, Bill and I stepped aside to call his brother and tell him we were thinking about his father at this special place. We owed it to Bill's dad to honor him at the same place on the course where the Elk appeared on Father's Day. Then, after bidding Julie and Ed's kids farewell, I set off from the summit and left Ed to spend some time relaxing with his family.

As I rode, I remembered that Ed had had a conflict about joining the team because of his previous commitment to chaperone his son's Boy Scout troop on a three-day hike in June. Now he'd been gone a week already. He was planning to leave once we hit Kansas and be replaced by Bill Sickenberger, who was coming in from Virginia. I learned later, though, that after Julie and the kids had spent time with the team and seen how everything was working, she told Ed there was no way they were going to let him leave the race before the finish line. Julie found another father from the Scout troop to fill in for Ed, who then had his business computer shipped ahead to Wichita so he could work while in the RV during the day. Ed used mobile access points to connect to the office, took conference calls in the RV, and often did driving duty on the night shift. It was a great gift that Julie shared with the team.

Shannon's dad, Andrew Eastman, wrote an email that my crew read to me that day:

> *Len, I got your voicemail for Shannon. I passed it along and she was thrilled. Congratulations on making it through the Rockies. What an accomplishment and leading the pack too! Happy Father's Day, from one father to another. I am so proud of what you are doing for so many children. You are a father to so many as a result of your efforts with Hopecam. Good luck on the road ahead. You have a lot of people cheering for you.*

By eight, with the slight wind at our back, we headed east to our next destination, Kim, Colorado, population 72. The meteorology team really proved its value during this stretch. WeatherBug's team leader called John and told him that the 5-mph tailwind that was pushing me east was going to kick up into a 15-mph tailwind at around 1 a.m. and last until about 9 a.m. the next day.

It would be best to either ride all night and rest the next morning or go down early. We decided to sleep in Kim inside the RV at 11:00 p.m., wake up at 2:30, and put in a big day on Monday.

The logistical challenge was there were no hotels in Kim, only camp grounds. Our team had to drive 54 miles east to the town of Walsh for everything: gas, ice, water, and hotel rooms. Using some creative chore-ography, the advance vehicle shuttled between Walsh and Kim, supplying the RV and follow vehicle with what was needed. After we all got settled, Kaitee massaged me in the cramped RV as I slept, while Wayne tuned up my bike in the windy moonlight in the campground parking lot where we stationed for the night.

## Lesson 7

Compared to yesterday's events, the descent through Cuchara Pass was a smooth ride. Everyone was feeling good, calling loved ones, and celebrating Father's Day on the road. We had made it through the desert heat and climbed through oxygen-thin air over the Rockies. Ahead of us were the Great Plains, Ozark Mountains, Ohio Valley, and Appalachian Mountains.

Like Shannon Eastman, I was fortunate to have a village—my team, our sponsors, and all the others who helped make this experience possible—supporting me, a village that could very well make the difference in this race. The WeatherBug meteorologists were watching over our path 24/7 with updates on the wind and temperature. The emails from people following our path on the Internet were coming in at over 50 per day wishing us well. Ed's family had driven three and a half hours to cheer us on. Eric at the bike shop took a gamble to support us with new wheels.

Even with the pressure we put on ourselves to complete our mission of finishing the race and raising awareness of childhood cancer along the way, it was good to build in some rest periods to renew and refresh our connections to families and to each other. Like the Hopecam children who are connected to classmates during chemo, the clear message on Father's Day was that as much as it often felt like we were on a long-abandoned stretch of two-lane highway in the middle of nowhere, we were not alone. There were legions of people helping and supporting us, including our families, who sacrificed and made do without us. There were many dads on our crew, but with the exception of Ed, they did not get to celebrate Father's Day together with their children this year. Bill would not be celebrating Father's Day with his father this year, but we both knew that Bill's dad was watching over us, probably proudly sharing a beer with my dad.

Life has taught me that support comes from all quarters—the material and the spiritual, the physical and the invisible. It takes a village, and as Daisaku Ikeda wrote, the true worth of a leader rests on one thing: how many people you have fostered to carry your vision forward.

*Happy Father's Day, Len and all the Team Hopecam Dads! Each of you is amazing. Thanks for taking such good care of Len and keeping us up to date on this adventure. We start and end our day with a visit to the website. It is the next best thing to being there.*

*—Terri Sutton*

*Hi Len! Heroes come in all shapes and sizes. I have had the joy of having Shannon Eastman in my life. She has truly shown my family what real courage, tenacity and resiliency is. Every time we see her beautiful smiling eyes and (post cancer) curly hair, she lights up our hearts. You, by doing what you're doing, are the same type of hero in my mind. God bless you and may he be always in your heart to get you over hills and through valleys, whether on your bike ride or your amazing journey through life. Thanks for giving so selflessly to help these kids. Go Len!, xoxo*

—Margo Graham

*Congratulations on crossing the desert and scaling the mountains. Per the Irish prayer, may the wind be always at your back. We are proud of our son, John, helping you achieve a HUGE accomplishment.*

—Bob and Marianne Moore

# DAY 6
## June 18, from Kim to Maize

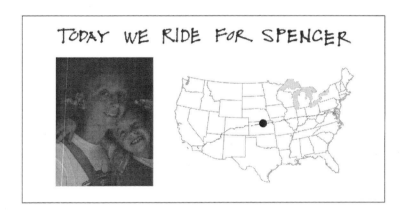

3am . . . 6am . . . 9am . . . 1pm . . . 3pm . . . 10pm . . . . 4am

CO | KS

Walsh    Montezuma    Pratt    Maize
Kansas

Ulysses    Greensburg

Kim
Colorado

70 mi — 124 mi — 174 mi — 240 mi — 271 mi — 348 mi

N

TODAY WE RIDE FOR SPENCER

| START | END | START | FINISH | DISTANCE | TOTAL MI | ELEVATION |
|---|---|---|---|---|---|---|
| Kim, CO | Walsh, CO (CDT) | 2:40 AM | 6:15 AM | 68.50 | 1,270 | 449 |
| Walsh, CO (CDT) | Ulysses, KS | 6:17 AM | 9:12 AM | 54.00 | 1,325 | 87 |
| Ulysses, KS | Montezuma, KS | 10:12 AM | 1:00 PM | 50.30 | 1,375 | 301 |
| Montezuma, KS | Greensburg, KS | 3:02 PM | 7:53 PM | 66.00 | 1,441 | 1,035 |
| Greensburg, KS | Pratt, KS | 8:14 PM | 10:13 PM | 31.70 | 1,473 | 106 |
| Pratt, KS | Maize, KS | 10:17 PM | 4:04 AM | 77.20 | 1,550 | 988 |
| Day 6 Sleep Break | | 4:04 AM | 7:21 AM | | | |

## CHAPTER 8

# "I COULD HAVE HAD A V8!"

*Whether you believe you can or believe you can't, you're probably right.*

—Henry Ford

THE TAILWIND THE WeatherBug team had predicted arrived in the predawn hours and our team scrambled so we would waste not one minute of this opportunity. Our morning team rolled out of bed at 2:30 a.m., looking forward to our first 300-mile day on an almost-entirely downhill course into the Great Plains.

Our strategy of shortening our sleep to ninety minutes in the evening was paying off; we could take advantage of downward-trending temperatures and gain ground on other racers. *Something big could happen…Len could win RAAM for his age group,* John posted to our blog that day.

Yet though you could sense the rising tide of excitement. We had the Great Plains ahead of us, and Kansas would not be easy. Interviews with many of the past competitors in the race had warned me of the boredom of the Great Plains, and Kansas in particular. Personally, I couldn't wait to get to Kansas and get out of the high altitude in the Rockies. Have you ever heard the phrase "You do something long enough you can do it in your sleep"? That was my experience in the Rockies. Falling asleep on the mountain descents made me long for the Kansas flatlands. Our crew members had also heard catastrophic stories from friends who knew first-hand how tough that section of the course was. RAAM athlete Randy Mouri, who'd been so helpful to our team in planning a strategy for the race, had shared stories of the hail storm he encountered—with hail as big as golf balls that dented his bike helmet.

"I refused to stop," Randy said with passion, "because the storm came with a 30-mph tailwind!"

*John calculating arrival times*

My own sister Laurie kidded me about the bad karma of being called "Tornado Len" while riding through Tornado Alley, reminding me that on our week-long Forkas family summer vacations growing up in suburban Cleveland, it typically rained five out of seven days.

It was going to be a day of faith and doubt fighting it out, even on a visceral level. After five days of repeated and continual physical stress, the body reverts to survival mode. This means it slows down the burning of fat for fuel and retains higher amounts of water, which causes swelling. Cortisol levels rise, which hijacks the transport of amino acids—the building blocks of protein, essential to building and repairing muscle—from the muscles to the liver. As a result, the body burns muscle instead of fat.

Ken and Greg had already thought of this and had started hiding amino acid supplements in the fruit shakes they were giving me. The taste was terrible, but we had faith in their knowledge and skills—and could see the proof of their expertise: I was exercising at extreme levels, burning 500 calories an hour, and yet weighing the same as I did in Oceanside before we started the race. How was that possible? It had to be the liquid nutrition that I was ingesting every hour.

As Ken said, "It's not a shake, buddy, it's medicine disguised as a smoothie."

*Kansas = Wind, Heat, & Dust*

\*

Rocketing through eastern Colorado on the Front Range, the colloquial term for the land between the foothills of the Rockies and the Great Plains, was like a dream. It was easy to think we'd sail through this day. We were averaging 20.8 mph, which we later learned was the fastest split for the entire race. At this point the horizon is flat, a tablescape of grain elevators and silos with few trees and buildings that top off at two stories. My heart rate was a third slower as we dropped a half mile in elevation over 50 miles. Although it was almost imperceptible, it felt like we were on a down ramp. All the pain and suffering climbing up and over the Rockies was finally rewarded here in Kansas until our next two enemies emerged: wind and heat.

There wouldn't be much else to think about on the long straight road taking us eastward as the sun continued to climb to its forecast peak of over 100 degrees. As we tracked further east into the state, the idea of sailing through the day eventually evaporated. The winds for which the Great Plains are known began to kick up dust. They were blowing at a consistent 20–30 mph, and at one point my crew handed me a surgical mask to block breathing in the dust blowing from dried-out farm fields. Kansas has at least one dust storm every year, the most famous being the 1930s' Dust Bowl, the great man-made (due to poor land use) ecological disaster. This is what it must have felt like then, when consecutive droughts destroyed farm crops and displaced millions of American farm workers. Kansas was left with more than 6,000 ghost towns. The brutal heat we were experiencing today, combined with the high humidity, would go on to set national records, and I could see in the faces of my crew that they, like the Wicked Witch of the West, were melting. Only we didn't have the benefit of a full bucket of water thrown at us to cool us off. The heat and humidity made it harder to regulate my core temperature. The ice-filled socks we were using to keep me cool dripped down my back, but this time the water wasn't evaporating before hitting my shorts.

As if the wind and heat were not enough, I was developing a painful case of saddle sores. Other racers had told me to be prepared for this, but very few athletes talk openly about them for good reason. They hurt like hell and you cannot see them without a mirror and no one wants to ask for help putting medication on them. Who would take that unpleasant job?

In the many endurance races I'd done, this was the first time I felt myself give into pain. These little sores, each about the size of a quarter, felt like sitting on a bed of needles. With each push of the pedal I'd feel a sharp, stabbing pain. Imagine going out for a jog with a blister on each heel. Not much fun. Now imagine that it's not a jog, it's not even a marathon, but a 20-hour run. Now imagine after today you wake up, the blisters are still there and you have five more days in front of you. How depressing is that thought? Nothing had prepared me for this overwhelming feeling of hopelessness. Stiff neck? No problem, just stretch every hour and ask Kaitee to work on me more during the twice-daily sleep breaks. Cramping calves? No problem, just add more electrolytes, increase my cadence to flush out the lactic acid, and put out less power until it clears.

Over the years we all learn strategies on repairing the physical problems. How was I going to survive this torture, which was embarrassing, excruciatingly painful, and miserable?

At that moment we were grateful to have a paramedic, whom we'd recruited, on the team. Surely dealing with the unpleasantness of saddle sores wouldn't rattle a seasoned first responder. Ken took on this task without even a grimace. The treatment options included a numbing ointment called Lanacane, antibiotic gels, and anti-friction creams called "Brave Soldier." The key was to make sure the sores didn't get infected.

Randy Mouri, the "race Sherpa," had recommended all of these products and we purchased enough for three RAAM races. The numbing ointment lasted about six hours. Sometimes when the pain medication wore off before a scheduled stop, I rode standing up. It was easier than enduring the pain.

Another technique was to wear a pair of bike shorts turned inside out as a base layer. Over that would be the normal padded bike shorts as an outside layer. That way the two bike short "pads" would be touching one another, lessening the friction on the skin.

I supposed I could borrow Spencer Goold's perspective—think about this newest challenge as one of the four seasons we experience each year. Spencer was today's Hopecam child. We filmed a two-minute dedication for the day from Montezuma, Kansas, in the early afternoon. Spencer is an inspiring example of faith and hope, in the midst of what he believed was only the winter season of his life.

When Spencer received his leukemia diagnosis, he posted this quote from NFL player Danny Wuerffel on his Facebook page: *I just happen to be in a tough season right now. It's winter for me. I trust a new and joyous season is on its way.*

That Monday, Spencer, a high school senior, was waiting for the results of a bone marrow test that would determine if cancer cells had returned after being in remission since May, when he'd been released from the hospital. Bone marrow tests hurt. For days. Just knowing that you're going to have the test makes most people shudder. The quote Spencer posted epitomized the spirit with which he tackled his leukemia—with faith, positivity, and hope.

*

In the conditions we were facing, where it seemed that nature and the course were conspiring to keep us from reaching the finish line, we took pleasure in simple things to keep us motivated. One—our early afternoon sleep breaks in the RV. They gave us a respite from the wind, heat, and humidity and cooled down my core temperature. Taking an ice-cold shower to wash off the road grit and stale sunscreen from nine hours of cycling and putting on a fresh set of clothing was something to look forward to. Two—the follow van itself was a key safety advantage on days like today, when fully loaded cattle trucks whooshed past us at 75 mph. Without the van with flashing red lights mounted on the back roof following the rider, the truck drivers would have a hard time seeing the cyclist at that speed, especially in the early morning when trucks were riding east facing directly into the sun's bright glare.

While I rested, a crew member called race headquarters to report our arrival at this time station. We had to be careful not to call in the arrival time at the time station twice. It's common for two different crew-members to call the hot line to make absolutely sure that our location has been properly reported. That mistake can cost you a fifteen-minute penalty assessed at the end of the race in a "penalty box" in Mount Airy, Maryland, just 50 miles from the finish line.

There are many other opportunities to rack up time in the penalty box, such as not making a complete stop at a stop sign or red traffic light, disobeying local traffic laws, drafting behind vehicles or other riders, improper water bottle exchanges, and so on. Not allowing vehicles caught behind the follow van to pass is the most egregious. Also, there's a no tolerance policy toward alcohol due to the risks of a sleep-deprived crew.

"There should also be a penalty for consuming too much beef jerky and glazed doughnuts," one of my crew said drily.

The other things that kept us motivated were surprises that would, when you looked back on them later, seem magical. For example, Ed Cepulis discovering Wayne, our gifted bike mechanic, at almost the last minute. My guardian angel, or Trevor Blake, or Alex Green or whatever power stopped me from crashing over the edge of the mountain in Colorado. Kenny finding a horseshoe on the road outside the Thunderbird Restaurant in People's Valley, Arizona. "We've got all the luck we need right here," he'd said, smiling.

Then there was Jon Nelson, a farmer who lived on Route 160, standing at the end of his driveway waiting for us to pass today so he could hand me $50. Jon flagged me over, his arms waiving broadly to catch our attention and I stopped, with the van pulling up alongside me.

"I want to support Hopecam," he said as he cheered us on.

Nelson is a cycling enthusiast who follows RAAM as it passes through each year. He'd read my profile on the RAAM website, then clicked through to the Hopecam link. Using the button that said "Find Len," Jon tracked me during the race and estimated when I'd be passing by. Jon made our day. Here was a total stranger who wanted to help our cause. It was such a strong example of what we were praying would happen—that word would start to spread about Hopecam's mission.

The GPS tool had become instrumental for our weather team and, as we inched closer to the finish line, for supporters like Jon who wanted to follow our progress minute by minute. It would become a pivotal piece of our strategy for racing RAAM, and part of that strategy was deciding whether to keep it on or off depending on how we felt about our competitors knowing where we were.

\*

On the bike there was not a lot to listen to other than messages my crew was broadcasting from the follow van, the rumble of the diesel-engine cattle trucks, and an occasional long and dull whistle of a freight train. So I listened with my eyes. The landscape reminded me of the scene in the Tom Hanks movie *Castaway*. The character delivers a Fed-X package to a woman living in the heart of Texas, an artist who creates wind sculptures. In the Kansas flatlands, we must have passed more than 200 of them—sculptures whose parts depended on the wind for movement—of every form and shape imaginable, from abstract to more representational. Statue-like creatures. Clocks with spinning arms. All had blades, wings, or some other element spinning in the 25-mph wind.

*The Kansas landscape*

As the evening faded to pitch-dark blackness, the only light on this desolate highway came from my headlight and the lights from the follow van. I got to craving a V8, something a RAAM volunteer back in Arizona had offered me a few days ago. Compared to the liquid nutrition I'd been drinking, it tasted incredible.

So incredible, in fact, that the next day I'd asked my crew to pick up some V8 so I would have something different to drink at night. Because V8 is an all-in-one "liquid nutrition product" packed full of vitamins, sodium, and other useful ingredients, it is one of the few items I can consume that won't slow me down. Plus it tastes great and complements my liquid diet.

"We're on it, Len." Greg said minutes after I asked at the Arizona stop.

But morning came and went and still no V8. I asked again.

"We're on it, Len."

Again, no V8s in the cooler. I asked for the third time, with no result.

Today, three days later, I asked for a V8 one more time. It was about ten at night, and we were approaching Pratt, Kansas. Greg, who was on the nutrition shift that night, said Ken would get them soon. It seemed my team was passing the buck. They either didn't want to give me a V8, or hoped I'd forget about it.

I rolled ahead, waited five minutes, then motioned for the van to pull up beside me. Maybe they weren't really hearing me. I was hot, thirsty, caked with dust. What would happen at work if my team kept postponing an important assignment, or more importantly failed to follow through assuming someone else will take care of it? Small oversights can snowball into large problems. There would be unforeseen consequences. The issue I was most concerned about was the lack of ownership of the request for the V8. No one stepped up to make sure it was going to get done. I thought back on the problem with the lights not being adequately charged in Arizona. If that kind of thing happened again I would be stopped dead in my tracks.

I needed to use this as an opportunity to make an important point. So I snapped.

*Greg and the V8*

"Greg, I'm not trying to be a jerk but you know that I am stuck with a liquid diet. This powder you are feeding me is getting old. Five days straight. You know that V8 is good for me. You told me it was okay to drink V8. I'm bored and Kansas is wearing me out," I said. "I have been asking for three days for a V8. You keep promising me that it's coming. Get...me...a...$@}+#...V8!"

About 30 minutes later the V8 appeared. By that time I'd lost my appetite for it and in fact I learned later that it gave me acid reflux, so I could not even drink it for the duration of the race. I regretted losing my cool over a lousy can of tomato juice. At the time it felt good to vent, but I knew that it was a rotten call to explode like that. It would have been much more productive to bring everyone together, face to face and asked why it was taking so long. We had solved the communication problem, we had solved the dead battery problem, and we had solved the problem of keeping the RV neat and clean. Just as before, someone would have taken ownership and accept responsibility for getting to the solution within a reasonable timeline.

Regardless, after this incident, I never had to ask twice for anything. It's important to support the efforts of your volunteers, but holding your team accountable for problem solving is also part of leadership. Yet even though I felt justified by making a reasonable request emphatically, it showed a lack of respect and I vowed never to do it again.

\*

With 270 miles under our belt, Pratt would have been a totally appropriate place to rest for the night, but the temperature was a balmy 79° F, 20° F cooler than five hours earlier. My crew felt good, I felt good, and we pressed on.

Wayne switched from driving the RV to navigation support in the front seat of the follow van. This was a critical role because my crew worried most about accidents at night. Riders have a tendency to fade, and my day had started twenty hours earlier with only an hour-long mid-day sleep break. We had heard the horror stories of riders falling asleep on the bike and weaving into oncoming traffic. We'd watched *Bicycle Dreams,* learned about Bob Breedlove, a 53-year-old pediatric surgeon and five-time RAAM finisher who'd been killed in a head-on collision in RAAM 2005. Other riders had been struck from behind by passing cars by drifting away from the shoulder into traffic.

There is a lot of pressure on the night shift to keep the rider as well as the van driver awake. Wayne did not disappoint. He played song after song to inspire me, every so often grabbing the microphone of the PA system and saying, "Rock on Len, rock on!" We called his performance "Radio Free Wayne."

Earlier on the shoulder of US 54 in Kansas Wayne had scored an incredible find… a Def Leppard CD. Although it looked beat up it worked perfectly enough for Wayne to add it to his playlist. Along with the music, Wayne read jokes, stories, and well wishes.

*"Hey Len. I heard your ruby slippers are speeding you through Kansas,"* sent from Kelly Johnson.

*"We are seeing the new Madagascar movie. Keep up your great job and see you at the finish line,"* sent from Shannon Eastman. She sent messages every day and the crew was falling in love with her.

*It is not the will to win that matters, everyone has that, and it's the will to prepare to win that matters— a quote from Alabama Coach Bear Bryant,* sent from my neighbor Ally Weingast.

Finally at 4:04 a.m. we rolled into the parking lot of the Holiday Inn Express in Maize, Kansas, after circling around a construction detour. As we walked toward the hotel, I saw my friend Cassie Schumacher, who was competing solo. Solo women started the race a day before the men.

When we talked in the parking lot, Cassie seemed to be extremely fatigued. Her crew chief, a young short woman in her thirties, was trying to get her focused. Cassie is a strong rider and had paid her dues. The year before, Cassie volunteered as a race marshal, enforcing the rules on the course for twelve days. She knew every mile of the terrain. She had beaten me in the ADK 540 race by two hours in September. But here in Kansas, you have to have all the puzzle pieces. Preparation, crew, nutrition—and all the rest has to come from willpower.

"Hang in there, Cassie," I told her. "Take it one time station at a time. You can do this."

Later we learned that Cassie dropped out of the race 200 miles further,

What Spins the Wheel | 149

near the eastern Kansas border. We suspected her will to keep going was beginning to fade when she said, "Len, I don't think I can finish this."

That worried me. The minute these kinds of thoughts start moving from your brain to your mouth, it's almost impossible to recover. Verbalizing your goals to others is one of the strongest techniques to keep you focused on fulfilling a personal commitment. The opposite is true when you verbalize negatives. If you say it, you believe it. This power of "pre-commitment" is a very effective tool for accountability. Want to lose weight? Tell fifty friends that your goal is to lose ten pounds in ten weeks. Watch what happens in ten weeks. You will be asked if you met your goal. We are more likely to hold true to our goals when we have pre-committed to the goal. Our friends, by simply asking if we reached our goal, are quietly holding us accountable. If you say it, you believe it. If you say it, you need to be prepared to be accountable. In 2013, Cassie returned to RAAM and finished the race.

Whenever pain or fatigue begins to erode my confidence, I do whatever possible to ignore negative thoughts. Many professional football players will tell you that there's a difference between pain and injury. Maybe it sounds insane, but pain is mostly in my head. As long as I am not injured or making the condition worse by continuing to cycle, I am going to keep pedaling forward. A former RAAM athlete had a saying: If it will heal in a year, just keep moving.

So we kept moving, taking strength from remembering we were doing this for Hopecam kids, taking inspiration from the faith and hope exhibited by kids like Spencer Goold.

## Lesson 8

Traveling across the Great Plains taught us that coping with adversity was a core competency for both rider and crew. The physical environment all around us changed quickly from a breezy downhill descent in the early morning hours to a flat, sizzling hot, and windy afternoon, where we would be plagued with painful saddle sores, crosswinds, and absolute boredom. We discovered that although we had little control over our environment and the physical wear and tear on my body, we could develop mechanisms to cope with the situation. For the boredom, we engaged our bike mechanic Wayne to act as DJ during the nighttime shift. To address the pain of the saddle sores, our paramedic applied numbing antibiotic cream. To repair the muscle damage from five days on the bike, our nutrition team mixed in amino acids in the lunchtime protein milkshakes.

Coping with adversity is made easier by putting "pre-commitments" in place that would hold us accountable if we ever allowed thoughts of quitting to enter our minds.

These dual lessons of accountability and coping with uncontrollable circumstances defined this day as we soldiered through the Great Plains. The landscape was not as dramatic as that of the previous days, but we found challenges all the same, and we overcame them as good teams do.

*Love you! Thank you! Keep going. Shannon says don't forget to drink water or your brain will turn into a raisin. Stay safe. Keep smiling but don't eat any bugs.*

—Miss Chris Doyle (Shannon's friend) Age 8

*From my three nephews: a) Nick: Why did the children eat their homework? Because the teacher said it was a piece of cake! ; b) Thomas: What vegetable can't you eat on a boat? Leeks!; c) Ian: Why did the chef go to jail? Because he was caught beating an egg! We hope you enjoyed this free entertainment for this evening. Have a successful ride tonight!*

—Laurie Forkas

*It is by riding a bicycle that you learn the contours of a country best, since you have to sweat up the hills and can coast down them. Thus you will remember them as they actually are, while in a motorcar only a high hill impresses you, and you have no such accurate remembrance of the country you have driven through as you gain by riding a bicycle (Ernest Hemingway).*

—Mike Maloney

# DAY 7
## June 19, from Maize to Weaubleau

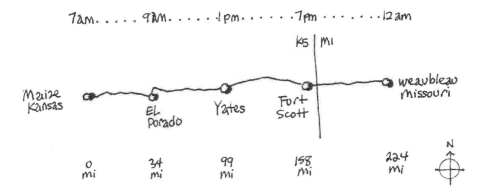

7am . . . . . 9am . . . . . 1pm . . . . . . 7pm . . . . . . . 12 am

KS | MI

Maize Kansas — El Dorado — Yates — Fort Scott — Weaubleau Missouri

0 mi — 34 mi — 99 mi — 158 mi — 224 mi

N

TODAY WE RIDE FOR STEFANO

| START | END | START | FINISH | DISTANCE | TOTAL MI. | ELEVATION |
|---|---|---|---|---|---|---|
| Maize, KS | El Dorado, KS | 7:21 AM | 9:31 AM | 34.20 | 1,584 | 464 |
| El Dorado, KS | Yates Center, KS | 9:32 AM | 1:19 PM | 64.60 | 1,648 | 1,194 |
| Yates Center, KS | Ft. Scott, KS | 3:00 PM | 6:56 PM | 59.00 | 1,707 | 1,012 |
| Ft. Scott, KS | Weaubleau, MO | 7:16 PM | 12:22 AM | 66.90 | 1,774 | 2,781 |
| Day 7 Sleep Break | | 12:22 AM | 4:40 AM | | | |

# CHAPTER 9
# DON'T FEED THE BEAR

*Remember teamwork begins by building trust. And the only way to do that is to overcome our need for invulnerability.*

—Patrick Lencioni

TODAY WE WERE past the halfway mark—we'd gone more than 1500 miles. Additionally, we were halfway through Kansas. We did not, however, anticipate that Kansas would feel hotter than the Mojave Desert.

"When I see temperatures in the nineties," John was fond of saying, "I look for swim trunks and a pool, not a bike ride."

Kaitee was working to redistribute the water that had collected in puffy pockets all around my knees, which had swollen overnight. In the midst of all this, a special guest had arrived from Wichita. It was my friend Bill Sickenberger, who flew in from Reston to join our crew for the second half of the race. It was great to see Bill. We had trained together for one of the qualifying races in Florida. RAAM was Sickenberger's idea in the first place.

John walked into the hotel room to check on the crew and me and handed me a hot plate of scrambled eggs, bacon, and toast. Solid food at night before bed—my body broke it down into energy. Solid food for breakfast was intended to give me a good base from which to start in the morning. I was alert from having rested, but a big meal in the morning had an obvious impact on my performance. It caused me to start slower than normal for the obvious reason: blood went to my stomach to digest the food, instead of to my muscles. We could afford that risk in the early morning because I was mentally awake.

"We have a murderous wind today," John said.

There's a reason *The Wizard of Oz* was set in Kansas. Only Texas has a greater potential capacity for wind power. Today we'd be riding toward Yates Center, one of the biggest wind farms in Kansas. The wind would be unrelenting. It only stops if something like a line of trees or a building stands in its way.

*Crew member Bill Sickenberger*
*joins the team*

"And Paul Millar is about an hour ahead of you," John added.

"I'm not racing Paul Millar," I said. We happened to be going back and forth with Paul and his team, and my team had been friendly with them at the places where we would intersect, like at gas stations to refuel the three vehicles we traveled in, or at one of the 56 time station stops where we would check in with race officials regarding our location.

Paul and his team, the racers from Ontario, Canada, had a reputation for being pleasant guys and great sports. He'd competed and finished RAAM in 2011 as part of a two-person team, and set a division record with his partner Mark Herbst. Like me, Paul was raising money for children with cancer. Although I had not met Paul, I was looking forward to our paths crossing in Missouri.

The weather had blessed RAAM in 2011—which was rare in the 31-year history of the race—and I couldn't help wishing we'd raced that year instead. This year was setting heat records all across the U.S. The National Oceanic and Atmospheric Administration (NOAA) was declaring 2012 the third-hottest summer on record.

*Blow dryer from competitor*
*Holger Roethig's team*

We were twelve hours behind the pace we'd anticipated. Still, I savored the solid breakfast as I got ready to head out and the crew prepared to do that day's laundry. Once again my nutrition team would be mixing ice-cold liquid fuel most of the day. And that was challenging. Once you got used to the taste of the carb-protein-salt in them, powdered drinks were just plain boring. Six days of powdered formula—even more boring.

Greg and Ken were my bartenders on alternating eight-hour shifts, mixing my drinks, handing them to me on their carefully calibrated schedule, and expecting each bottle to be drained in fifteen-minute intervals. They logged everything. They weighed me at lunchtime and at night. They owned the nutrition job. Firefighters are trained, regimented and apply a military style of discipline to the role. When it was above 90° F, they diluted the drinks to different strengths based on my sweat rate, always reminding me to keep my intake schedule consistent. During the race it's easy to get so tired you forget to drink. And then you don't race well.

Racing well takes a lot of concentration. Racing long distances at the top of your form is hard. Most of the nutrition that fuels your body has to be liquid. You have to look at liquid nutrition like shoveling coal into a furnace. You do it regularly so your performance power stays even. Nutrition makes or breaks the RAAM. We found it worked best to consistently consume 350 calories an hour. Solid food has to be consumed in portions under fifty calories, with a maximum of fifty calories of solid food an hour. Altering this plan slows your speed and makes you fatigued and drowsy.

Ken and Greg often had to refuse me solid food so I would maintain my speed and stay alert through the 20-hour race days. Many athletes complain about hallucinating as the race wears on—Jure Robic, the gonzo Slovenian who won back-to-back RAAMs in 2004 and 2005, reported being shadowed by bears, aliens, and bearded horsemen, for example, and Muffy Ritz, who finished second in the women's division three times, said she saw imaginary flea markets along the roadside for miles. But unless the athlete sleeps less than three hours per night, most of that comes from poor nutrition.

At lunch my reward might be a 200-calorie half-sandwich of tuna salad followed by a brief nap. Every hour I could eat anything I wanted. So long as it wasn't more than fifty calories. The trouble was, I get hungry when I am bored. I crave sugar, like a toddler. When I get sleepy and don't want to go down for a quick nap, I want enough sugar to push me past that mental dullness and fatigue.

"Len, you're like Yogi Bear. You come up to the window of the van and ask for food," Ken said. "We all know that you are big, lovable, and very persuasive. But we learned in Arizona that we aren't doing you any favors by giving you what you want. You need to eat solid food once an hour, but no more. The rest has to be liquid."

"And never more than fifty calories an hour."

Ken didn't want my body to draw too much blood from my brain, leaving me dull and unfocused. Otherwise, I got an ice-cold twenty-ounce bottle of Skratch or Infinit, the custom nutrition products that had been developed to fuel endurance athletes.

Think about it. How often do you take a trip to the fridge just because you are bored and want something to take your mind off the problem you've been working on at your desk? Now imagine twenty hours of pedaling a bike and craving mental relief in the form of food. For six days straight. Enduring every kind of wind except a tailwind.

*Nutritionist and paramedic Ken Gates*

The nutritionist's job was the pressure seat. He had to respond quickly to whatever request came at him, whether it was for a piece of chocolate or fruit or a bottle of water, because minimizing downtime for the rider was the priority. It was challenging to do that hour after hour, on top of keeping fruit slices clean and free from bacteria and mixing the drinks while the caravan constantly crossed through shifting weather patterns.

I knew Ken had a hard job. But I didn't want liquid. I was getting sleepy after starting the day in Maize at 7:00 a.m. It was noon, about an hour from a designated sleep break and I wanted sugar. I didn't want to take a five-minute nap, like I always take when I am dozing off. Chocolate would pop me out of my trance. So I decided to motion for the follow van to pull up next to me. Within a few seconds we are traveling side by side, the back window rolls down, and there's Ken's smiling face, eager to help. I asked him for the chocolate. It was my second food request within the hour.

"Uh, no, Len, you're going to have to wait thirty minutes before I can give you that chocolate," he said.

"That was the deal, and by the way, you have to finish that bottle of Infinit." The window rolled up and the van slowed down and resumed the follow position about 20 yards behind my tire.

"*Really?*" I thought to myself in disbelief. He has to be kidding! Whenever I am upset I taught myself to count to one hundred before saying anything. At that moment I counted to five hundred. At the end of my countdown, I motion to the van to pull forward. The van appears and the window rolls down. I decided to tell Ken something he probably wasn't expecting.

"Ken, let's take a minute and assess the situation," I said. "You're half my age, I started this charity, I'm responsible for paying for this trip, and I asked you for a piece of chocolate. Do I have that right?"

"Yeah, that's right," Ken said, matter-of-factly.

Ken calmly looked at me like you would a kindergarten child who was revving up for a tantrum. He was getting as comfortable confronting me as he was sitting in the tight quarters during an ambulance run or in the back of the follow van arranging the bins filled with gear, supplies, and food. Greg had not only seared the story of the Arizona burrito incident in his brain, but also his anger at having almost been run over by a car when the incident happened.

And then in a flash it occurs to me: the firefighter culture he and Greg know is a lot like the military. Authority is not questioned. You follow orders, and you do it with no fuss. It must have taken a lot for him to stand up to me. What's more, he and Greg had fought John hard for this responsibility. A rider's nutrition was critical, and if they failed at this, their necks were on the line. They had to come down hard on me.

I wanted that chocolate. In fact the better description of this scene is that I didn't want to take my nap, I wanted my candy, and I didn't want to drink my formula. When deprived of many of life's luxuries after five straight days on a bicycle, little things that we all take for granted get magnified. I was acting like a toddler. And if I overruled Ken, I would demoralize him. And for what? A 50-calorie sugar high? It was really stupid for me to ask.

"I'm good with that. I'm not going to second-guess you. Once I delegate something to you, I am never going to take it away. Don't tell me what I want to hear, tell me what I need to know," I continued. "When you and Greg joined our team to handle my nutrition, I put 100% of my trust in you to keep me on target. You are doing a great job."

I gave Ken the empty water bottle and said, "Let me know when I can have the chocolate."

Sometimes leadership means you learn to suppress your power of authority and prolong your pain or boredom. In this case, I wanted everyone on my team to know that I respected them so that they could continue to do their job with confidence. This meant that I could continue to do mine. My job was to ride the bike. Honor their roles. Trust their skills.

Thirty minutes later the van pulled up with my chocolate.

*

By this, the seventh day of the race, the crew was fully engaged in watching the position of the other athletes, and not just focusing on my goal of crossing the finish line on Saturday night.

In addition to going back and forth with Paul Millar, we were also trading places with a Brazilian rider named Claudio Clarindo, a three-time solo finisher who was just 1,000 feet behind me. The crew, who often played music from the loudspeaker on the follow van, was blasting Bon Jovi: *Whooah, we're halfway there...whooah, we're livin' on a prayer.*

We could tell how far Clarindo was behind me by watching his crew leapfrog past my crew at fifteen-minute intervals. I was averaging 17 mph as the gap widened between us. Looking ahead, I saw race director George Thomas on the side of the road. Seeing George on the course meant that the leaders of the race were not far away.

It was 12:20 p.m., 95° F, and I was completely depleted. What was I thinking, hitting it so hard to stay ahead of the Brazilian? The effort to stay out in front was simply not worth increasing my speed.

We rolled into the time station at Yates Center, Kansas. I needed a nap to recover from the heat and the exhaustion of a seven-hour, nonstop, chocolate-deprived morning.

Wayne and John had decided to use this time station stop to perform surgery on my bicycle. Wayne had concluded that the frame would not stand up to the steep descents awaiting me in West Virginia. My favorite Zipp 404 wheels were not the problem. The problem was that on my main bike, I had a very expensive piece of equipment—a SRAM Quarq power meter—a specialized crank connected to the pedals. The Quarq allowed me to see how many watts of power I was producing. I needed to have that crank installed on the backup bike.

*Wayne performs surgery on the bike crank*

Normally this procedure takes a few hours in a bicycle shop, as long as you have the right tools and equipment to make the change. Wayne would have to perform the swap while I took my sleep break in the heat of the day—in under ninety minutes. Neither bike would be rideable during that time. The pressure would be on Wayne to finish the job quickly.

But Wayne, too, was suffering from sleep deprivation. "It was hard for me to function," he later admitted. "I had to prove my mettle under a microscope with everyone watching."

The difficult part would be pulling off the pedal cranks and swapping them between the bikes—the ninety-minute time frame was a huge constraint.

*Wayne secures the bike on the roof rack on*
*another wind-filled day in Kansas*

The crew had set up the folding Hopecam tent to give Wayne shade while he worked in the intense heat. Both bikes were prepped and placed onto racks. Wayne meticulously arranged the tools he needed to swap the cranks. Our good fortune, at least, was to have listened to Wayne's insistence weeks before the race began of using identical bike models with identical parts rather than my original plan to bring my seven-year-old Trek 5900 as a backup bike and purchase only one new bicycle.

This was a risky move. If something went wrong, both bikes would be out of commission. John had to trust Wayne's skill to execute this maneuver. Otherwise, it could cost our team a big delay.

"Do your magic, Wayne," John said as he escorted me into the noisy RV, its rooftop generator cranking at full blast to cool the inside to 78° F. Wayne worked with the precision of a heart surgeon to prepare for this transplant, with Ed providing support under the shade of the Hopecam "MASH" tent.

"It was a wonder to witness," Ed said later that day with pride. After all, Ed had recruited Wayne to join our crew and felt a strong sense of commitment to helping Wayne perform his job. Ed's neck was on the line as well, because he personally vouched for Wayne. When the last screw was turned and the crank checked out, it was a joyful moment at the time station parking lot.

At 3:00 p.m., I climbed down the stairs of the RV. Wayne smiled broadly and held out the bike for me along the side of the road until I got on—his ritual after any bicycle tune-up.

I thanked him, as was my routine, this time with a big bear hug for the hard work he was doing to make sure that every bolt, every screw, was tight and ready for the next ten hours of punishment.

*

Departing Yates Center, Kansas in the mid-afternoon was again uplifting. I'd escaped the most intense heat of the day. Wayne was still working under the tent fitting the crank to the backup bike, and he anticipated it would be another two hours before that bike would be ready to be placed on top of the follow van. If my primary bike broke down—or if Wayne had missed something during "surgery"—we'd be delayed again. We trusted him. My job was to let my team members do their job, so I could do mine.

Even though we'd gotten a reprieve from the worst heat of the day, its cumulative effects were taking their toll. Our goal of crossing the finish line on Saturday night was beginning to slip. We would have to make it to Camdentown by nightfall to stay on schedule and get to our resting point beyond the Missouri border.

Now, as we headed east, the lonely and desolate road became more populated. Large cattle trucks and concrete trucks blew past me in that ever-present wind, and I could hear the clickety-clack of train wheels on the tracks that ran parallel to the highway. The drivers of the follow van had a daunting task—besides protecting me from these huge passing vehicles and handing off water bottles, they often pulled alongside me so the navigator could profile the topography of the race course that lay ahead.

The members of the Irish team led by Joe Barr, whom I had spoken with just before Pagosa Springs, Colorado, were among those applauding other teams as they passed by. Joe had been hospitalized in Colorado with hypoxemia (oxygen deprivation associated with altitude sickness).

It was great to see how a competitor who had to drop out of the race because his long-term health was at risk was cheering with his crew for other athletes. They would continue to cheer for every racer, all the way toward the finish line in Maryland.

Our crew was again in high spirits, and the town of Fort Scott was beautiful with its American flags flying everywhere in preparation for the Fourth of July. As I approached the bridge over the Marmaton River, I rode past my crew, lined up along the span singing the words to the Village People song "Macho Man" as I rode past. This was my sister Laurie's doing. She sent me an oversized singing greeting card for my 50th birthday that played that song. Amy captured the sequence on video and uploaded the YouTube video to our blog that evening. Although we all shared a laugh as the sun set in Fort Scott on a picture perfect afternoon, we could see the fatigue beginning to show on the faces of our crew.

The crew had finally gotten comfortable with acknowledging how tired they were, Ed told me, and began to cover for each other when needed. "If we didn't rest, the team would suffer," he said. "We knew we had to recharge, although some people were going to burn it to the end."

After we crossed into Missouri, one of the official RAAM photographers and film crew from race headquarters in a white van caught up to our crew. They wanted to do a moving interview—on a very challenging winding and twisting road, while dark was falling. Missouri Highway 54 was dangerous with its heavy traffic and fast-moving cars, potholes, and no shoulders alongside the road. Drivers get frustrated with cyclists because without shoulders for cyclists to move to, locals can't safely pass a cyclist without crossing the road's center line. The interview lasted about a minute.

Pretty soon the road became one big parking lot on both sides. A well-to-do landowner was putting on his renowned annual fireworks show. He was also celebrating his 50th wedding anniversary, and this year's fireworks show, his gift to the community, was not to be missed.

I thought that Stefano Rocca, whom I'd called that morning, would love the event. He loves life—runs, plays, explores with his younger brother all day long (and night, too, if his mother would let him). Getting a Hopecam computer had been a big deal for him. He loved being able to set a "secret" password for his Skype account.

At first he was afraid to let his classmates see him with no hair, but within a few minutes he became the class clown, making funny faces and jokes to ease the tension. When he returned to school after treatment, his first days back were not so overwhelming. The webcam had eased much of the nervousness about returning to school while still being bald and undergoing treatment.

Today when I'd called, Stefano was visiting Hershey Park. I hoped he'd get to see some fireworks, and like someone in our crew said when we pulled over briefly to watch the show, that he'd have a life that was "all about collecting great memories." Like the one we were making, taking a deep breath and enjoying the beauty all around us, even though we were in the middle of a race. Stefano later wrote me an email that my crew read to me: *Keep your eyes out for mountain lions. Pumas are my favorite animals. My username on Skype is PumaRocca!*

Stefano connected with his friends at school via Skype, using the computer Hopecam provided. We all laughed hearing Stefano's message.

As we watched the grand finale, we wasted no time getting far ahead of the crowd exiting the show. We didn't want to have to share the road with everybody who'd been partying.

We were all looking forward to this rest break. I crested the hill to the abandoned gas station that marked the entrance to the town. The cabins we would stay in that night, unfortunately, were 18 miles away from the course. They were rustic and musty, but for me a hot shower and a bed with a blanket just about anywhere felt like heaven. When we arrived at the time station stop, I'd seen a tall rider from Hungary tucked into his sleeping bag on the road next to his van, his crew of four—the minimum you need to ride this race—milling about.

I took a seat on the raised island where the gas station pumps were located and slowly lowered my back to the ground, and waited while the crew set things up. At times like these, I liked to remember the Marines' saying *Don't Run when you can walk, Don't Walk when you can stand, Don't Stand when you can sit, Don't Sit when you can lie down, Don't Lie down when you can sleep.* Sleep was like water in the desert. If you find it you take it, no matter what.

Soon we were checked in at Pomme de Terre Lake's Clear Light Inn. We hadn't made it to Camdentown, but it was a sure bet that if any of our competitors were using the "Spot Len" locator, they were envying our arrival in Weaubleau.

## Lesson 9

The importance of trusting your team to take ownership of their jobs was never more evident than today, watching Ken and Wayne in action. Dan Pink's book *Drive: The Surprising Truth About What Motivates Us* mentions three characteristics that are essential in every work environment to empower team members to do their best: autonomy, mastery, and purpose.

Ken and Wayne both were given the autonomy to do what they knew best when it came to nutrition and maintaining the bicycle respectively. No one second-guessed their judgment or ability, because they were masters at their trade. They had proven themselves before being asked to join the team, and well before we left Oceanside. Over the course of six days, they had demonstrated competency and single-minded dedication to performing their jobs. It would have been devastating to take back that task by being critical or second-guessing them for doing the job we had asked of them. Delegating fearlessly and honoring their contribution to the team was not easy. I wanted that chocolate. I was tired, cranky, didn't want to take my nap, and wanted my candy. RAAM had reduced me to acting like a toddler. But to be a good leader you have to let go, especially when it's hard. Empowering your team is trusting your team.

*Greetings from Hopi land. I had the opportunity to meet and talk with a few of your crew members in Flagstaff. My husband and I had just missed seeing you...I just wanted to wish you well and may the Lord bless and keep you safe on your ride. Asquali, Koo-na-ah (Thank you in the Hopi and Tewa languages).*

—KJ Sahmie

*Fantastic progress, Len! Must feel good to be past the halfway point, not to mention at the head of the pack. Everybody is psyched about what you're doing. If it's any consolation, the weather ought to get a little better as you head east, unless you're bringing the heat with you!*

—Patrick Phillips

# DAY 8

June 20, from Weaubleau to Hamel

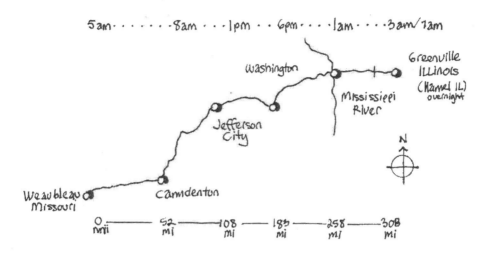

| START | END | START | FINISH | DISTANCE | TOTAL MI. | ELEVATION |
|---|---|---|---|---|---|---|
| Weaubleau, MO | Camdenton, MO | 4:40 AM | 8:25 AM | 52.40 | 1,823 | 2,637 |
| Camdenton, MO | Jefferson City, MO | 8:25 AM | 12:44 PM | 56.90 | 1,880 | 1,573 |
| Jefferson City, MO | Washington, MO | 12:44 PM | 5:53 PM | 74.20 | 1,957 | 2,414 |
| Washington, MO | *Mississippi River* | 7:10 PM | 12:41 AM | 75.80 | 2,029 | 1,740 |
| *Mississippi River* | Greenville, IL | 12:44 AM | 7:00 AM | 43.80 | 2,075 | 873 |
| Day 8 Sleep Break | | | | | | |

# CHAPTER 10
# A MISSION-DRIVEN PURPOSE

*The best things in life make you sweaty.*

—Edgar Allen Poe

OUR PLAN OF racing in the RAAM to increase Hopecam's visibility and therefore its reach was working. As we hit the Midwest, the crowds cheering us on at each time station stop were growing, as was interest in our organization. Of course, when I refer to crowds I'm not talking about throngs.

In Camdentown, for example, we met Eric Johnston, local coordinator for the time station stop 32. Like other volunteer race supporters, Eric was an expert at the race logistics and got to know who was competing by following the links to their websites. Eric told me he had read my website and was impressed by Hopecam—and even more impressed that I was in first place. "I never imagined you would be such a good athlete," he said.

Eric wanted to find out how he could get his local school board to promote Hopecam. We gave him a race jersey and Bill and Steve stayed behind to talk to Eric and to refill the ice and water coolers in the back of the van while I headed out toward Jefferson City. Eric said, "I wanted to meet Len and I wanted to meet some of the guys from the kids' teams, like Paul Millar."

Like Jon Nelson, who'd handed us $50 for Hopecam as we passed his farm on Rt. 160, Eric was another example of people hearing about us through our blog, Facebook page, and other communications, and then getting behind the Hopecam mission. People along the racecourse gathered at the time station stops and wanted to take pictures with our crew. We tried to share our mission with as many people as possible on the course. John called it "making friends and kissing babies." He said, "I wanted to keep sending the message about why we were doing what we were doing."

*Eric Johnston, Time Station*
*Captain, Camdentown, MO*

We learned later that the number of people following our race blog was growing, too. We were getting close to 1,000 hits a day. That was more than had come to the Hopecam website since its inception. By providing continuous updates of our expedition, we gave people a fun way to connect and watch the outcome unfold. By posting Amy's videos on the blogs, including the daily "Hopecam dedication" to the child we were riding for that day, we gave people a reason to care.

Charlotte Jennie Reynolds—her family called her C.J.—was today's Hopecam child. Charlotte preferred books to stuffed animal toys, and loved greeting customers at the kids' gym that her parents owned. At three-and-a-half, C.J. was diagnosed with a large, aggressive brain tumor. Unfortunately, the protocol failed and C.J. died. The family had used the Hopecam computer to keep in touch with family all over the United States while she was being treated, and when she was in the final stage of her life, friends and relatives Skyped with her or emailed videos of themselves reading books to her.

Like many surviving families, C.J.'s parents started a foundation (cjstuf.org) to provide financial assistance for families of children with chronic and life-threatening illnesses. Her father had written us a letter before we'd departed on the race.

*We don't cure anything, we don't fund research, we don't solve huge problems. What we do is make an unbearable situation a little more bearable. Thank you, Team Hopecam, for helping make our unbearable situation a little less so.*

Messages like these and the ones we were getting from supporters reminded us of why we were here, doing what we were doing, even as we powered through the heat, wind, sleep deprivation, and sheer tedium of pedaling. My crew liked broadcasting these messages over the loud-speaker, usually at night, when it also helped all of us stay awake.

Many times there would be long pauses between the words of the message. This wasn't dramatic effect by the navigator. It was the navigator, and every crew member in the van, getting choked up by the challenges C.J., Shannon, and all the kids like them and their families faced.

\*

If we made today's goal—the Mississippi River—we'd be two-thirds done. The early morning at 77° F felt balmy compared to what we'd experienced the previous 1800 miles. The road was filled with gently rolling hills and beautiful views of trees. We hadn't seen forested areas since we'd left Trinidad, Colorado, more than 600 miles and two days ago.

By 10:00 am, though, the heat and humidity were rising and my saddle sores were really hurting. I had to pull over and ask Ken for more numbing medication. That was a first. The pain was unbearable. It takes a lot for me to stop, and the stabbing pain as the sores rubbed against the bike shorts felt like salt in a wound. The hotter it got the more I would sweat, and that sweat would accumulate in my bike shorts and the pain would slowly begin to amplify. I'd started wearing two pairs of bike shorts to add more padding and eliminate friction. At least the sores were being "managed"—that is to say, not getting worse—but that was little consolation. These two little quarter-sized blisters were destroying me. We had endured the Mojave, the altitude of the Rocky Mountains, the unrelenting winds across the Great Plains, the unending rolling hills of the Ozark Mountains, and now these sores were so painful I wondered if I could continue. That's how bad it was. And the heat was once again increasing, making the pain even worse.

*An ill-fated attempt at a haircut*

Our next scheduled stop was Jefferson City, Missouri, but getting there felt like an impossible task. I was simply spent. Though I'd become more acclimated to the heat, I was beginning to get overheated. I thought about all the riders who had done the race before and noticed they all had one common denominator: shaved heads or buzz cuts. You can see where this is going.

I asked Bill to call ahead and have the people in the advance van buy a pair of battery-powered shears so I could cut my hair. There would be no end of teasing about this. "Forkas, you're the only guy out here using hair gel in the morning," John said.

While all this was going on, John was busy instructing the driver about how to mark turns so we wouldn't lose any time at intersections. In contrast to the wide vistas of the West, the roads in the Midwest were narrower and there were more turns closely spaced together. Marking turns is akin to choreography—leaping ahead of the rider, parking on the roadside at a critical intersection, and having one of the crew stand and point in the direction of the turn.

Sounds pretty simple, right? Now imagine that in eleven days, our team will make hundreds of turns. Some at night. Some in heavy traffic. As the race wears on, fatigue sets in. The further east we travel, through more populated areas, the more turns there are, and they are often back-to-back. We were getting closer to the outskirts of St. Louis, closer to the Illinois state line. Turns were appearing more frequently.

Enter a little self-created distraction. At our next time station stop, Bill appeared with the shears. "Bub, are you sure you want to do this?"

"I'm melting, Bill. Let's go."

He sheared broad swaths of hair from the left side of my head. About three minutes into the process, he handed me the shears. I tried to even out the sides. The heat must have been affecting my mental state. How on earth would a haircut in the middle of Missouri make any difference whatsoever on my performance? So far, this was the only time I had "lost it" mentally.

I took it as a wake-up call that I was starting to melt down. Living on a bike can do obscene things to the body—and to the mind—but the most common problem is cumulative sleep deprivation. Many solo riders hallucinate as the race wears on. It was finally happening to me, I thought, as I set down the shears. Maybe I needed to sleep more at night or take more naps during the day. I didn't want to be one of those racers who saw mailboxes in the night jumping out at them.

The crew insisted I go down for a longer sleep break while Wayne tried using a box cutter to carve away some of the bicycle seat to relieve the pressure on my saddle sores, and Ed experimented with how to attach the two American flags he'd purchased (more distraction) to the vans.

"The Germans have a flag, the Swedes have a flag," he insisted, and found some twist ties that he decided would work. "We live in America, we need a flag."

We had a glorious start to the next leg of the course: the stately white dome of the Missouri state capitol building and the glistening Missouri River to the east with its hundreds of barges ferrying up and down the waterway carrying stockpiles of grain and other cargo. The next seventy-two miles would follow alongside the river, up and down a series of undulating hills laid out like a roller coaster. In this 97° F, shadeless heat, and everyone so incredibly bored with the race at that time, I had to do something to mix it up. So I started doing intervals. Intervals are quick high output sprints that max out your heart rate. Push as hard as possible on the downhill to build momentum on the uphill. My heart rate hit 163—not a good idea in that heat and humidity. But I did them anyway just to break up the monotony.

*

In general it was unusual to see other riders on the course, but every once in a while, we'd find ourselves in the same place. One of those spots was the Revolution Cycles bike shop in the small strip mall in Washington, Missouri, where time station 34 was located. Right in front of the shop was a large inflatable swimming pool. It was simply too inviting. We had to stop. So did a lot of other racers and crews.

John had been saying if we play this right, we could win our age division in this race. The team had been taking excellent care of me—Kaitee and Greg using massage and active release therapy to move the fluids in my muscles around and work out the knots so I could remain flexible, Greg and Ken managing my nutrition so I'd be racing at the top of my form. Ed, Joe, and Bill were handling the driving and navigating while Steve was busy running errands, writing the blog posts, capturing short 30-second videos and feeding them to the blog. Amy was working tirelessly filming, editing, narrating, and producing two-minute videos of the events that transpired each day. Amy also filmed the daily testimonials for the Hopecam child we were riding for, as we described where we were, who the child was, and how Hopecam had benefited his or her life.

My wife Elizabeth watched these videos every day and could see the subtle physical changes that were slowly emerging in me as the race wore on. "I could see the fatigue in his face, the way he looked into the camera, how tired he looked," she said, "but his speech was clear and articulate as he described where he was and all about the child he was riding for. Len was still mentally sharp after eight days."

At lunchtime, we called these children to let them know we were thinking about them, and how much they inspired us each day. We called the parents of the children who were no longer with us, like the Reynolds family and the McClain family.

Many teams were surprised we were rookies and yet doing so well. When we arrived at the time station and asked if we could jump in the pool, we got the nod from three German crew members taking a break from supporting racer Holger Roethig. They asked me who I was crewing for.

"I'm not crewing, I'm racing," I said, splashing in the ice-cold water.

They shook their heads in disbelief. "No way! You don't look like you are racing!"

I took that as a compliment, wished them well, and headed into the RV for a quick change of clothes. I just needed a brief respite before riding to cross the Mississippi that night.

While we were there, the crew fielded questions about the inner workings of our team, the training, and how a rookie RAAM rider could do so well. The experience turned out to be a special moment for the crew. We were leading, well ahead of our twelve-day cut-off. Although we were about twelve hours off the aggressive schedule we'd set for ourselves at the start of the race, the crew was in a great mood, knowing home was in closer range. The Annapolis finish line was only days away.

\*

We beat the cutoff for the next time station by more than a day. Our lead against Paul Millar, the Canadian who was also riding to raise awareness about childhood cancer, had widened at that point and the bulk of the pack was six hours away. We were gaining on the leaders and slowly reeling past, one by one, even the younger riders as we steadily rolled east.

One of those younger competitors was Dr. Wolfgang Mader. Our team watched his even, mechanical pace over a four-hour stretch. His power output was consistent whether he was riding a flat or a hilly section. In contrast, when I came to a hill I would put out a short burst of power right before the base and use that momentum to carry me up the hill. Dr. Mader was steady and slow. No quick moves, everything very deliberate. I thought, "I can learn from this guy."

Mader and I frequently arrived at time station stops simultaneously, but he did it at a much more even pace. Having studied Dr. Mader's style, I decided to ride more like he did. Steady, easy, not crushing the hills. Take them slowly and keep the cadence even.

The turns needed to navigate St. Louis and make our way over the Mississippi were tricky. Some stretches felt like driving through an industrial zone in my hometown of Cleveland—semi tractor trailers on one side and roaring interstate traffic on the other. The map indicated we had to make a dozen turns in fewer than four miles. It was a labyrinth with few markers to guide our way, and at times the crew said it felt like they were going around in circles. It was dark, everyone was sleepy, and we made a wrong turn that took us a short distance off course. But finally, at 12:45 a.m., we crossed that major milestone into Alton.

We had a couple more hours to go before arriving in Hamel, where we'd stop for the night. We had crossed the desert, the Rockies, the Great Plains, the Ozarks, and the mighty Mississippi. By tomorrow night we'd be halfway across Indiana and into the home stretch.

How were we doing so well in the race when we were only rookies? When the German crew had asked that question of my team, my crew had said it plain and simple—the training rides with their careful planning, prepping, and practicing that gave everyone confidence about confronting the course, and how all the people on the team worked with and helped each other.

I also believe it was our willingness to be beginners and learn from our own and others' experience. The constant course corrections. The doggedness of persevering under adverse conditions. Building in accountability, validating and appreciating each other's skills. Not magic, not lucky charms, not haircuts.

For me, the critical underpinning was that we had a team that felt more like a family than a crew, people who embraced not just a mission but a mission-driven purpose. When you have that, it bonds the individual team members and in the process, changes them such that they end up changing others. The clearest example I can think of happened earlier that day, shortly after I'd ridden off with my new iPhone holder that Wayne had so ingeniously built and attached to my handlebars.

*Impromptu conference: Where to stop for the night?*

The RV had made a quick stop at a local bike shop so Wayne could refill needed supplies, particularly the rear lights, which kept rattling off the bike. I had brought four flashing tail lights and all but one had managed to fall off the bicycle. At the shop, he stocked up on spare tubes, handlebar tape, and other parts.

Then as he pulled out of the bike shop's parking lot, an elderly couple in a late-model American sedan drove up alongside the RV, rolled down the window, and began to berate Wayne for the unsafe race course.

"The bicycles should have a different route! It's unsafe, cars can't pass, and it's creating massive traffic jams," they said. "You need to stop and take a different route immediately!"

Wayne patiently tried to explain that we were in a competition and had no power to change the direction of the course. He reassured the couple that he'd communicate their concerns to the race officials.

This did not stop the driver's tirade. "I had to slam on the brakes several times, almost causing an accident because of the cyclist ahead of us!" she said.

Again Wayne waited patiently while they vented. They went on for another five minutes complaining about how disruptive all these cyclists were to their community.

Then he said, "Okay, I've listened patiently for five minutes to your explanation of the problem. I would like for you to take two minutes to listen to me and for me to share with you our cause, which is Hopecam."

He handed them the 4 x 6 cards we carried that explained our mission and our journey. The couple read the card and did a complete turnaround.

"We'll pray for your team and your rider. God bless all of you!"

It would have been so easy for Wayne to dismiss this couple for being "grumpy senior citizens." But by taking the time to allow them to share their experience he was able to completely win them over to our cause.

"Yes, we were trying to get a guy across the USA, and that couple, well, they just wanted to be heard," Wayne said. "But our mission was Hopecam. I wasn't fully sold on the mission at first. I was just a mechanic. I figured Len was like a lot of racers looking for a charity to help him pay for an expensive bike race. But when I saw him talk to random strangers, I saw his commitment to the mission."

"It was so rewarding to dedicate our time and energy to it. Our team was unified toward that goal: to raise money and awareness. And in doing that we were trying to get Len across the USA."

*One of Missouri's magnificent sunrises*

## Lesson 10

On this day we learned that others were beginning to understand our mission: Eric Johnson, who knew about our cause well before we arrived in his time stop in Camdentown; the folks at Revolution Bicycles, who talked with us when we each took a dip in the pool that they had set up in the parking lot in front of their shop; and Wayne, our originally skeptical bike mechanic, who became a true ambassador for our mission, explaining patiently why we were following the guy in the orange and white spandex outfit. We had understood from the start that we might need to "educate the public" and so we set those wheels in motion by letting people know we were "Team Hopecam"—we wrapped our van with our logo, we set up media interviews in advance, we installed the "SPOT connect" locator so people could follow us. We also took the time to talk with people on the course so they could get to know us and what we were about, even though we were in a race and had a goal to achieve.

We had also tackled more hardships, including the twisting, rolling, unrelenting hills in the Ozark Mountains. I suffered with saddle sores so painful that they made me cry when the numbing cream slowly wore off in the rising heat. And the heat made me so desperate that I began to hallucinate thinking that a buzz cut at lunchtime would forever cure me of overheating.

Despite these obstacles, we persevered, learned from the people around us, and were open to continued innovation and improvement. Like many high-performing teams, each day more elements fell into place. We developed routines and patterns but more importantly after a week of our team running smoothly we began to look out for one another, insisting that some take longer rest breaks to catch up on much needed sleep. Our bonds were growing stronger. We were more and more like a healthy family.

*Thanks for this priceless gift of supporting these innocent children like Stefano Rocca in their struggle. Keep up the great challenge in testimony of your commitment.*

—Sofia Enggren

*Len! You have no idea of how word of your fearless adventure has spread! Because I'm a blabbermouth and absolutely CANNOT believe a human being can do what you are doing. All my friends ask for progress reports. I am praying to the wind Gods to knock it off, and sending all my best vibes that you stay strong. You can do it Len!*

—Julie Savoie

*Len, we are following your efforts here in DC and are all rooting for you to meet your goal in Annapolis!*

—Anthony Balestrieri

*Hey Mr. Len—this is Hannah with a joke for you. What's the scariest animal in Alaska? A Cari-BOO.*

—Hannah Ruthie Weingast, age 5

# DAY 9
## June 21, from Hamel to Bloomington

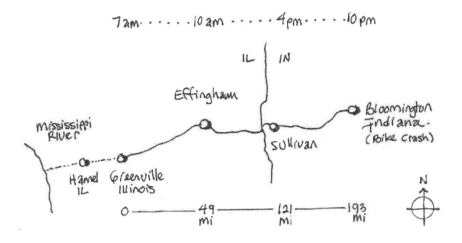

7am · · · · · 10 am · · · · · 4pm · · · · ·10 pm

IL | IN

Effingham

Mississippi River

Bloomington Indiana. (Bike crash)

Sullivan

Hamel IL   Greenville Illinois

N

0 ——— 49 mi ——— 121 Mi ——— 193 mi

TODAY WE RIDE FOR JUSTIN

| START | END | START | FINISH | DISTANCE | TOTAL MI. | ELEVATION |
|---|---|---|---|---|---|---|
| Greenville, IL | Effingham, IL | 7:04 AM | 9:45 AM | 48.90 | 2,125 | 936 |
| Effingham, IL | Sullivan, IN (EDT) | 9:45 AM | 3:59 PM | 72.90 | 2,197 | 1,040 |
| Sullivan, IN (EDT) | Bloomington, IN | 4:22 PM | 10:52 PM | 72.70 | 2,265 | 2,948 |
| Day 9 Sleep Break | | 10:52 PM | 3:09 AM | | | |

# CHAPTER 11

# SEA CHANGE

*Discouragement and failure are two of the surest stepping stones to success.*

—Dale Carnegie

TODAY I WAS looking forward to meeting old friends in Sullivan, Indiana, revisiting the state where I had attended college. Aside from Julie Cepulis' surprise visit in Colorado, these would be the first close friends that I had seen during the race, aside from those on my crew.

But first we had to get out of Illinois. The next time station stop would be Greenville. Downtown Greenville's Village Center in the early dawn reminded me of the movie *Back to the Future*—the same brick buildings with the same large clock and prominent steeples. I love riding through small towns like these. It's true Americana and a good way to stay grounded. Many of the towns we'd passed showed signs of the recession: white-washed windows, buildings needing paint and repair. We always rely on economic data to determine the trends of our global economy, but a lot can be gleaned from the look of the cities tertiary to the major metropolitan areas.

I hadn't ridden this section of the course in my practice rides, and it all felt new. Our team was rocketing through Illinois, courtesy of a tailwind that pushed my speed to 19 mph. My resolve to ride slower and easier, like Dr. Mader, faded away in the excitement of catching this tailwind and seeing old friends. Everything felt great, and I felt once again like blowing out a time trial pace on this one section of gently rolling hills.

Or maybe we all wanted the race to be over and figured that speeding up would get us there.

Then on an uphill section my wheel hit a pothole in the road. My iPhone fell out of the case Wayne had built for me and tumbled down the pavement behind me. Without thinking, I grabbed both brakes and spun around to go back for it.

My team in the follow van was not pleased.

"What are you doing?" John yelled out the passenger window.

"iPhone on the pavement—going back for it."

I will admit, I'm addicted to my iPhone, and yes, I sometimes check my emails and texts while riding the bike, though I try hard to resist the urge to text and pedal. I reached the phone just before a dark sedan almost flattened it. It was a close call—for the iPhone and for me. Surprisingly, the phone had no damage. I picked it up, placed it in my back pocket, and returned to the race. About twenty minutes later, on a flat stretch of road, the follow van pulled alongside me.

"Len, you almost got yourself run over chasing that phone of yours," John said. "You have got to stay focused and put that thing away."

"All right, John, but that's my link to rest of the world. It's how I call these kids I'm riding for each day. But you're right."

Connecting is really important to me, and of course the need for connection was the impetus for Hopecam. We were dedicating today's ride to Hopecam child Justin Condoluci, the nephew of one of my neighbors, Alison Weingast. Justin was eight when he was diagnosed with acute lymphoblastic leukemia (ALL). After three years of chemotherapy, he thought he'd beaten cancer, but six months later he relapsed. News of a relapse hits hard. At least when you're diagnosed, there's a protocol. You know that you're following the same protocol that has cured 80% of children with that type of cancer. When children relapse, they get kicked into the 20% category. It's one of the most heartbreaking moments in their lives.

Justin's new treatment plan—an intense regimen of high-dose chemotherapy and twenty-two rounds of radiation—would take place seventy miles from home. In this unfamiliar environment, staying connected to family and friends was even more important. Despite the rigors and side effects of treatment, Justin kept faith in beating cancer.

The success of our efforts in RAAM—both the race itself and of course taking Hopecam to a wider platform to help more children like Justin—would depend on the connections we were fostering with each other on the team, with our donors, and with the supporters (including families, friends, and friends of friends) we were accumulating day by day. In addition to the increasing crowds of our supporters at time station stops, messages were pouring in on email, the Hopecam blog, and Tumblr. Just knowing that, and having my crew read them to me over the van's loudspeaker, was incredibly sustaining. RAAM finishers Randy Mouri and his wife Susie were huge supporters of the effort. They emailed at least once and often several times each day, sending praise (*If Hopecam wasn't on the map before, it certainly is now. Love the video updates, Amy. Awesome job you all.*), encouragement (*Tough climbing ahead that will seem twice as steep as experienced in your practice ride. Keep the focus, team.*), and advice (*If you have another hotel stop scheduled along the course I'd suggest an ice bath just below the hips.*)

So of course I felt I needed my phone, I wanted to see that support for myself. Seeing the actual messages made it more real.

Wayne had worked hard to find a solution to my addiction to being connected. The phone's GPS and weather apps let me know where we were and what was going on. And having the phone let me listen to audio books while I rode or have long conversations with the crew when it wasn't too windy and the road was straight and smooth.

But John really was right. We had come so far. It would be foolish to lose focus now.

I peeled off the layers of tape that had been used to strap the case to my handlebars, finally placing the case in my back pocket to be returned to Wayne later that day.

For probably the hundredth time in that race, I refocused myself. Ride the bike. Just ride the bike. But put the hammer down: my closest friends from college—guys who had supported each other during demanding hours in the design studio and who had all become successful architects in southern Indiana—were waiting for me.

*

Being able to see close friends for the first time during the race really felt like a metaphor for inching closer to the finish line. The temperature was a brutal 99° F at 11:00 that morning, but the terrain was flat, we had a mild tailwind, and finally there were trees—and shade. I couldn't wait to see my friends. I knew that they all were taking the afternoon off work to see me, meet my crew, and be a part of the experience.

*Meeting college friends from Indiana*

We rolled into Sullivan, Indiana, at 2:00 p.m. My crew had set up the Hopecam tent and several chairs for the visit, and Wayne once again worked diligently on the bike while I cleaned up in the shower and washed off the accumulated grit and caked-on sunscreen from the day's riding. It felt great to put on some fresh street clothes and a pair of flip-flops, even for just a few minutes, after nine days of racing. We talked about the race and the extreme heat, then my friends agreed to meet me at the next station stop in Bloomington, where another former roommate who lived near the Kentucky border would join them.

I could see from the looks on the faces of some of my crew that they were not happy about this next rendezvous. They appreciated the idea of me encountering friends; riding the bike was, as I'd known at the beginning, sometimes a lonely job. But I think they preferred getting back to doing what they knew best—keeping the team moving head at 15 mph. Pitching a tent in a dusty gas station parking lot, creating a working space and a small area to relax under the shade of a canopy, then breaking it all down and packing it up without leaving anything or anyone behind couldn't have been much fun. For some it must have felt like a traveling road show: bad food, little sleep. Worst of all the crew could consume no alcohol. The penalty is immediate disqualification of the rider, with no exceptions. No one was going to risk that consequence.

I was excited by the visit, though, and so instead of taking my normal sleep break, I quickly got dressed, asked my med team to help with medicating my saddle sores (which were simply not going away), and jumped back on the bike. But as it turned out, skipping my sleep break might not have been such a great idea. Though you might think of Indiana as flat, Highway 54 features rolling hills. When I had passed through here in April, it was cool, early morning, and my legs were fresh. Today, with a 5:30 a.m. start and thirteen hours of high velocity riding at an average speed of 19 mph behind me, I was feeling fatigued.

By supper time, the climbs were getting steeper and steeper, so several times I jumped in the van and took five-minute naps—three times between 5:00 and 8:00 pm, an unprecedented number for me. I was spent. My legs were heavy and it was hard to stay awake. I was finally feeling the effects of prolonged sleep deprivation, but more importantly I had underestimated how tough the hills surrounding Bloomington were, and how stupid it was for me to push so hard to get to Greenville. And I had underestimated the value of after-lunch naps. By the time I was five miles from the time station stop, all I wanted to do was lie down and sleep for an hour.

Soon the familiar buildings of the Indiana University stadium and campus came into view. Then something unexpected—construction. The traffic was compressed into two lanes with no shoulder. A freshly poured concrete apron and new curb lay to the right; orange construction barrels and steel rods everywhere pierced the Thursday night dusk.

In a few minutes I'd be placing a call to Justin and I knew that my phone battery was dead. Bill and Joe were able to hand me a charger that I quickly snapped to the phone. Then as I placed the phone in my back pocket, I hit the section of pavement that meets the curb and my bike slid out from underneath me. I broke the fall with my right hand.

It scared the heck out of my crew. They pulled over into the construction zone on the left, protected by the orange barrels.

"I'm fine! I'm fine!" I said to them as cars streamed by between us. Luckily I'd been riding slowly and was able to land without any damage to my hand or my bike.

But the traffic in Indiana was not fine. Because my crew was following me closely for the five minutes before I fell, a long line of cars—at least thirty—had backed up behind them. There was no place to pull over except in the construction area. We were doing the best we could, but no one was letting my van jump back into traffic, so I told the crew that I would meet them at the time station stop one mile up the road.

I got back on my bike and started riding again. About three minutes later a driver, probably angry at the delay, decided to brush close to me as he passed. I jerked to the right, barely missing getting hit by his passenger side mirror, but then caught that edge between the pavement and the curb and went down again, this time striking my right knee on the freshly poured concrete curb. This time when my bike slid underneath me, my feet did not disengage from the clipless pedals in time for me to catch my balance. I went down with a thud and mashed my leg just below the knee joint.

My knee had a large scrape the size of a grapefruit and a hole in it the size of a silver dollar. The hole was bleeding quickly. This time I was shaken up. My crew recognized that and quickly pulled over. I could not tell if I was more affected by the fatigue that had accumulated during the day or by the crash itself.

Kenny walked toward me with the med kit and fumbled through

the many packets of cleaners and bandages, looking for the hydrogen peroxide.

"Ken, it's not that bad. I can ride on it. Let's just patch it up at the time station stop."

The stop was less than a half-mile away. Since traffic was not my friend I decided to ride the sidewalk until it ended at the edge of the construction zone. I then walked the bike over the gravel and rejoined the stream of cars making their way through Bloomington.

It was getting dark and hard to see, but I was able to navigate past the many cars heading south and finally find my crew in the parking lot. For the second time that day they were not happy with me.

*An injury from crashing in traffic*
*outside Bloomington, IN*

Joe and Bill had radioed the news of the crash, so there were many worried faces, including those of my college friends. The crash was my first big mistake. The story was that I was texting while riding or dialing a friend or relative, but this time it was not true. The construction, poor visibility, no safe pull-overs, and motorists who were rightly frustrated by the delay caused by my route were why I crashed. And maybe the fatigue. I had underestimated the impact the heat would have on me, and I was overconfident.

It was almost ten at night, and I needed to be patched up. The tissue around my knee was all mashed in; the hole could not be stitched. The blood streamed down my knee and over my calf. My college friends had been waiting for me and I apologized for not being able to spend more time with them.

We decided rather than push on to Greensburg we would lay up in Bloomington. I said goodbye to my friends. Ken began cleaning out the wound with hydrogen peroxide and did his best to patch up the knee with the bandages we had on hand.

Within twenty minutes my crew had secured hotel rooms and brought me a delicious plate of pasta from a local Italian sub shop. No sooner had I gotten settled so Kaitee and Greg could start working on me when John walked in the room, a "fatherly" look on his face.

He sat down next to me. "Len, we're in first place and we are going to win this race, but we can't do anything stupid. You're going to have to give up the cell phone for good."

For the second time that day, John was right. I needed to maintain 100% focus on these last 700 miles of the race. I handed over the phone.

Ken patched me up again. Then after dinner and a big slice of apple pie with a large scoop of vanilla ice cream, I quickly fell asleep. As usual, Wayne fixed up the bike and inspected it for damage. He ended up replacing the tires, because the sidewalls had been scraped when they hit the curb. Fortunately, the wheel rims were not damaged.

*

The speculation about what had caused the crash fueled rumors about what had really happened, but the truth is I had pushed myself way beyond my limits that day and did not take a needed rest break in the afternoon as I had done in the past. Yes, I was looking forward to seeing friends; that excitement kept me pumped. But mostly I was overconfident and underestimated the effect of the mid-day heat. I had forgotten the fundamentals.

The crash was a wake-up call for our team. Despite the damage to my bike and me it was probably one of the best things that could have happened. Distraction has consequences. It's a stupid mistake that can be avoided. In 2011, for example, Gerhard Gulewicz reportedly took off his jacket while pedaling in Indiana. The jacket got caught in the spokes and this threw him off the bike, breaking his collarbone. Race over!

Just as in Colorado when I almost went over a guard rail after falling asleep while pedaling, my crash grounded us in the reality of the dangers of RAAM. As Steve put it, at any moment I could be "one squirrel away" from life and death. The crash refreshed the importance of sleep breaks, not getting separated from our follow vehicle, and not chasing after "bright shiny objects."

*John's parents visit from Ohio*

"We got into the competition of the race and promoting our cause," one of the crew members told me later. "But what everyone forgot was that the number one job was keeping you safe on the bike—we actually got away from that somewhere in the middle of the race."

John's view was that we'd learned a lot after a week of racing, most of it good—but that we'd also accumulated some bad habits with the confidence of having come this far.

"We got used to the widely spaced turns of the west, where we would remain on one road for hundreds of miles," John said, "and now found ourselves unprepared for the tightly spaced turns of the east, where you could have four or five in a mile. We took it for granted that your reserves are endless. We kept thinking we could do more. But we learned there are consequences to overconfidence.

"We are over 80% done with the race, which sounds like we are almost done," he added, "but that represents over 600 brutal miles through the Appalachians, and a lot could go wrong."

Randy Mouri had said the same thing. The eastern hills we'd ridden in our practice rides could feel twice as steep.

After we went down for the night in Bloomington, I felt an emotional sea change in the crew. We needed to be smart and careful, John warned. "If we are, we can finish this race in beautiful shape," he said. "If we are not, the race can end in an instant."

## Lesson 11

The most important lesson that we learned today was that we had forgotten the fundamentals. We were overconfident. We needed to review what we had done each and every day to get so far without major mistakes. One: We rode slow and steady. Two: We took rest breaks and slept in the afternoon in the cool air conditioning inside the RV to escape the heat and cool down my core temperature. Three: We religiously rode in front of the follow van, allowing it to protect me from traffic. Four: Most importantly, I focused on the road in front of me, nothing else.

What did we do in Illinois and Indiana? We rode fast and hard early at an unsustainable pace. I skipped my afternoon nap in the cool temperature of the RV and sat outside talking with my college pals in the 95º F heat. I underestimated the distraction of the cell phone mounted on the bike and nearly got run over when it bounced off my bicycle handlebars. And finally, by allowing myself to be separated from the follow van, a car came too close, causing me to crash the bicycle into a construction zone curb and leaving a permanent mark on my right leg. This series of poor choices resulted in us not reaching our destination for the night, costing us an unnecessary four-hour delay.

When you're "in it for the long haul," mistakes are inevitable. That's your opportunity to regroup and turn discouragement and failure into success by refocusing on the fundamentals.

*Are you allowed to eat something and if you are is it regular food?*

*—Ian Cox age 9*

*What a marvelous team you have formed. They have allowed you to do what you trained so ably to do, ride strongly and safely across the USA. Pretty soon you will smell the Chesapeake and it will draw you in like the sirens. So proud to support your mission.*

*—Dick Michaux*

*You are an inspiration to me and my family...and all of those families who are dealing with pediatric cancer. On behalf of the Kennedy/Weingast Clan...a huge heartfelt thank you for your selfless act of courage and perseverance. We are SO proud of you, Len! Keep going. Never give up. You have love, support, and prayers pushing on those pedals for you.*

*—Katie Kennedy*

*First, I wish you the best. I waved to you this morning from the lane at my farm in Indiana, eight miles before TS #41. (Oxford, OH) God speed you. My family wishes you well in this race and the awareness that you create.*

*—Pamela Drake*

# DAY 10

June 22, from Bloomington to Athens

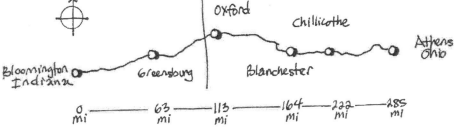

3am · · · · 8am · · · · 11am · · · 2pm · · 8pm · · · · 12am

N

IN | OH
Oxford
Chillicothe
Athens
Ohio

Bloomington
Indiana
Greensburg
Blanchester

0 mi — 63 mi — 113 mi — 164 mi — 222 mi — 285 mi

TODAY WE RIDE FOR IAN

| START | END | START | FINISH | DISTANCE | TOTAL MI. | ELEVATION |
|-------|-----|-------|--------|----------|-----------|-----------|
| Bloomington, IN | Greensburg, IN | 3:09 AM | 7:29 AM | 63.80 | 2,328 | 1,631 |
| Greensburg, IN | Oxford, OH | 7:52 AM | 10:57 AM | 50.20 | 2,377 | 1,699 |
| Oxford, OH | Blanchester, OH | 10:58 AM | 2:18 PM | 50.80 | 2,428 | 1,913 |
| Blanchester, OH | Chillicothe, OH | 2:40 PM | 7:41 PM | 58.20 | 2,486 | 2,017 |
| Chillicothe, OH | Athens, OH | 7:51 PM | 12:05 AM | 63.20 | 2,545 | 2,242 |
| Day 10 Sleep Break | | | | | | |

# CHAPTER 12
# WHAT HIGH-PERFORMING TEAMS DO

*Our greatest glory is not in never falling, but in rising every moment we fall.*

—Confucius

M Y CREW WAS afraid that I had sustained permanent damage to my knee without realizing it. When you crash, adrenaline flows through your body and masks pain. Fortunately, Ken had cleaned me up thoroughly and I could ride without any pain. Because the bandages fell off within a few minutes of departing Bloomington, we found ourselves looking for an all-night CVS at three in the morning. We bought different types of dressings, Ken patched me up again, and I was soon back on the bike. Again the bandages quickly peeled off in the wind. Then, within an hour, the entire injury scabbed up. Amazing what a little 15 mph wind will do to the body! With a thick brown scab growing over the injury, though, I wouldn't have to worry about it getting infected.

We continued our ascent toward Columbus, Indiana, home to Cummins Diesel Corporation. The company had taken such pride in the city that they funded the construction of several signature buildings—city hall, a performing arts center, libraries, and other municipal buildings—commissioning their designs from some of the most renowned architects in the world, such as Cesar Pelli, Phillip Johnson, I.M. Pei, and Frank Gehry. I had studied architecture in school, and my college had supported many trips to Columbus.

The inspirational scenery combined with the momentum of being on a winning team was terrific. We'd recovered from the fall and had gotten a good night's rest. Friday was a new day. Randy Mouri was feeding us intelligence on the other competitors in our division, and we learned that our lead over the next competitor had widened to more than eight hours. We were getting so much support: Mouri's guidance, emails from people such as Shannon Eastman's aunt, and even a farmer who said she had waved to us that morning from the lane at her farm in Indiana, eight miles from Greensburg. There was a real sense of anticipation.

We could not help but smile. We were fifty miles from the Ohio border. Soon I'd be arriving in my home state, then in Oxford. Ed, Bill Vitek, John, and I all grew up within 45 minutes of one another outside Cleveland. We had all met either in college or in Virginia. Ed blasted one of our favorites, The Pretenders' "I Went Back to Ohio, but My City Was Gone" through the loudspeakers as we entered the city. Oxford is home to Miami University, a beautiful campus filled with three – and four-story Georgian-style buildings. Many of my high school friends had gone to college there. To top it off, we'd gotten good news today about Spencer Goold, the Hopecam child we'd honored earlier in the week. He'd received the results of his bone marrow test and had gotten a clean bill of health.

When we stopped for a break, we did our daily Hopecam dedication. Today it was for seven-year-old Ian Vandenberg. Since birth, Ian has been battling health issues that have made school attendance not possible. Hopecam stepped in to help Ian when he started the first grade in 2011. His classmates said they miss him being in that empty seat, so it's been as important to them to be able to connect with Ian as it has been for Ian to connect with his classmates. We're hoping that Ian, too, will get the good news of improving health like the one that Spencer got that day.

As we continued on course between Dayton and Cincinnati and passed through Lebanon, I noticed a cyclist riding just ahead of me. To many athletes riding for 10 straight days, the opportunity to break the boredom and talk to another person on a bike would be a welcome sight. RAAM's strict rules, however, preclude a racer from riding near any other cyclist. An unfair advantage can be gained by being "paced" by another rider, and it's tempting to draft unfairly. Unless the other athlete is a registered RAAM racer, you take a 15-minute penalty. I kept approaching the rider, thinking *Wow, he looks really familiar*, curious who it might be.

*High school friends Len Forkas and Kevin*
*Larsen meet on the race course*

As I passed him, focused on pulling ahead, I heard a voice from behind. "Hey, do you mind if I ride with you?"

"Sorry, dude. It's illegal. I'm in a race."

"Hey Len, how are you?" he called out.

I nearly fell off my bike. When I was in school, Kevin Larsen had been a close friend. He was a frequent first-place finisher in track and cross-country events. He was also an endurance athlete and had run the Boston Marathon and finished Ironman distance events over the years. In high school, I had looked up to Kevin as an elite athlete and cheered him on. Here he was cheering for me.

I immediately pulled over to chat. Kevin and I had re-connected through Facebook, though I hadn't seen him in ten years. It pained me that I could only stop for a few minutes, especially since he lived five minutes from the race course and had ridden out to meet me.

Seeing Kevin riding alongside me reminded how much I missed the company of a friend to share a bicycle ride with. RAAM was lonely. My crew had each other and they had down time, where they could relax, talk over a meal, and call home. My downtime was sleep. I could talk with my crew during the ride but that was usually for a few seconds as I handed off a bottle to the person sitting in the van that pulled up alongside me. There weren't any long deep conversations. I had to keep my eyes on the road. One pothole could send me over the handlebars. I still couldn't believe that Kevin would take the time to leave work, change into his bike gear, and surprise me by riding up alongside me. He made my day.

We said goodbye and promised to meet again at our 35th high school reunion in September.

*

Because I'd rested well in Bloomington the night before and because Ohio's cooler temperatures weren't as draining, I skipped my sleep break. Instead, I took the usual five-minute catnaps in the front seat of the van. The combination of the tailwind, temperatures, low humidity, and flat terrain made for an excellent day. I was moving at a 16-mph pace and a heart rate of 100, and everything felt great.

I was experiencing the sense of flow that Mihaly Csíkszentmihályi wrote about in his book *Flow: The Psychology of Optimal Experience*. Csíkszentmihályi's theory is that people are happiest when they are in a state of flow, meaning when a person is so completely absorbed with the activity he or she is doing that it seems effortless. It's being in the groove, being "in the zone." The brain science is that flow operates similarly to the section of your brain called the basal ganglia. This region allows your body to perform functions almost subconsciously. It's like driving a car or hitting a golf ball without consciously thinking about it.

This state happens when you are engaged in activities that you control and that are goal-related and meaningful. "The ego falls away," Csíkszentmihályi wrote. "Time flies. Every action, movement, and thought follows inevitably from the previous one, like playing jazz. Your whole being is involved, and you're using your skills to the utmost." This is the only rational explanation for anyone doing the same repetitive motion all day for 20 hours and hardly stopping for ten consecutive days.

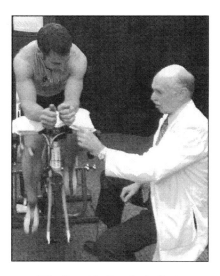

*Bike fit with Dr. Andy Pruitt*
*ten weeks before the race*

It was great to be experiencing flow this late in the race, when you might reasonably expect energy and focus to be fading. As Maslow would have described it, I was self-actualized and fully immersed. All my most basic needs were being met and I had placed on the sidelines all other distracting thoughts. I was at peace on the bike. Efficiency, form, function were all synchronized, freeing my brain to dream of other things. Often this is when I get my most creative and lucid ideas. This feeling is so freeing and so fulfilling. I realized as I approached Chillicothe, that I have sought it out in many forms over the years.

Yet avoiding injury from this kind of repetitive muscle use was of primary concern, which we'd known since well before we reached the starting line. The time I spent with Dr. Andy Pruitt at the Boulder Center for Sports Medicine in April when I was training for RAAM was a good example of how we approached this risk. The Center works with elite athletes, and Pruitt is considered by many one of the most respected "bike fitters" in the world. He sets up the bicycles in his laboratory for many of the most well-known cyclists, making micro-adjustments for speed, efficiency, and injury prevention. He also knows a lot about RAAM. I had traveled to his lab so he could analyze my cycling gait on his three-dimensional computer model connected to six "capture" cameras. Based on this analysis, Dr. Pruitt makes many small but critical adjustments to the bike, such as realigning handlebars or seats, lengthening the spindle of a pedal to accommodate the frame of the rider, or shifting the cleats on the bottom of shoes to prevent a foot injury. Among other things, he approved of the electronic drive train with push button shifting (Shimano DII) to avoid carpal tunnel syndrome, a condition that dogs many ultracyclists. I went to him because these items fit in the pre-race Bucket Two (things I could control). But he also helped me understand that though I'd competed in many endurance races to prepare for RAAM, I had made the right decision to delegate the bicycle set-up to an expert.

Learning to delegate is an example of the need to unlearn behaviors that have worked in the past but will not work in the present, an idea presented in David Rock's book, *Your Brain at Work*. Rock says that often we are influenced by the actions and thoughts that preceded us. We sometimes carry forward a certain approach that has worked in the past, when what is needed is a fresh approach. The process of unlearning requires being able to step back, separate yourself from the environment you are in, and watch your behavior as if you are a distant, detached observer.

Unlearning familiar behaviors is a constant struggle for leaders, who are used to having answers and taking charge. I knew from my own experience at the start of the race, when Ken and Greg were fitting out the follow van, for example, how difficult it was for me to refrain from giving advice. I believed in trusting my team, but I didn't always succeed in unlearning my own "old-faithful" leadership behaviors. It can be a struggle to strike a good balance between trusting yourself and trusting others to whom you've delegated responsibilities. It takes wisdom to discern when and how to negotiate changes in that balance—and forgiveness when mistakes happen. Because they will. My team was getting good at "forgiving my trespasses." But there were times when they also had to forgive each other.

This happened a lot when we had to navigate turns, for instance. We got lost three times during the race, each time missing a critical turn. The first time we went a half-mile in the wrong direction and a crew from the Czech Republic chased us down to tell us we were going the wrong way. The second time was near the Mississippi River crossing, where we went a quarter-mile the wrong way. But the third time, near Ohio, we traveled three miles in the wrong direction uphill in the heat.

As upsetting as it was, making mistakes is a part of racing. John had once said RAAM is a rolling string of mistakes that require goodwill and team spirit to forgive. I knew that every time we'd gotten lost before, the crew had felt terrible about causing me to waste precious time going in the wrong direction and exerting energy needlessly. So I tried to make it a point to help us all recover quickly from the setback, even taking advantage of every second to get some well-earned sleep in the van. I was an expert at falling asleep in less than 45 seconds. I said, "We are getting tired, we are going to make mistakes. Let's just try hard not to make so many of them, or catch them before they get too big."

I was thinking about the V8 incident. I had thought that the team either passed the buck on who'd be responsible for fulfilling my request or hadn't really heard me. But later I found out there were a few things I didn't know.

Greg had delegated getting the V8 to Ken, who'd just finished a shift in the RV. He grabbed his signature camouflage design baseball hat and walked into the convenience store without his phone to purchase the drinks.

Meanwhile Wayne drove off in the RV with Amy, Kaitee, and Steve Gurney. At first Ken thought it was a prank. He calmly waited for the

RV to return, pick him up, and get back on the road. No such luck. The crew in the RV didn't realize Ken was missing until two hours later, when they pulled to the side of the road to watch the amazing colors of a Kansas sunset.

Wayne was the first to notice. When he mentioned it to the others, they all figured that Ken was in the advance van eight miles further east, making arrangements for hotel rooms in Maize.

He called ahead to verify. No Ken. They called Ken's cell phone. No answer. Wayne began to worry. Where could he be?

Meanwhile, another RAAM crew who were also at the convenience store had let Ken borrow a phone. They were also hospitable enough to offer him a drink and some food.

Ken had no money and hadn't memorized anyone's cell phone number, so he called the fire station in McLean where he worked with Greg to ask for his number. No one had it because Greg had transferred to another station. Ken called that station, and because Greg was new, no one could readily find his cell phone number. Finally Ken called RAAM race headquarters and they patched him into crew chief John Moore's number. John then called the RV.

Wayne turned the RV around and drove back to pick up Ken. Trouble was, Wayne wasn't sure which convenience store it was, and so that caused further delay until he got the right information.

"I hope Ken has a good sense of humor," Steve said.

When the RV arrived in the store's parking lot, Ken was sitting in front of the store on the curb, his baseball hat tipped low over his forehead.

"He doesn't look very happy," Amy said.

Nobody knew what to do or how to handle the situation—whether it was best to apologize, to act embarrassed, or to joke about it.

Ken wasn't saying anything, so Wayne decided to break the tension. "Hey, we thought you switched teams on us," he said.

Ken started explaining, talking fast, obviously upset. "I didn't have anyone's phone number, because my phone was in the RV!" For whatever reason, when Wayne called the number, it didn't ring, or they didn't hear it.

"I'm really, really sorry about this Ken," Steve said.

Still, a lot of silence.

Finally Ken said, "I have the V8."

\*

As the sunlight was fading, we arrived in Chillicothe ("Principal Town" in the language of the Shawnee Indians), the first capital of Ohio when it joined the union in 1803. We then pushed north past Dayton, and up and over some rolling hills on our way toward Athens, the home of Ohio University. OU was another college that many of my friends from high school attended. I had visited them during our college days and, on this Friday night, as I pedaled past the stop signs at midnight with all the late-night revelers moving from bar to bar, I laughed at the contrast. I had started my day at 3:00 a.m. in another college town, Bloomington, Indiana, and pedaled my bike 286 miles virtually non-stop for 21 hours. It was time for the nightly routine of shower, food, and massage by "bad cop" Greg on my IT bands and "good cop" Kaitee on my neck before falling asleep for a well-earned three hours. We had a big day tomorrow—finishing Ohio, entering West Virginia, then getting through mountains even more challenging than the Rockies on our way toward Maryland and the finish line.

Although we had made the mistake of getting lost this day, riding 3 miles in the wrong direction uphill, we learned that no matter how well prepared they are, every team is going to make mistakes. The key lesson is to learn to forgive one another and move on, and not lament the error or point blame. When Ken was left behind at the convenience store for several hours, he had to learn to forgive his teammates. The core values we had subscribed to in recruiting our team paid off. Positive, selfless teammates don't hold grudges. They forgive one another and learn not to repeat mistakes.

## Lesson 12

High-performing teams learn that they are going to make mistakes along the way, and that it is natural to screw up once in a while. We are all human; mistakes are part of life. The key is learning from the mistake, forgiving one another, then moving on and not holding a grudge. There were plenty of times when I got cranky and wasn't very pleasant. I had to pray that my team would forgive me when I became difficult and that I would learn to forgive them as well when we got off course. But more importantly, as evidenced by abandoning Ken, they had to learn to forgive each other. Because that's what high-performing teams do. They forgive one another.

*Hi Len...my sister Rose-Ellen told me you're facing the home stretch now...always know that you have tons of supporters cheering you as you ride. Having that support and encouragement makes all the difference, doesn't it? That's how our whole family felt when Shannon was going through her chemo and radiation treatments. Knowing we were never alone and showing her that tangibly with the use of her computer through Hopecam...well, as the commercial says, "priceless!" We're cheering for you down here in Florida!*

— Colleen VanSuetendael

*Hi Len, The phrase "it's like riding a bike!" takes on a whole new meaning!!!! We are all so proud of you here on "Yellow Pine Drive." We are with you every mile of your journey!...Thank you for all you have done in bringing hope and connection to all those children! Like all those children, our wish for you is; that you free-wheel home safely to the finish Line!*

—Suzanne Christie

*Hi Len, it's Shannon. I see [you're] in Ohio and only have 500 miles to go. Keep pedaling! You can do it! I wanted to tell you that I signed up for Tae Kwon Do. It starts tonight. I'm so excited and when you get home I can show you what I learned tonight. Stay safe. See you soon.*

—Shannon Eastman

# DAY 11
## June 23, from Athens to Cumberland

4am. . . . . . . .9am. . . . . .2pm. . .9pm. . . .1am

Cumberland Maryland

OH | WV

Athens Ohio

Ohio River

Ellenboro West Virginia

Grafton

Keyser

N

0 mi — 66 mi — 131 mi — 201 mi — 240 mi

TODAY WE RIDE FOR CAMERON

| START | END | START | FINISH | DISTANCE | TOTAL MI. | ELEVATION |
|---|---|---|---|---|---|---|
| Athens, OH | Ellenboro, WV | 3:47 AM | 8:47 AM | 66.00 | 2,612 | 2,990 |
| Ellenboro, WV | Grafton, WV | 8:58 AM | 1:45 PM | 64.60 | 2,677 | 4,415 |
| Grafton, WV | Keyser, WV | 3:15 PM | 9:15 PM | 70.10 | 2,747 | 6,425 |
| Keyser, WV | Cumberland, MD | 9:56 PM | 12:42 AM | 38.90 | 2,776 | 2,373 |
| Day 11 Sleep Break | | | | | | |

# CHAPTER 13
# THE WILL TO FINISH

*The difference between a successful person and others is not a lack of strength, not a lack of knowledge, but rather a lack of will.*

—Vince Lombardi

LOGIC LEADS A rational person to believe that the Rocky Mountains, with its soaring elevations of well over 10,000 feet, would be significantly more difficult to navigate than the Appalachians. But the Appalachians are a lot more challenging.

Why? For the same reason that clearing snowy mountain roads in Colorado is easier than clearing snowy mountain roads in West Virginia: road grade. Plows cannot push significant amounts of snow on a grade steeper than six percent. The average grade in the West Virginia Mountains is eight percent. Also, Colorado roads have significantly wider shoulders. In West Virginia, few roads have shoulders at all, the pavement quality is lower, and the hills average 300 to 1,000 feet from bottom to peak.

Riding through them is like going 15 rounds with Mike Tyson. The hills, like a punch from Tyson, just keep coming at you. You descend one steep hill, accelerating over 40 mph, then reach the bottom and slog up at 8 mph, all the while trying to keep a steady and even pace and distribute power evenly. Over and over, up, then down, then up, then down. It's mentally exhausting; they just keep coming and coming and coming.

This was "our home turf"— our team had been training in these mountains for the past three years. Last April we'd knocked off a 730-mile section in less than forty hours, part of the time in pouring rain. Yet we would need every bit of strength and energy we had to get through these hills. Our inspiration came from the family of Cameron McClain, the Hopecam child we were honoring.

Cameron, a first-grader who was homebound more than a year, was one of the first recipients of Hopecam. After a successful bone marrow transplant and a period of remission, he relapsed and had to undergo a second transplant. He was only eight years old and did not survive. Cameron's father later became a member of Hopecam's board of directors. He believes that his unique perspective as both a school administrator and a parent can help serve the effort of finding ways to continue connecting home and school when children are undergoing treatment for serious illnesses.

I will never forget the moment Cameron's grandfather appeared at my office toting a laptop carrying case. I had known John McClain for many years as a distinguished professor at George Mason University.

"John, what brings you here?" I asked.

He told me he was returning a computer Hopecam had given his grandson. "He passed away a month earlier and I wanted to make sure another child could use it."

That's when I realized that Cameron was John's grandson. I'd never put the two last names together before. If anything could help me get through the Appalachians, it would be the memory of the strength shown by Cameron and his family.

Thankfully, it was a cool 60° F. Our team was in first place in our division with an eleven-hour lead and only 500 miles to go. It looked like we were going to win our division—something our team never considered when we set off ten days earlier.

But we had one small problem. I was losing weight dramatically. This was a surprise, because from the start of the race my weight had held steady; for the first few days I had even slightly gained. Since leaving Indiana, though, my weight was dropping two pounds a day.

Ken and Greg couldn't figure out what was happening. "Either your metabolism is super high or you have minor organ failure," he said.

This mystery put Greg and Ken under a lot of pressure. It's the uncharted territory thing. There is no baseline for knowing how your body will react, because you've probably never trained for more than four or five days in a row. Who could, if you have a family or operate a business, unless of course you were a past professional cyclist, or had attempted RAAM previously, like many of my competitors? We were clearly in uncharted territory. We didn't have control over how my body was going to respond. We simply had to deal with it the best we could.

This didn't stop Ken from worrying, though. He took his job very seriously. "The people I work with as a paramedic don't choose to have me do my job," he said. "I just arrive on the scene. It's a huge responsibility."

But I *had* picked him and Greg…which maybe doubled the pressure he was feeling.

My body was burning roughly 500 calories per hour while cycling. I had been consuming 350 calories an hour, which is the maximum that my body could process into fuel while exercising. The nutrition plan was designed for a 150-calorie deficit every hour. At night I would consume another 500 calories in solid food to "catch up," which would be converted into fuel while I slept. When I awoke, another 500 calories for breakfast.

Noticing that I was losing two pounds daily after day six, Ken and Greg changed the nutrition they were feeding me from 350 calories an hour to 600 calories an hour, adding extra whey protein in the smoothies at break time. They did not inform me of this decision and even though every drink they mixed began to taste different, and I was still losing weight, I didn't question or challenge them. Unfortunately, my nutritionists didn't remember that I was lactose intolerant and the extra milk-based protein was making me incredibly gassy. I was so flatulent that it was noisy to be around me. Thankfully, there weren't any other cyclists near me during the day. The smell would have chased them away.

As it turned out, there was a little naiveté in increasing my calorie intake so much. After nine days of sleep deprivation, and two firemen doing the work of three, the fatigue was taking its toll on all of us. My nutrition teammates were in full panic mode. The decision to increase the calories and give me lactose protein was a painful experiment, because at the time no one really knew why I had gained weight in the first part of the race and then so precipitously lost it toward the end. It didn't make sense: I was burning 10,000 calories a day and taking in 12,000 calories, sleeping three hours a night. Something was destined to happen and it was not likely to be good.

What I later learned was that when the body is under duress, like the kind you experience riding 20 hours a day on very little sleep, it goes into triage mode. First it holds onto water. After four to five days, when you're burning more than you're ingesting, the body first burns fat, then muscle. Then it goes for the organs.

"We could have cost you the race and your life," Ken told me later. "If you would have gone into organ failure, I would have been responsible for your death."

We had thought the answer to staving off organ failure was more calories, but we overestimated the amount. My body couldn't process that much food into useable energy and let's just say that I was taking a lot more bathroom breaks in this last part of the race.

*

We rode wave after wave of the hills leading to Ellenboro and then to Grafton in blessedly cool temperatures. This part of the course—Route 50, a major east-west thoroughfare—was milled pavement like the kind we'd encountered in Arizona. It's bumpy and dangerous—often sewer manholes and water valves would be left sticking up a few inches above the road level. The race officials allowed the cyclists to place their bikes on the bike racks and be driven over this section of the race course in Arizona to avoid injury because of the unsafe road conditions. After riding across this same type of pavement for roughly 2 miles, we called the race director to request safe passage across this construction zone. We pulled over and waited a few minutes while the race officials mulled over our request. Minutes later they gave us the okay. As we proceeded we noticed another athlete riding the pavement—Stefan Schlegel, a 34-year-old German. We pulled alongside his follow van to notify his crew that he did not have to ride across this three-mile section.

Within a few minutes, we cleared the construction area and my team brought my bike down from the roof. I felt a little guilty for being transported comfortably while Schlegel was riding up and downhill, so I waited until he passed me before riding again. I figured I at least owed the guy the lead. The decision to request permission to drive and not cycle this three-mile section would later end up haunting me. Finally, after many left and right turns, we arrived in Grafton, where we exited the major highway and escaped the huge tractor-trailers buzzing past my ear, to head out on old US 50, a narrow two-lane stretch of highway with lots of alligator skin-like pavement and narrow shoulders.

There we saw our friend Holger Roethig, another German and fellow RAAM racer, sitting by the side of the road in a lawn chair with his feet in a bucket of ice-cold water. He was getting ready to get on the course just as I was coming in for a quick shower and more pain-numbing medication for my saddle sores.

Our crewmembers had spent a lot of time with Roethig's crew. They were laid back and had a great sense of humor. That goes a long way to making the tedium of the race tolerable, even enjoyable.

Roethig's crew pointed to the empty chair next to Roethig and invited me to sit down and soak my feet.

It felt good to relax that way. It was also great to talk to Holger, a six-foot, three-inch giant, who kind of reminded me of Big Bird, the Sesame Street character. I decided to tease my crew. "Hey, where's my footbath, boys?"

"Write it down," John said. "We'll get one for you in next year's race."

Roethig left to continue the race and I ducked into the RV for a shower and a brief rest. It was a nice gesture for Roethig's crew to invite me to sit a while and reflect on the race, especially since the upcoming miles were going to be more brutal than the last. There were a number of monster climbs in this section, among them a 1,000-foot climb at an eight percent grade, then the next hill even higher at 1,200 feet.

Roethig knew what that could mean. The course had forced him to drop out two years earlier, and he had returned to conquer it.

The RV lurched up the hills in low gear as it snaked up the narrow passage. Then, as the crew approached the midpoint of the ascent, we noticed the tail lights of our friend's follow vehicle. He was standing along the side of the steep road section, hyperventilating and a little slurred in his speech. His crew asked if Ken, our paramedic, could check him out.

"Holger was physically OK," Ken said later. "The symptoms he was having were from sleep deprivation and stress. He was nervous about the same feelings returning from two years ago, the ones that forced him to stop. He needed to forget those awful feelings and persevere past them." His symptoms occurred after he had passed the exact point where he had failed in 2010.

This particular stretch of hill brought back memories for me as well. I had ridden it in the middle of the night in April, in a cold and dreary rainstorm. I was freezing wet and dodging potholes with fogged-up glasses, watching each curve for its bright yellow sign that indicated a left turn. Dozens of these signs. Never ending. Right turn, left turn. Is this some kind of joke? How to cope? Once again the race course was trying to destroy me.

Every muscle, every joint, every part of my body was begging me to stop as I lurched up this hill so steep that if I slowed down any more my bike would tip over. My calves felt like rocks. I made myself look down at the road in front of me. Why? It's simply too painful to see the hill ahead. If I don't see it, I don't think about it. I played a few games, like countdown. I stood up on my bike and took ten strokes, then sat down for ten pedal strokes, then repeated the pattern. I'd play count up—take twenty pedal strokes, then stand for ten, twenty-one pedal strokes, then stand for ten, twenty-two, and repeat this pattern until I reached fifty. I can't tell you which is more painful, the mental fatigue or the physical fatigue.

My mind drifted. *At least it's not raining. It could be worse.* Those four words are the common denominator for everyone who has had to power past or fight through an incredible hardship. Ten-year-old Trevor Blake, fighting cancer, honored on day four of the race, is delivering toys to children in the cancer wards inside hospitals all over Virginia and Maryland because "They have it worse than me, they are still stuck in the hospital."

*Rapid weight loss worried the
crew and family at home*

In the end, any race is about not what's left in your legs or in your lungs but what's *in your mind*. Your will drives your actions. Finishers succeed through a combination of nutrition, rest, and training, but I believe most of all that the race is won or lost mentally. You've got to want it more than anything in your life and you've got to believe you can do it. Unless there is something physically failing in the biomechanical workings of the body, succeeding is a matter of the will to not give up. U.S. military training instructors call this "grit," and it's a key determiner in how teams are selected.

The only thing that would have forced me to stop would have been crossing a physical boundary that would have created irreversible damage that would have precluded my ability to compete again. This was my family's biggest fear. My wife Elizabeth mentioned this concern to John a few days before the race. We were having breakfast together and John had asked Elizabeth if she was worried about me doing RAAM.

"Len's will is so strong that he often ignores physical warning signs," she told him.

"I'm not going to let anything happen to him," John reassured her.

But that didn't stop Elizabeth from worrying. She watched the daily videos that Amy was producing. She said she could see my face slowly changing, growing gaunter as I started losing weight after the fifth day, and she noticed how my eyes kept squinting from the sensitivity to the bright sun. She consoled herself by remembering I was in good hands, that so many members of my crew were long time friends that she could trust to look out for me.

The reason I did not invite any family members to join the crew was for this precise reason. After a week of nonstop cycling, close relatives begin to see the fatigue accumulate on your face as you begin to lose weight, and they then worry about the risk of irreversible damage from putting so much stress on the body. Elizabeth was right about my strong will to finish. It was grounded in the promises I had made before the race began. If you have a goal you truly wish to achieve, there is no more powerful way to strengthen your resolve and stick with the actions that are needed to achieve the goal than to *make yourself accountable to others*. The will to finish this race was instilled in me by virtue of the stories of the children to whom I had dedicated each day. Many of those kids and their families knew I was riding for them. Many knew I would call them. Some waited for that call. The ideas of stopping never entered my mind. *How would I explain quitting* to all the families that had supported me and all the contributors who had sponsored the race, and especially my crew?

\*

With two monster climbs behind me, I set my sites on Keyser, the last city in West Virginia before reaching Maryland. As if to give me a reward for making it this far, I saw friend and fellow Hopecam board member Steve Wiltse parked alongside the road waving to me. Steve had a summer home in nearby Deep Creek, Maryland. I pulled over and snapped a few pictures with him before continuing. It was close to sunset, and knowing people who lived near this part of the race route made everyone and me on my crew feel as if we were almost home.

We had a steep 2,000-foot descent into Keyser through a series of switchback hills. In the past twelve hours we had climbed 10,800 feet over 130 miles. By the end of the day, we would climb up three miles of mountains over a distance of 240 miles, more than any comparable stretch in the Rocky Mountains. Not only were we keeping the same pace throughout the race, we were climbing the hardest, steepest sections at the same pace as the when we crossed the flats in Kansas and Missouri. All the encouragement that my friends had given me years before—"Len, you get stronger as you go further"—were ringing true. We were matching the same speeds on day 10 as day 3.

We arrived in Keyser a little after nine. It was just getting dark. The stretch between Keyser and Cumberland is short, less than forty miles, and I would have one more rest break before the final push to Annapolis. We had debated taking a long break in Cumberland but the hills between Cumberland and the point where the race curves into Pennsylvania for a bit at Hancock were murderously steep—more than 4,000 feet over forty miles.

These hills comprised the toughest stretch in RAAM, and it was the stretch I knew like the back of my hand. Though I knew Cumberland very well, we had to navigate a challenging, circuitous series of turns to approach the bridges that spanned the railroad tracks and streams that surround the city. Anxiously tackling the 400-foot rolling climbs, I came to the light where the spaghetti-like confluence of local bridges and roads mapped out on the course appears. John was behind me, navigating through the labyrinth.

"Stop, Len, you need to go right at the bridge," he said.

"No, John, I don't think so. I remember it being straight in April." Maybe it's instinct, maybe it's all my architectural training, but I have very good visual recall. I didn't remember a right turn, not here, not at this intersection.

"No, it's a right," John said. "Stay to the right."

I had been making it a point not to second-guess my crew chief. Plus

I had been riding since 3:47 a.m., when we departed Athens. It was well past midnight and mentally I was already in bed resting up for the last day. So I followed John's instructions. But I felt very much lost in the dark. We had to be going in the wrong direction—I just knew it.

About two minutes later the loudspeaker sounded. "Len, pull over, we're going the wrong way," John shouted.

Unfortunately we had entered the "on ramp" to Interstate 68 and could not simply turn around. I got off the bike and John and Greg mounted it to the van's roof. They drove me back to the spot where we had veered off course. Essentially we had traveled for twenty minutes in an eight mile loop to get back to the exact spot where we had taken the wrong turn.

This was the fourth time we had been lost. Each and every time I had held my breath and said, "Don't worry about it, I'm resting now, let's just find where we need to go." It was late, everyone was tired, and getting the approach right in Cumberland was very, very confusing.

As I hopped out of the van to start again, my hands shook. It was 59° F, my core temperature had gone down during the rest, and my body was shivering, not so much from the cold as from the accumulated fatigue of the day. The feeling was normal and familiar—I'd felt it while running a fifty-mile ultra-marathon for more than ten hours. Familiarity takes away fear. I knew with the same certainty that let me survive the Mojave Desert that I would make it through.

We arrived in Cumberland at 1:20 a.m. I was cold, stiff, and ready for a hot meal and a warm bed. This last sleep break would be quick, because I had only 224 miles left to go, and I was anxious to get home.

## Lesson 13

The willpower not to give up was most evident on day ten. My team's nutrition strategy was beginning to show weakness. Experimenting with the nutrition led to some dire consequences, I was passing gas constantly, and this was the moment we realized that with 200 miles to go, our team was in completely uncharted territory. In addition, the effects of sleep deprivation were beginning to appear in our entire crew. The mental fatigue of crossing the Appalachian Mountains is the final fatal punch that the course has to offer as it attempts to demolish the racers. The cumulative effects of desert heat, thin air and high altitude of the Rockies, the crosswinds and the searing heat in the plains, and now the steep Appalachians were setting us up for a knockout round.

All of these challenges can be thought of as metaphors for the challenges one faces in life, or for business situations where unexpected challenges surface, making it impossible to do "business as usual." Two things helped us through:

The accountability inherent in having made so many promises to so many children, donors, and crew members that we would finish the race. It helped me ignore what my body was telling me, which of course was "PLEASE STOP."

"Grit." Mental perseverance must match physical ability. We used third-party accountability to create self-induced fear, making the price of quitting so high that it would be unbearable to experience. That in essence is why giving up was so impossible to imagine.

*I recently read that we should do more than is necessary to be kind. What you are doing is a variation of this — what is more than is necessary to be kind... and amazing. Thank you for bringing so much inspiration to these families. And now—for your musical entertainment... 99 bottles of beer on the wall... 99 bottles of beeeeerr...*

—Wendy Shang

*Way to go, Len! You are an amazing man doing an amazing thing. Cancer can be a very lonely time when people don't know what to say and they tend to leave you alone a lot. Allowing kids to keep in touch with other kids at school is a rare thing to be able to do. I pray for you and others like you that show such strength. Many prayers to your team also! My mother is a cancer survivor and I appreciated any and everything that people did to support her as I know all the kids you are helping appreciate all you do. Peace.*

—Lucy Cusack

*A message to get you to the finish line from my sister Terri: "A good laugh and a long sleep are the two best cures for anything" (Irish proverb).*

—Jeanne Ing

# DAY 12
## June 24, from Cumberland to Annapolis

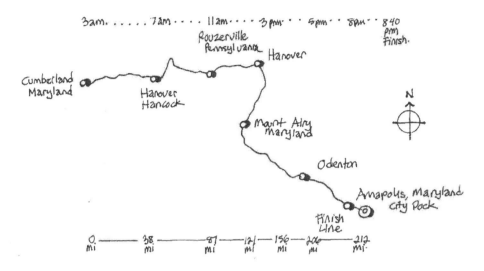

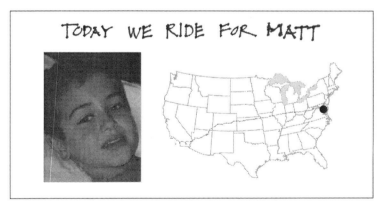

TODAY WE RIDE FOR MATT

| START | END | START | FINISH | DISTANCE | TOTAL MI. | ELEVATION |
|-------|-----|-------|--------|----------|-----------|-----------|
| Cumberland, MD | Hancock, MD | 3:16 AM | 7:08 AM | 37.80 | 2,813 | 4,138 |
| Hancock, MD | Rouzerville, PA | 7:10 AM | 11:00 AM | 48.80 | 2,861 | 3,167 |
| Rouzerville, PA | Hanover, PA | 11:12 AM | 2:32 PM | 34.10 | 2,902 | 2,059 |
| Hanover, PA | Mt. Airy, MD | 2:45 PM | 4:52 PM | 35.00 | 2,938 | 2,001 |
| Mt. Airy, MD | Odenton, MD | 5:20 PM | 8:10 PM | 50.10 | 2,978 | 2,096 |
| Odenton, MD | Annapolis, MD | 8:13 PM | 8:40 PM | 1.00 | 2,987 | 2 |
| Annapolis, MD | Finish Line | | | 5.30 | 2,993 | 119 |

# JUST ONE MORE FINAL PUSH

*It's not the fastest guy who wins the race. It's the guy who slows down the least.*

—Unknown

DEPARTING CUMBERLAND AT three in the morning on the final day of the race reminded me of my college days, taking that last final exam before summer break. Just one more final push and the exhilaration will follow. The sleep rest was short lived at less than two hours, as I was anticipating home. No more hotels, massages, and changing clothes in a cramped RV. Heading up the last four remaining hills in western Maryland in the early morning darkness felt as normal as waking up at home and doing a familiar training workout.

There are four major climbs between Cumberland and Hancock: Polish Mountain, Rocky Gap, Green Mountain, and Sideling Hill. All are about 10% grade on the way up and have wickedly fast down hills. I was happy to hit these hills and wanted desperately to cross the finish line before sundown. My family and countless friends and supporters were all waiting for our arrival.

My family had spent Saturday night in Annapolis helping prepare for the finish line celebration. My sister Laurie had made a special trip from New York with her husband David and three boys to spend the weekend in Annapolis, and my sister Debbie, who now lived in Virginia, was also there waiting to cheer for me at the City Dock. The Hopecam team had planned a welcome reception at the hotel where the banquet would take place and more than 80 supporters would be there wearing orange and blue t-shirts sporting the Hopecam logo. Our crew could feel the anticipation as well, especially the Washington, DC-based crew whose family members had been driving out to meet them at different sections of the race course.

*Cheerleading support on the final day*

But what my crew saw on my face was fatigue—a pained expression John said he hadn't seen at any point previously during the race. For eleven days I'd been constantly trying to stay focused and tamp down those demons that chase each other around in your brain begging you to stop. Part of your brain is listening to all these cues from the pain and another part is working hard to ignore it. The more than 500 emails we received from supporters made a difference in ignoring the pain messages. And during the night rides, when my crew was reading them to me, they helped me take my mind off the drudgery.

Now we were on the final push. The morning's route was east out of Cumberland toward Hancock, and then to a remote time stop called

Rouzerville in Pennsylvania, where we'd turn almost due north, then east again to the base of the Catoctin Ridge, one of the last mountain ranges in the Appalachians.

Despite my longing to get home, despite the commitment I had to Hopecam, I could feel that my body was just going through the motions. My pace was slower than normal. The time splits between Cumberland and Hancock were among the slowest of the eleven days. At first this seemed logical, because we were ascending almost a mile of uphill elevation over forty miles of roadway—the most difficult stretch in the entire race. But the time splits on the rolling hills between Hancock and Rouzerville, the easier section, began to register at 13 mph when my normal speed was closer to 15 mph. My head was heavy. For the first time, the hills began to look different. I was beginning to dread them. They felt like thousands of small pinpricks. The pain was more mentally exhausting than physically tiring.

The crew also saw that I was fading and they were not going to sit idle and bear witness. They used the colorful poster board, markers, and chalk brought to them by Bill Sickenberger's wife Phyllis, who'd driven up from Reston, to make signs and to write inspiring anecdotes or messages on the pavement. They shared these materials with the supporters who had been tracking our progress on the "Spot Len" GPS device so they could show up along the route and at the different time station stops.

John Slidell, a long-time friend who had supported my fundraising goals by arranging the opportunity to share my story with several real estate professionals in the DC area, had been waiting more than an hour at the time station stop in Rouzerville. He watched several other crews roll in and out of the stop.

"Most of them looked exhausted," he said. "Then your crew rolls up. They are writing words of encouragement on the pavement with chalk. They are carrying brightly colored signs with your name on it. They are like a team of cheerleaders ready to go out at the halftime break."

At that moment I realized the benefit of having treated the team members to hotel rooms with hot showers instead of camping on the side of the road, as some crews do, and the wisdom of assigning specific roles and shifts with frequent breaks so they could have personal downtime.

John handed me a cold Slurpee he had purchased from the convenience store. I looked at Greg. With a wink, he gave me the okay to take a cool sip.

\*

Cresting the Catoctin mountain range, which is 30 miles north of Camp David in Frederick County, Maryland, reminded me of the April training ride and, of course, in Colorado, where I nearly lost it hurtling down the hill, my bike shaking uncontrollably. It was a grinding climb and a steep descent. This time, though, I was on the backup bike. I felt confident I would be safe, and we cleared the descent without incident. We rode through Gettysburg's battlefields and approached the city. A long line of cars, ambulances, and fire trucks, though, blocked the road, and we called the race officials for advice about the best alternative route. I used the time to take a 15-minute rest break in the RV. The delay ended up costing us 30 minutes and none of my nearby competitors experienced this wait.

Unfortunately, I had added to that tension. Despite my confidence in Wayne's "surgery" on the backup bike, he and John hadn't been comfortable with the idea of me riding the backup bike during the steep descent. So that morning Wayne had placed a phone call to Scott Stewart, a longtime friend and fellow endurance athlete. They asked him to stop by my house and bring my third bike, a Trek 5900, to the team.

Scott already had a long drive planned that weekend—he was taking his daughter to visit a college in the northeast and his time was very tight. The team didn't know that; I did. Scott was nice enough that he would agree to their request. That meant he'd have to drive a total of at least 22 hours in one weekend.

When I learned of what had happened, I was mad. It wasn't strategy this time; it was real anger. They were inconveniencing my friend, for what I could see as no good reason. I thought Wayne was being overcautious, that he was worrying because the bike was looking a little wobbly when going more than 35 mph.

I called John on my cell phone. "Call it off or find someone else," I insisted. "The backup bike will be fine."

I figured I would just ride more slowly, keep the bike at 30 mph, which was still pretty fast.

*Words of encouragement from the crew*

The team knew how angry I was but the damage had been done. Unknown to me, Scott was already within range of our location. Now the team was put in the unfortunate position of keeping that information from me, because I'd been so clear about what I wanted. They ended up hiding the bike Scott brought in the storage compartment of the RV.

If only someone had said, "I know you're upset, but what's done is done. He really wants to see you." I think they were worried about my mental state, which they could read on my face. I was squinting from sleep deprivation and from the constant staring into the horizon, which made my eyes not only photosensitive but also temporarily farsighted.

Reflecting on it later, I realized I had made a grave mistake and regretted what I had told my crew. Wayne was looking out for me. He had seen discoloration on the bike, which he interpreted as micro-cracks, and was worried about my safety. It was his professional opinion, and I had broken my own rule of second-guessing my crew by criticizing a major decision that had already been delegated: the care and treatment of my gear, and the advice of my mechanic.

*Final 100 miles*

Everything about delegating responsibility that was so important to me for the entire race I'd reneged on, in one small outburst. In the end, I deprived myself of a chance to see my good friend, and I deprived him of something he really wanted to do, because the crew didn't want me to know he was already on his way. It was, though, like most such mistakes, an important lesson.

Under that cloud we pressed on. In mid-afternoon, we took a break at a time station stop located at a gas station. I was dying for an ice cream sandwich and the nutrition team gave me the nod. I sat with my feet propped up in the RV, the AC blasting in the ninety-degree heat, savoring every bite.

*

Our crews changed shifts for the last time in Hanover, Pennsylvania. Greg took over the nutrition seat in the back of the follow van. Bill drove and John navigated. This crew would get me through the complicated turns as we passed through suburban Washington, DC, and the accompanying late afternoon weekend traffic, all the way to the finish line in Annapolis.

We were in tenth place overall but two other racers were within twenty minutes of me, gunning for the tenth-place spot. One of them buzzed past me while we were stopped, so I jumped back on the course once again, heading south toward Mt. Airy.

The terrain was pastoral—large expansive farms with towering silos and groomed fields of wheat, corn, and beans flanking the road, small farming towns dotting the rolling hills that, with the cross winds, were draining my energy. Up 200 feet, down 200, up 100, down 100. I was alternating between 8 mph and 30 mph for what seemed like an eternity.

At one point John pulled up beside me. "Are you feeling OK? It looks like you're really dragging right now."

"John, I am spent. I've hit hill fatigue," I said. "I am just sick and tired of these hills."

Every pedal stroke was painful. I was out of gas and losing the little bit of momentum gained from the downhill as the uphill started. So I would start with a fast descent and push extra hard on the downhill to carry me through the climb. By the time I reached the top, my speed would fade to 6 mph. Where was Dr. Wolfgang Mader when I needed him? He had made it up and down the hills in Missouri so effortlessly. He was 12 hours behind me, probably suffering in West Virginia, I thought.

Soon I heard the growl of a motorcycle next to me. Great, a race official checking up on me. But when I turned my head, I saw a sign on the windshield saying, "Go Len." It was my friend Jim Long on his Harley ready to escort me the remaining sixty miles to Annapolis. I pulled over, gave Jim a big hug, and introduced him to my crew. He was the leader of a father–daughter group called the Indian Princesses that our girls had been with for more than eight years. All during the race he and other dads from the group had sent the crew and me messages of encouragement. Jim, our chief leader, came up with the name "Kiwidinok" which is Cheyenne for "wind." He'd been our virtual cheerleader, praying daily for our safety during the race. With Jim leading the way and the inspiration from the signs my crew had created, like "Free Beer Ahead," to spur me on, I started stepping up the pace. It was as if Jim had known the exact moment to show up and help motivate me. That is a true friend, sacrificing his afternoon and riding 60 miles to intercept me on a bicycle.

By the next time station, my tire passed over some glass on the pavement as we crossed Interstate 70 and flatted out. The follow van pulled over and Greg unscrewed the spare wheel from the roof rack. In fewer than two minutes we were rolling again, right into the Mt. Airy time station, located in front of the aptly named Mount Airy Bicycle Company. We didn't expect to stop here, because we had no penalties that required our team to sit in the "penalty box" administered by the race officials. But when I saw friends from work cheering loudly at the parking lot and chalking more inspiring messages on the pavement, I pulled over and began to dismount to start shaking hands and giving out hugs to the dozen or so friends that had made the effort to come cheer for me.

John said, "Get back on the bike, we have to go."

*Competitor Stefan Schlegel*

The rest of the crew loudly objected, thinking it was a mandatory stop for all riders.

John spoke again, very plainly. "See that guy at the top of the hill? He's about to pass Len for tenth place."

I spun the bike around, quickly said farewell and got to it. Within a few minutes the racer flew past me—Stefan Schlegel again, speeding away at 20 mph.

By now my lead over the other competitors in my age group was locked in. We were 12 hours ahead of the second-place athlete in my division. With under fifty miles to go, I was holding a steady 14-mph pace, which would have put me at the finish line just before dark. But in a field of 47 solo athletes from 20 countries, I was in tenth place overall. This was no small feat for a team that was content on making it before the cut-off. Weary from the 3 a.m. start, I looked slowly toward the van, which again was pulling up beside me. The window rolled down and there was my crew chief.

"Forkas," John said, "don't tell me you're going to let that German kid steal tenth place from you?"

Schlegel was an accomplished, elite 34-year-old cyclist and Ironman competitor from Mannheim, Germany. He was 18 years younger. He has not just ridden past me. He blew past me. There are moments in life that define who you are. This was one of those moments.

More importantly, have you ever had a friend that knows exactly how to phrase things so that they turn on a switch in your brain? John was that person. Fellow endurance athlete, fellow Clevelander, he was "calling me out." John knew that I would regret letting this happen without a fight.

This was a defining moment. I was being asked if I was a dog or a cat by my crew chief. I took a deep breath and started pushing faster and faster until Schlegel's follow van appeared on the twisty two-lane road ahead. The sun was beginning its final descent and a heavenly tailwind was gently pushing me closer toward the German. As I began to bear down, the red tail lights became visible.

I passed Schlegel on a steep uphill climb and raced ahead over the rolling landscape of Maryland's Montgomery County. I peeked behind me waiting for my follow van to pull up at a safe distance and give me some indication how far away the next turn would be. Sprinting ever faster to increase the gap between Schlegel and me I descended a steep hill with a stop sign at a four-way intersection at the bottom of the hill. No sign of Schlegel. No sign of my van. I had no cell phone—I'd given it up in Indiana. What to do? Which way to go? The course directions were in the follow van.

When I needed them the most to mark down turns for me as I am chasing down my German competitor, my crew was celebrating with fans at the time station stop. I had just pushed harder than I ever thought possible to overtake him, and here I was at a stop sign, deciding to gamble and go straight or wait for my crew.

How ironic that I own a wireless company and started a charity to connect kids with their classrooms during cancer treatment—and now I had no ability to communicate with my crew.

I waited and caught my breath. The seconds seemed like minutes. On the horizon a cyclist appeared, a white van following behind. Schlegel whizzed past me again. Just behind his van were John and my crew. They could not safely pass the other van due to the curvy roads and were equally frustrated at being stuck behind my competitor. Finally John said over the speaker "Go right at 108."

I cranked up the pedals and started my second chase after Schlegel. Five minutes later I was able to see the tail lights of his white van. I smiled and waved at his crew as I passed him for the second time that day, nodded at him as I passed, noticed the puzzled expression on his face as he kept pace with me.

Slowly I increased my speed and settled into a steady, consistent 20 mph pace to put as much distance as possible between the two of us. My thighs were aching. With John and my crew behind me now, things were back on track. I looked ahead and saw the turn for MD Route 108. I banked a slow sweeping turn to the right and headed south.

The follow van began honking wildly. At the same time the loud-speaker blasted "STOP! STOP! Turn around!"

I hit the brakes and made the U-turn. "What are you talking about? You said turn right at 108?"

"No," John said. "No, I said eight miles straight!"

As I prepared to turn back onto the racecourse, I watched Schlegel whiz past me once again, his van a close distance behind. Not again!

One more time I turned on the power. It took everything I had. I could hear my bike frame creaking as I pushed harder and harder on the pedals. Within minutes I caught Schlegel for the third time. Now his face looked confused. He must have thought I was playing a cruel game with him, a cat and mouse thing, tormenting him.

"Great work, Stefan. Best of luck," I said sincerely while approaching him.

Then, for the first time in that entire race, I pushed my bicycle beyond any physical limits I'd experienced in the past eleven days, putting so much torque on the bike with my legs and upper body that I thought one of two things was going to happen. I was either going to snap the chain or crack the carbon frame.

*Finish Line: My son Matthew cheers (far left) while my nephew Ian (right) hands over an ice-cold beer. (Photo courtesy of Pawpro Media)*

Over the next twenty miles we hit speeds of 30 mph. How was this possible? After 2,950 miles of continuous riding, this race is ending with a time trial sprint? This was a defining moment for our team. It was the moment when I refused to let my age define who I was and what I was capable of doing. It was my metaphor for how to live your life, run your business, or approach a problem.

The incongruity of it all was highlighted when, on the right side of the roadway, a guy took a picture of me with an iPad. "Hey, Richard!" I said. It was another friend, Richard Boales, who lived nearby and who had been following our team.

Finally, when I arrived in Laurel, about thirty miles from the finish line, I started to breathe normally and resumed an 18-mph pace, consistently looking over my shoulder for signs of Schlegel. This last section of the course would take us over I-95, one of the most heavily traveled highways in the eastern United States. The traffic lights on this section were brutal—between I-95 and I-296 on Routes 216 and Route 198, we stopped at no fewer than a dozen. On the final five miles before the finish line I looked to my left and there was Randy Mouri in a white car with the sticker "Race Official" on the side. Randy was a race marshal and was there to escort me the last few miles of the race.

"Randy, I can't believe you of all people are here," I said.

"About time you finished this race," Randy replied.

I crossed the finish line at mile 2997 at the Rams Head Tavern, beating Schlegel and recapturing tenth place in the race overall.

My family and several of my friends rose from where they'd been sitting on a grassy embankment and cheered as I sped past the line en route to the gas station where all racers stop and clean up before being escorted to the City Dock finish line by Randy Mouri.

As I exited the gas station, Schlegel and his crew were arriving. I congratulated him. "Well done, Stefan."

His crew chief, a tall blonde with brilliant blue eyes, looked straight at me and smiled. Extending her hand, she said, "Len that was a great race. Congratulations." We pulled out of the parking lot and headed down the road into town with Randy in an official race escort car, passing rows of historic townhouses, shops, and restaurants set close to the cobblestone streets. My crew had duct-taped a newspaper-sized American flag on the back mount of my bike seat and handed me a smaller flag to hold as I pedaled through the wet city streets. I was the only American to finish in my division; only four of the race's 28 finishers were American. And, of course, as in the majority of my childhood family vacations, it was drizzling—the only rain we had experienced in 3,000 miles and eleven days.

Cameras flashed and music played as we paraded into the city. One by one, my friends and family came into focus. I stopped, stepped out of my clipless pedals, and raised the bicycle over my head. My journey was over.

*With son Matt at the finish line*

I had raised more than $300,000 for Hopecam, placing first in my division and tenth overall in a field of forty-seven solo athletes from twenty countries.

I began greeting my crew and my supporters. My nephew Ian greeted me with a cold beer. Greg and Ken gave me a bar of Hershey's chocolate. Then I found and hugged my wife Elizabeth, my daughter Viena and, finally, my son Matt, to whom I had dedicated this last day of the race for Hopecam.

## Lesson 14

The final push to any goal can feel harder than everything else that led up to that point. That's when the faith others have in us can create a turning point. By seeing in others what they can't see in themselves, we can inspire people to achieve more than they ever thought possible. That's what John, my team, and all our supporters did for me. They taught me that power is in the mind as well as in the body. It allowed me to do what I'd never done before: surpass my physical limits and push through.

*Well Done Hopecam!*
*Now get some well deserved rest Len and crew.*
*You'll have some great stories to share in the*
*months to come.*

—**Randy and Susie Mouri**

*Mr. Len, Thank you so much for doing this for all of*
*the children like me who cannot go to school, and*
*our only interaction with peers is by being able to*
*connect to school thanks for Hopecam! Love, Ian*
*van den Berg*

*Last day!!! Beautiful cool morning helping you*
*home. Fight the exhaustion, keep pedaling, and you*
*will have accomplished an amazing feat.*

—**Lisa Rother**

*The Poor Clare's are estimating 4:00 pm Laurie:*
*6:25 pm, Nick: 6:15 pm, Ian: 6:20 pm, Thomas: 6:25*
*pm, David: 7:25 pm, Debbie…. Yes she showed: 7:45*
*pm. Please tell Len that we just bought him a black*
*dog cap as we understand that Bill should not quit*
*his day job to become a barber.*

—**Laurie Forkas**

*Congrats on an amazing achievement! Thank you*
*for Hopecam and the amazing people who make it*
*great! You rock Len! Warmly, Alex Green and family*

*Safe at last. Len, you orchestrated a perfect plan*
*and with a well-tuned/trained and motivated team.*
*Congratulations on achieving your goals and in such*
*a classy manner recognizing everyone but yourself.*

—**Dick Michaux**

# FINAL THOUGHTS

Years ago, after my son Matt had gone through treatment, I read Sir Ken Robinson's book, *Finding Your Element*. Robinson suggests that using your strengths in such a natural way that things begin to flow is the key to creativity, happiness, and transformation. Reading and thinking about his message forced me to look deep inside myself and think about how I was able to use my strengths to reach a goal—first, helping Matt, then later, helping other kids with cancer.

During RAAM, I was in my element. I'm not fast or agile. My cycling technique isn't tuned to maximum efficiency. I'm not an exceptional athlete. I am a father, husband, business owner, and someone who wants to make a difference. My son is alive. I owe it to these children to help them. If there is anything that differentiates me from others, it's that once I set a goal, I don't quit. How fortunate I am to have found happiness doing something that I love and using it in a way that benefits others.

I often think about my experience in RAAM and the experience Matt and all the Hopecam kids go through fighting cancer: the impossible journey, the physical toll, and the teams of supporters who surround us all. But in the end, the toughest bicycle race in the world cannot even compare to what children with cancer go through during treatment. I could have stopped at any time and come back next year to try again. These kids don't have the option of quitting. They have to reach the finish line.

As difficult as it was for me to cross that skybridge to the hospital, it was Matt who had to reach the finish line. But that short walk from our old lives to our new ones changed us both forever.

Each of us is on a different journey. And no one should have to make that journey alone.

Even if there is no immediate crisis we have to deal with, it seems that all of us are striving to make a difference in the world. By looking deep inside ourselves, we can identify which unique and God-given gifts we can use in service to a meaningful goal. That's how we create opportunity out of crisis, and spin the wheel from negative to positive. That's how we walk the skybridge across that dangerous and unknown abyss that connects our old and familiar life to what's waiting for us on the other side.

# APPENDICES

## THE HOPECAM TEAM

*Left to Right: Brian Daum, Jen Bond (Hopecam Director) Ken Gates, Greg Wood, John Moore, Wayne Smith, Len Forkas, Bill Vitek, Kaitee DeMonti, Ed Cepulis, Bill Sickenberger, Steve Gurney, Amy Doherty, Joe Knill*

Competing in RAAM was transformational for me—my team accomplished an "impossible" task because we had the right people and the right purpose driving us forward. Each day we were confronted with challenging problems to overcome. You could compare the experience to ascending Mount Everest. If Everest is like a puzzle with all its pieces nicely forged and the outlines preassembled, the climber's task only to put the pieces in the correct places, RAAM is like assembling the puzzle blindfolded.

For example, RAAM does not offer a wide variety of mountain guides whom you can pay to get you to the finish line. You have to pull it together yourself. Fortunately, I met Randy Mouri, who'd completed the race the year before. He gave me volumes of resources—navigational manuals, training plans, nutrition plans, schedules, and contact information for previous RAAM riders he consulted before he entered the race. I interviewed those riders, searching for the deal breakers lurking in the thousands of details required to execute a well-ridden race.

The most important theme that emerged from these interviews was "attitude first, skills second." Your team will make or break you. I had a great team, and in the end their faith in the mission, their skills and their selflessness allowed me, an outlier, to succeed where others had failed. Meet the Hopecam Support Crew, the team that motivated, strategized, navigated, and kept me cycling to the finish line.

### John Moore, Crew Chief

Native Clevelander, endurance athlete, former tank mechanic in the Marine Corps. Lives in Boulder, Colorado, with his wife and two teen-age children. John and I have completed numerous 24-hour mountain bike races, ultra marathons, and Ironman triathlons together. John has held senior management positions at such companies as Cisco and Juniper Networks and currently works at Hewlett Packard.

### Bill Vitek, Second Crew Chief

Native Clevelander, best man at my wedding, and an avid skier in Denver, Colorado, where he lives with his wife and two college-age children. Bill has completed several "Leadville to Copper" bicycle races for Children's Hospital of Denver. An entrepreneur and nationally respected, award-winning landscape architect, Bill is co-founder of "Dig Studios," a Denver-based design company. Bill balances his passion for creating, enhancing, and preserving sustainable places with his business sense about landscape architecture.

### Wayne Smith, Bike Mechanic ("The Wrench")

Originally from Lake Tahoe, California, and chief mechanic at Boulder Full Cycle Bike Shop. Wayne has been working on bikes for twelve years and jumped at the opportunity to do any job at 15 miles per hour. You will find him playing Ultimate Frisbee, or skiing, or doing what he can to travel—which made RAAM a good fit. Wayne enjoys a good road trip and has supported the University of Colorado Bike Team during numerous competitions.

### Kaitee DeMonti, Massage Therapist

Born and raised in Stafford, Virginia, and, at 21, the youngest person on Team Hopecam. Kaitee has been a competitive dancer since the age of four and loves to travel. After completing high school in 2009, she spent spend three months in Germany and Romania, earned her massage therapy degree and graduated in December 2012. Katiee used her massage therapy skills to similar to how a prize-fighting medic patches up a boxer in the ring during intermissions.

### Greg Wood, Physiologist and Nutritionist

Firefighter and EMT originally from "south of Boston," who lives in northern Virginia with his wife and two daughters. Greg is a member of the exclusive Fairfax County Urban Search & Rescue Team and founded Franchise Fitness, LLC, in 2006. Greg's expertise in nutrition, stretching, and active myofascial release techniques proved invaluable. With a Master's degree in physiology, Greg was capable of closely monitoring my health as the race wore on, knowing which nutritional supplements were needed and when, to keep me from falling apart.

### Ken Gates, Paramedic and Nutrition Expert

Born and raised in Fallentimber, Pennsylvania, now residing in Front Royal, Virginia, and working as a Fairfax County, VA, firefighter and EMT, a career he began at the age of fourteen. When he is not rescuing people trapped in cars or buildings, Ken pursues interests in athletics, personal fitness, weight training, and power lifting. Ken joined the team on the second training ride between Indiana and Maryland in April 2012. He coined the phrase "Pretend Len is a bear in a national park and DO NOT FEED Len solid food."

## Steve Gurney, Driver and Blogger

Native Washingtonian, now living with his wife and two children in Reston, Virginia, Steve is a cyclist and co-founder of the Reston Town Center Grand Prix Bicycle Race. Steve participates regularly in a variety of master's-level sports, including cycling, swimming, rowing, snowboarding, and triathlons. He organized the team's first 500-mile training ride in Oceanside in March 2012. Steve was a longtime writer for the Washington Post, and in 1990 he created the Guide to Retirement Living SourceBook, a publication to help people care for aging family members. He's spent his life working with nonprofit boards and regional and national organizations on aging to help maximize their exposure and help find solutions to their challenges.

## Ed Cepulis, Driver and Navigator

Native Clevelander lives with his wife and three children in Boulder, Colorado. Ed is a "weekend warrior" athlete who enjoys biking, hiking, and skiing. He has been mountain biking with Len and crew chief John Moore for over 15 years, and has participated in several 24-hour mountain bike races and other similar endurance events. He introduced the Hopecam team to bike mechanic Wayne Smith. Ed works in the high tech industry, where he has held marketing and sales leadership roles for more than twenty years.

## Joe Knill, Driver and Navigator

Born in South Bend, Indiana, and raised in New Orleans, now living with his wife and two daughters in Reston, Virginia. A triathlete and century bicycle ride organizer, Joe has completed a number of Olympic-distance triathlons, 5K-/10K-/10-mile road races, and multi-day bike rides. Employed by Northrop Grumman, Joe has served in a number of leadership positions, most recently as a program manager for Defense and Civilian programs.

**Brian Daum, Driver and Navigator**

Pittsburgh native, now living with his wife and two children in Reston, Virginia. Brian has been a competitive swimmer since childhood, earning multiple gold medals and two Pennsylvania state high school championship titles, and now competes with the Reston Masters Swim Team. He has spent the past twenty years in director- and executive-level financial positions with fast-growth public and privately held companies, including his most recent position as Chief Financial Officer of SAVI Technologies Inc. Brian reluctantly left the race on Day 5 due to a work conflict in Durango; Bill Sickenberger replaced him on Day 6 in Kansas.

**Bill Sickenberger, Driver and Navigator**

Multi-lingual (Portuguese, Spanish, French) guitar player, triathlete, and Reston, Virginia, resident with a wife and two college-aged children, Bill has completed more than forty triathlons, including several half Ironman competitions, and three marathons. He was the catalyst for the RAAM experience. Bill has spent his career working with and successfully growing emerging companies. He is currently serving as CFO of worldwide logistics company MSI.

**Amy Doherty, Videographer**

Mother of three from McLean, Virginia, who writes and produces issues-oriented pieces, including the award-winning PBS documentary, Take Away This Anger. Amy produced the Hopecam video that describes what Hopecam accomplishes, as well as over two dozen two- to three-minute video clips about our RAAM experience. Often working 20 hour days at no expense to Hopecam, Amy filmed, edited, produced and posted daily updates on YouTube that linked to our blog. Amy played a pivotal role in telling the Hopecam story to the media and our followers about the day to day progress of our race crew. Amy's Company is Pawpro Media, a video production company based in Washington DC, which produces high quality, creative video content media for business. http://www.pawpromedia.com

## HOPECAM KIDS

Each day of the race was dedicated to a child who had been a part of Hopecam. Every day, usually during my mid-afternoon break, I called and spoke with the children or the families of the children to share what lay ahead of me. These children were with me during the journey. They inspired my crew and me. Their families and friends sent us more than 500 email messages during the twelve-day race, encouraging us along the way and deeply moving my crew with stories about how their lives were changed by being able to stay in touch with their friends during treatment.

When a **child** is diagnosed with cancer, keeping that child connected to friends and classmates is usually the last thing parents are thinking about. But medical teams and social workers understand the importance of connection, and they're usually the ones who refer the family to Hopecam. With Hopecam, a child with cancer is not just a child who was in class one day, then is gone the next. The child is a friend and classmate who is battling cancer and needs classmates' support. With Hopecam, the child's classmates can be "with" the child during treatment, just like the Hopecam children were "with" me on the ride, inspiring my journey.

Our mechanic, Wayne Smith, said it best. "When I was in the car with Amy and Steve, they showed me the biographies of the Hopecam children we were riding for. Len would tell me about a conversation that he'd just had with a Hopecam kid. It was not a publicity stunt. It was real, and the stories were real."

## Day 1: Oceanside California to Blythe, California

Alex Green was diagnosed with a Stage IV Wilms Tumor at the age of five. Shortly after going into remission, he relapsed. In April 2012, during a complicated surgery to remove as much of the tumor as possible, he was left partially paralyzed and unable to move his legs. Alex now uses a wheelchair but is determined to do whatever he wants to do, including popping wheelies and jumping from the ground to his seat using his upper body! Alex was at the hospital when I set out on the RAAM course, undergoing another round of chemo—and I was praying that I would have the same determination and strength during this bike race that Alex has shown during his treatment and surgeries. Today Alex continues to fight cancer and is undergoing chemotherapy treatment with the hope for achieving remission.

## Day 2: Blythe, California to Prescott, Arizona

Jessica, whose family is originally from Ghana, Africa, was a first grader when she was diagnosed with liver cancer and is now battling a relapse. She is Hopecam's first recipient of the iPad. When Jessica moved to the USA, her only friends were those she met from elementary school. Each day Jessica connects with her class and participates in the morning meeting. Her teacher says Jessica's classmates get excited "every time I say we're going to call her. It allows them to see her so their imaginations don't get carried away by the word 'cancer,' and the fact that one of their classmates has been sick." On Day 2, we rode through the Mojave Desert. I had dedicated my ride that day to Jessica. As I endured the desert temperatures of 110° F, pedaling into a head wind, we thought about the long road that lay ahead of her and her family. Jessica unfortunately lost her battle with cancer in March 2014.

### Day 3: Prescott, Arizona to Mexican Hat, Arizona

Daniel Shank-Rowe, nine years old, was undergoing treatment for T-cell cancer. He was one of our first "customers" to use Hopecam, and has spoken publicly about his experience in a way that makes Tony Robbins look subdued. As his mother told me in a letter I received the day before I was to start the race, "Daniel never had an opportunity to say, 'I don't want to do chemo this week' or 'I want the nurses to stop trying to get a needle into me.' I know you will find… moments [during the race] when…you will think; 'I can't do this.' I hope that you will think of each push forward as a testament to each painful procedure that our kids have had to experience." Daniel, high school freshman in full remission, was recently honored by the Georgetown University Lombardi Cancer Center for raising funds to support cancer research.

### Day 4: Mexican Hat, Utah to South Fork, Colorado

Trevor Blake was eleven and fighting neuroblastoma, a cancer of tissues that form the sympathetic nervous system, which controls body functions like heart rate and breathing. He was undergoing treatment for his third relapse. Trevor's dream is to bring a treasure chest full of toys room-to-room to hospitalized children so they can choose from it something to brighten their day. Trevor also loves RVs, and his parents bought one to help Trevor make the rounds to hospitals in Maryland, Virginia, and North Carolina. His selfless determination to help other children battling cancer has led to the start of a nonprofit organization called "Trevor's Treasures." On the fourth day of the race, I dedicated my trip through the Rocky Mountains to Trevor. I would be thinking about Trevor's determination to help fill the lonely gaps in these children's lives, much like the mission of Hopecam. We are saddened to report that Trevor lost his battle with cancer in 2013.

## Day 5: South Fork, Colorado to Kim, Colorado

Shannon Eastman was diagnosed with cancer at age four. After she was in remission and undergoing a routine check-up, she was diagnosed with another, different form of cancer. When school was in session, Shannon connected weekly with Hopecam, and during RAAM she wrote me messages every day of the ride, messages that my crew read to me, usually at night, over the follow van's loudspeaker. Compared to what a child like Shannon Eastman goes through to get cured from cancer, RAAM is nothing. Her family joined me at the finish line and Shannon put a medal around my neck at the grandstand. Shannon is eleven years old and cancer free.

## Day 6: Kim, Colorado – Maize, Kansas

Spencer Goold tackled his acute myeloid leukemia (AML) diagnosis with positivity, faith, and hope. The Hopecam computer was his lifeline to the outside world, helping him keep tabs on his Facebook and Twitter accounts and keep up with schoolwork. On May 31, 2012, Spencer was considered "in remission" and was released from the hospital for what his family hopes is the last time. Spencer is a freshman at James Madison University, and celebrating over two years of being completely cancer free.

## Day 7: Maize, Kansas – Weaubleau, Missouri

Stefano Rocca was ten during RAAM, and fighting leukemia. He is undergoing a three-year treatment cycle and has returned to school after many months at home and in the hospital. He was able to run Hopecam 5K with his dad and younger brother and he was our honoree for that race, which raised more than $20,000 for Hopecam. Today Stefano is a fourth-grade student and completing the final phase of his treatment. He is active in sports, hiking, climbing and running around with his younger brother.

### Day 8: Weaubleau, Missouri – Hamel, Illinois

Charlotte Reynolds was diagnosed with a brain tumor in 2009, when she was three-and-a-half years old. During her illness, the Hopecam computer was the family's lifeline to relatives in Virginia, Florida, Colorado, and New Mexico. Charlotte did not survive her cancer—she died when she was four—but when she was dying, the family held a reading vigil so her last days would be filled with her favorite things: books and music.

### Day 9: Hamel, Illinois – Bloomington, Indiana

Justin Condoluci was nine years old when he was diagnosed with acute lymphoid leukemia (ALL) in 2007. Three years of chemotherapy and six months later, he thought he had beaten it, but the cancer returned. Justin battled another three years of chemo treatment, completing his last phase in summer 2013. Unfortunately he relapsed a second time. He is currently 13 years old, and received a bone marrow transplant in fall 2013. His triplet sister Annie was a perfect match donor. We are praying that Justin remains in remission.

### Day 10: Bloomington, Indiana – Athens, Ohio

Ian Vandenberg is a seven-year-old in first grade. He has been battling life-threatening illness since birth and, due to related health issues, has missed a lot of school. Hopecam stepped in to help Ian when he entered first grade Ian is now in the 3rd grade and continues to be homebound undergoing medical treatment.

### Day 11: Athens, Ohio – Cumberland, Maryland

Cameron McClain was diagnosed with acute lymphoid leukemia (ALL) in 2003 and used one of the first computers from Hopecam to connect with his classmates when he was in first grade. Cameron lost his battle with cancer in 2005, and his father serves on the Hopecam board in his son's name to support other children and families that struggle against this disease.

### Day 12: Cumberland, Maryland – Annapolis, Maryland

Matt Forkas, my son, was diagnosed with leukemia when he was nine. His situation inspired me to found Hopecam and continues to inspire me to this day. Matt's treatment was successful, and now he inspires other kids who have cancer that they can get through it and thrive. In June 2013, at the age of 20, Matt climbed Mt. Kilimanjaro and raised $25,000 for Hopecam kids. Matt is a fourth-year student at Stetson University.

*Matt reached the top of Mount Kilimanjaro in July*
*2013, raising $25,000 for children with cancer*

# HOPECAM SPONSORS

Mr. & Mrs. David Flanagan
The JBG Companies – Stewart Family Foundation

\* \* \*

Rehab to Racing – Alan & Mary Delaney
Capitol Seniors Housing – Scott Stewart
Milestone Communications
Earth Networks: WeatherBug
The Wiltse Family Foundation
Spokes Etc. – James & Lynne Strang

\* \* \*

The John & Jacqueline Bucksbaum Foundation
The Bernstein Family Foundation
The International Association of Fire Fighters Union Local
2068
Fairfax County, Virginia
HELPCOmm Inc.
Life with Cancer
Lindsey Joelle Miller Memorial Fund.
March Family Foundation

\* \* \*

WeatherBug/Earth Networks
Mooring Financial Corporation
Hefler Performance Coaching
LF Jennings Inc.
Eisenberg Family Foundation
David Mayhood
The Boulder Center for Sports Medicine

# BIBLIOGRAPHY

Beck Milinda, Wall Street Journal. *"The Sleepless Elite"* April 2011

Baumeister, Roy F., and John Tierney. *Willpower: Rediscovering the Greatest Human Strength.* Penguin Press, 2011.

Christensen, Clayton. *How Will You Measure Your Life?* HarperBusiness, 2012.

Csíkszentmihályi, Mihaly. *Flow: The Psychology of Optimal Experience.* Harper & Row, 1990.

Collins, Jim. *Good to Great: Why Some Companies Make the Leap…and Others Don't.* HarperBusiness, 2001.

Duhigg, Charles. *The Power of Habit: Why We Do What We Do in Life and Business.* Random House, 2012.

Gladwell, Malcolm. *Blink: The Power of Thinking without Thinking.* Little, Brown and Company, 2005.

Lyubomirsky, Sonja. *The How of Happiness: A Scientific Approach to Getting the Live You Want.* Penguin Press, 2007.

Pink, Daniel H. *Drive: The Surprising Truth About What Motivates Us.* Riverhead, 2007.

Pink, Daniel H. "The Puzzle of Motivation." Presentation, TED Conferences LLC. July, 2009.

Robinson, Ken, and Lou Aronica. *Finding Your Element: How Finding Your Passion Changes Everything.* Viking Adult, 2009.

Rock, David. *Your Brain at Work.* HarperBusiness, 2009.

# BACKGROUND
# HOPECAM.ORG

*Hopecam uses technology to make a difference in the lives of children with critical illnesses by fighting loneliness, giving hope, and easing the transition back to a normal life.*

Hopecam helps children undergoing treatment for cancer and other life-threatening illnesses connect with their friends at school by using laptops, high-speed Internet connections, and web cameras. Recognizing the critical need for socialization with their friends and classmates, Hopecam seeks to bridge the lonely divide between children and their friends at school during this frightening time. Staying connected to school significantly reduces the stress of re-entry when treatment is completed and children resume a normal life.

Since its founding in 2003 as a 501(c) 3 charitable organization, Hopecam has formed partnerships with Children's National Medical Center, Inova Hospital, National Institutes of Health, Leukemia & Lymphoma Society, and Virginia Commonwealth University.

## DID YOU KNOW?

- It costs about $1,200 to connect ONE child.
- Hopecam has connected more than 6,000 children at home and in classrooms since 2002.
- Hopecam has never turned away a child that has requested a connection.
- On average, a child uses the Hopecam program for 1.5 years.
- We dream BIG—we want to reach every hospital and homebound child in the United States.

## HERE'S HOW YOU CAN GET INVOLVED:

Hopecam is a grassroots organization and we rely on the kindness, generosity, and energy of our supporters. There are many ways to get involved with Hopecam.

- MAKE a donation. Current cost to connect each child is $1,200.
- CREATE your own fundraising campaign (bake sale, school fundraiser, sports event, etc.).
- ARRANGE for a Hopecam speaker to talk to your service organization or business.
- DONATE an auction item for the Hopecam annual Fall Fundraising dinner.
- JOIN a committee to fundraise, market, or research technology for Hopecam.
- ASSIST with a fundraising event.
- FOLLOW us on social media and invite your friends.
- TELL schools, guidance counselors, and school nurses in your area about Hopecam.
- REACH OUT to social workers and child-life specialists at hospitals in your area.
- INTRODUCE Hopecam to foundations and other funders.
- SHARE pictures & stories about your own experiences using Hopecam as an alumnus or teacher.
- CONTACT your local media about Hopecam.
- VOLUNTEER to help us connect more children.

Our address is: 12110 Sunset Hills Rd., Suite 100, Reston, VA 20190
Telephone (703) 620 – 2555 ext. 101 • info@hopecam.org

# WE WANT TO HEAR FROM YOU

*What Spins the Wheel* is the story of how one man's dream to make cancer treatment less isolating for his son ultimately made a difference to hundreds of children who also experienced cancer and other life-threatening illnesses. In this book, entrepreneur Len Forkas shares the story of his journey from the worst day of his life—the day his nine-year-old son was diagnosed with leukemia—to one of the best days of his life, when he crossed the finish line as a sole competitor in the grueling, 3,000-mile Race Across America (RAAM), placing first in his division and raising more than $300,000 for Hopecam, the charity he founded to connect children undergoing treatment for cancer and other life-threatening illnesses with their friends at school using laptops, high-speed Internet connections, and web cameras.

But RAAM was more than a grueling way to realize a dream. It was a life-changing lesson. Len was able to effect significant change by applying what he had learned in business to recruiting, training, and working with the all-volunteer, 11-person crew who provided the support needed to complete the race. Much like Oceans 11 on a bicycle, this high-performing, mission-driven team came together to help children with cancer. Sports enthusiasts will enjoy the story of Len's journey, and business leaders will learn valuable lessons about how to use purpose, patience, practice, perseverance, and perspective—couched in stories about meticulous preparation, fundraising, and messaging; team selection and training; partnership and delegation; and accountability, validation, and forgiveness—to achieve more than they ever thought possible.

Could your organization benefit from these leadership lessons? Let us know how we can help. Here are some ideas:

- Engage Len Forkas to speak to your organization or team. Contact solutions@wwsg.com to arrange for Len to speak at your next event.
- Share copies of this book with your leaders and high-potential contacts. Print copies and electronic copies are available from www.whatspinsthewheel.com

# ABOUT THE AUTHOR

Len Forkas is the founder of Milestone Communications, a Reston, Virginia-based Company that owns and develops wireless towers in the mid-Atlantic region. Before forming Milestone in 2000, Len spent 15 years in the real estate development industry and held management positions at Bank of America, Weyerhaeuser Real Estate, and Oxford Development Company. Len earned an MBA from The American University and graduated from the College of Architecture at Ball State University. He lives with his family in the Washington, D.C. area. To contact Len, please email him at len@hopecam.org